INTERACT

WITH

INFORMATION

TECHNOLOGY

New Edition

3

Roland Birbal
Michele Taylor

Orders: please contact Bookpoint Ltd, 130 Park Drive, Milton Park, Abingdon, Oxon OX14 4SE. Telephone: +44 (0)1235 827827. Fax: +44 (0)1235 400401. Email education@bookpoint.co.uk Lines are open from 9 a.m. to 5 p.m., Monday to Saturday, with a 24-hour message answering service. You can also order through our website: www.hoddereducation.com

© Roland Birbal and Michele Taylor 2020

This edition published in 2020

Published from 2015 by
Hodder Education,
An Hachette UK Company
Carmelite House
50 Victoria Embankment
London EC4Y 0DZ

www.hoddereducation.co.uk

Impression number   10 9 8 7 6 5 4 3 2 1
Year   2024 2023 2022 2021 2020

Cover photo © *GraphicCompressor* – stock.adobe.com

Illustrations by Stéphan Theron, Val Myburgh and Wimpie Botma

Typeset in Glypha LT Std 45 Light 11/14 pt

Printed in India

A catalogue record for this title is available from the British Library.

ISBN: 978 1 5104 7398 0

Contents

Being IT safe – taking care of IT things (3)

✳ Objectives

At the end of the chapter, you will be able to:

❑ identify possible problems associated with computer hardware and software

❑ select from a variety of solutions to solve a problem

❑ record troubleshooting steps

❑ state the rules for personal safety in a computer room or lab

❑ state the rules for equipment safety and use in a computer room or lab

❑ identify emergency procedures in a computer room or lab

❑ explain how government agencies with responsibility for health and safety legislation carry out their mandate in relation to ICT/IT industry.

In *Interact with IT* Book 2, we looked at how to identify the ports on our computer and how to identify the cables that connect peripheral devices to the computer. We also looked at how to maintain and care for devices. In Book 1, you learned that some causes of hardware malfunctions or problems can be normal wear and tear of parts and circuitry, poor assembly by manufacturer, dust accumulation, extreme heat, humidity, power fluctuations and vermin. In this first chapter of Book 3, we will look at how to identify and troubleshoot basic computer problems and find possible solutions.

However, before we look at how to troubleshoot problems and find solutions, let us revise some rules for working in a computer laboratory. Obeying these rules is important to work safely and also to prevent some problems from happening.

✳ Avoid stepping on electrical wires or any other computer cables.

✳ Do not touch, connect or disconnect any plug or cable without your teacher's permission. Report any broken cables, sparks or smoke in the laboratory immediately.

✳ Place chairs under the desks when not in use and return any items used to their original place.

✳ Always shut down computers using the proper procedure 'onscreen', rather than directly using the on/off switch.

✳ Protect computers from dust by covering them with dust covers after use. Too much dust may affect the circuitry.

✳ Avoid using USB drives, CDs and DVDs that were used to store information in computers from outside the laboratory. These storage devices may contain viruses that can affect the computers.

✳ Do not pile anything onto the computer keyboard. Objects on the keyboard may damage the keys.

✳ Do not eat or drink in the computer laboratory. Liquids can cause short circuits or electric shocks, and the crumbs from food can cause malfunctions inside the computer.

✳ Do not change any of the settings in the computer.

✳ Do not install or attempt to copy any software without your teacher's permission.

Figure 1.1 Some computer problems may need a technician to do the repairs.

Computer problems

Troubleshooting is a form of problem solving and, in computers, troubleshooting means finding the source of the problem and coming up with a solution to fix it. Have you ever experienced any of the following problems?

* Your computer will not start up.
* Your computer screen goes blank.
* You send something to the printer, but it will not print.
* You plug in the projector, but nothing shows on the screen.
* You are not hearing any sound from your speakers.

In some cases, the solution may be very simple and you are able to resolve it on your own. However, some problems will need to be sent to a professional, such as a technician, to repair or resolve.

In this chapter, we will look at two types of computer problems:

* Basic hardware problems and how to fix them
* Basic software (Windows) errors and how to fix them.

Did you know?

The Windows operating system comes with a troubleshooting tool that helps with diagnosing and fixing common software problems. It is found in the control panel under System and Security.

You will also need to be able to tell the difference between whether it is a hardware or software issue. Although most problems you may encounter will be software problems, some will be related to hardware. There are also some problems that can be caused by either the hardware or the software. Table 1.1 lists the main computer problems and their causes.

Table 1.1 Computer problems and their causes (hardware, software or both hardware and software)

	Problem	Hardware	Software
1	The computer does not start up when the power button is pressed.	✓	✓
2	The computer is operating slowly.	✓	✓
3	An application is frozen.		✓
4	The computer is frozen.	✓	
5	The sound is not working.	✓	✓
6	The screen is blank.		✓
7	The 'blue screen of death' appears.		✓
8	The keyboard does not work.		✓
9	The computer keeps restarting.	✓	✓
10	The printer does not print or is not working properly.	✓	✓
11	The Internet (WiFi) is slow or not working.	✓	✓
12	The computer is not seeing the flash drive.	✓	✓

Figure 1.2 The 'blue screen of death' is caused by a software problem.

Note!

It is important to record the model and serial numbers of the device, in case you are unable to fix the problem and have to refer the device to a technician.

Some computer problems may need you to try many different approaches before you find the actual solution. It is important to record the various approaches you have tried, to prevent repeating them. You can use the simple form in Figure 1.3 to record your troubleshooting steps and solutions.

Computer Troubleshooting Form
Device name: [Insert the name of the device with the issue]
Date: [Insert the date]
Owner of device: [Insert the name of the owner of the device]
Model #: Serial #:
Possible problem type: Software ☐ Hardware ☐
Problem description:
What were you doing when the problem occurred? What software was open when the problem occurred?
Was there an error message? Yes ☐ No ☐
If Yes, what was it?
Has the problem occurred before? Yes ☐ No ☐
Option 1:
Did it work? Yes ☐ No ☐
Option 2:
Did it work? Yes ☐ No ☐
Option 3:
Did it work? Yes ☐ No ☐
Resolved: Yes ☐ No ☐ If Yes, date resolved:
If No, need to call a technician: [Insert technician's information here]

Figure 1.3 Troubleshooting form

Now let us look at each of the computer problems listed in Table 1.1 in more detail.

Problem 1

Problem 1 is that the computer does not start up when the power button is pressed. Table 1.2 shows some causes for why the computer may not start up and a few possible solutions.

Table 1.2 Some causes and possible solutions for a computer not starting up

Causes	Possible solutions
• The cause of the problem can be as simple as a loose cable or connector (USB, HDMI, power cord, network cable, mouse, keyboard, speaker, monitor, projector cable, and so on).	Check if all cables and connectors are securely plugged into the appropriate outlets.
	Check if your power strip, surge protector or UPS is turned on and has power, or is working.
• The power strip or power outlet is faulty. • The power cable is faulty. • The power supply button in the power unit is faulty. • The power supply is the incorrect type. • The battery is faulty. (If your computer is a laptop or portable computer that uses a battery, it may be causing the problem.)	Remember that a surge protector and UPS are designed to protect your equipment from power spikes such as lightning, which can burn or fry the electronic components in your equipment.
	Check to see if your screen or monitor is turned on. Although this may seem very obvious, sometimes the cause of the problem might be very simple.
	Check to see if the outlet has electricity. Plug something else into the outlet to make sure that it is not faulty.
	If you are using a laptop, check to see if the battery is charged. Plug it into an electrical outlet and then wait a few minutes and restart the device.

Problem 2

Problem 2 is that the computer and all its programs or applications are operating slowly. Table 1.3 shows some causes for why the computer is operating slowly and a few possible solutions.

Table 1.3 Some causes and possible solutions for a computer operating slowly

Causes	Possible solutions
• The computer is infected with a virus or malware.	Check for a virus or malware by running your antivirus scanner. Clean the virus if one is found.
• The hard drive is full and has no more space.	Delete any unnecessary files or save your pictures, videos and music to an external drive. Pictures, videos and music can take up a lot of space on your hard drive.
• The computer's hard drive is too fragmented. A fragmented disk is one in which the files on the disk are divided into several segments and stored in different locations. When the computer searches for a file, it has to look in several areas of the disk for the different parts of the file to put it back together into a single file. This process slows down the computer. Defragmentation puts the files back as one single file in a single location.	Run your disk defragmenter: • Click on the **Search icon** on the taskbar. • Type and select **Defragment and Optimize Drives** from the search bar. • Click **Optimize** (see Figure 1.4 on the next page).

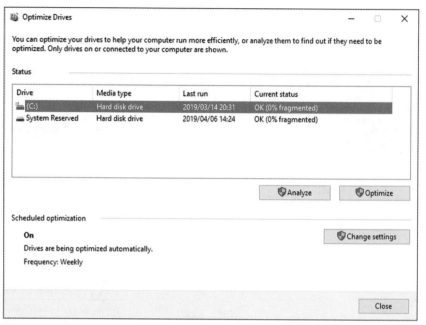

Figure 1.4 Defragment and optimise drives

Table 1.4 shows some causes for why only one application may be operating slowly and a few possible solutions.

Table 1.4 Some causes and possible solutions for only one application operating slowly

Causes	Possible solutions
• The computer is infected with a virus or malware. • The program or application is not functioning correctly due to a bug in the program.	Try closing and reopening the application.
	Check for any new updates to the program or application.

Problem 3

Problem 3 is that an application on your computer is frozen. Table 1.5 shows some causes for why an application or a program may become stuck or frozen, and a few possible solutions.

Table 1.5 Some causes and possible solutions for an application or a program becoming stuck or frozen

Causes	Possible solutions
• The computer is infected with a virus or malware. • The program or application is not functioning correctly due to a bug in the program.	Close the window or application and reopen it. If you cannot close window or application, try the next possible solution.
	Force the application to close. Hold down the Control, Alt and Delete keys together. Select the **Task Manager option**. Choose the appropriate application and then click on **End Task** (see Figure 1.3). Restart your application.
	Hold down the ALT + F4 keys together, which will shut down the window you are working in.

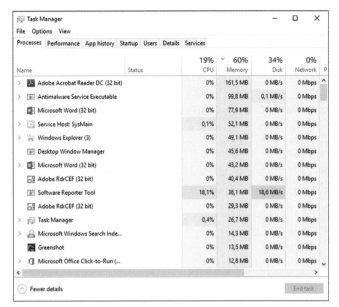

Figure 1.5 Task Manager

Problem 4

Problem 4 is that the computer is frozen. This means that everything on your screen is frozen, and the mouse and keyboard do not respond either. Your computer is completely locked up, and you cannot close or open any applications or even select the Shut-down option. You will need to reboot the computer. Table 1.6 shows some causes for why your computer may become stuck or frozen, and a few possible solutions.

Table 1.6 Some causes and possible solutions for a computer becoming stuck or frozen

Causes	Possible solutions
• The mouse has stopped working. • The computer system or system unit (the tower or chassis of a desktop computer that houses the CPU, DVD drives, motherboard, RAM and other components) is overheating. Some systems are very sensitive to changes in temperature. • Driver corruption errors have occurred. Drivers are a type of software that allows the hardware device to communicate with the computer's operating system. • Software errors have occurred. The application software is not running correctly. • The computer is infected with a virus or malware.	Check if the indicator light on the mouse is on, as well as whether the batteries in the mouse need changing.
	Check to see whether any of the air vents are blocked.
	Hold down the Control, Alt and Delete keys together. Click on the **Power button icon** that appears in the lower right-hand corner of the screen and select **Restart**.
	Press and hold down the **Power button** for 5 to 10 seconds to force the computer to shut down. Restart the computer after a few seconds.
	LAST RESORT (Only attempt this if other options fail): Unplug the power cord from the electrical outlet or if you are using a laptop that is not connected to an electrical outlet, remove the battery. Wait for a couple of minutes, reinsert the battery or plug in the computer and restart.
	Once the computer restarts, check your computer for viruses. Update your antivirus software and scan your computer.

Problem 5

Problem 5 is that the computer sound is not working. Table 1.7 shows some causes for why the computer sound may not work, and a few possible solutions.

Table 1.7 Some causes and possible solutions for the computer sound not working

Causes	Possible solutions
• The volume is low. • The cables are not attached correctly. • The speakers are plugged into the wrong port. • The speakers are defective.	Check to see if the volume level is up. Click the **Audio button (speaker icon)** in the taskbar. Double-clicking on the icon will bring up the audio controls. See if the volume control is muted or turned down very low. Adjust the controls or unmute the volume control.
	Check to see if the cables are securely attached to the computer and that the speakers are plugged into the correct audio port.
	Check if you can hear sound by using headphones.

Problem 6

Problem 6 is that the computer screen is blank. Table 1.8 shows some causes for why a computer screen may be blank, and a few possible solutions.

Table 1.8 Some causes and possible solutions for a computer screen being blank

Causes	Possible solutions
• The monitor is switched off. • The computer is 'asleep' (gone into standby or hibernation mode). • The connections between the computer and the monitor are loose. • The screen brightness and contrast is turned down.	Switch on the monitor.
	Move the mouse or touch the keys on the keyboard to wake up the computer.
	Check if the monitor cable is securely plugged into the computer and the back of the monitor. Check if the monitor power cord is securely connected to the electrical outlet and that the power light is on.
	Check if the computer is plugged in and turned on.
	Check if the brightness and contrast levels on the monitor are set too dark, so that you cannot make out anything on the screen. The brightness control is found on the monitor and on some keyboards.

Figure 1.6 Check that the monitor cable is plugged in if the computer screen is blank.

Problem 7

Problem 7 is that the computer shows a blue screen, which is known as the 'blue screen of death'. Although both software and hardware issues can cause this problem, it is mostly due to the hardware. Table 1.9 shows some causes for why the computer may show a blue screen, and a few possible solutions.

Table 1.9 Some causes and possible solutions for a computer showing a blue screen

Causes	Possible solutions
• The drivers are corrupt. • There are too many demands on the RAM. If too many programs are open, the amount of RAM is not enough to handle the memory requirements. • The hard disk is faulty.	Reboot the computer. Unfortunately, there is not much else that you can do. If this solution does not work and the problem re-occurs, then this means that the problem is more serious and you need to contact your technician.

Problem 8

Problem 8 is that the keyboard or mouse does not work. Table 1.10 shows some causes for why a keyboard or mouse may not work, and a few possible solutions.

Table 1.10 Some causes and possible solutions for the keyboard or mouse not working

Causes	Possible solutions
• The keyboard or mouse is not connected or is not turned on. • The wireless adapter for the keyboard or mouse is not plugged into the computer. • The battery in the keyboard or mouse is flat (has no more power). • The components in the keyboard or mouse are damaged.	Check to see if the keyboard or mouse is securely plugged in. Disconnect and reconnect it in the same port. If the keyboard or mouse still does not work, reconnect it in a different port.
	If you are using a wireless keyboard or mouse, check to see if the power switch is turned on.
	If you are using a wireless keyboard or mouse, check to see if the wireless adapter is plugged into the computer and that nothing is blocking the signal.
	Change the battery in the keyboard or mouse.
	Try another keyboard or mouse.

Problem 9

Problem 9 is that the computer keeps restarting (randomly rebooting) or crashing. Table 1.11 shows some causes for why a computer may keep restarting or crashing, and a few possible solutions.

Table 1.11 Some causes and possible solutions for why a computer keeps restarting or crashing

Causes	Possible solutions
• Your computer is overheating. • Your computer is infected with a virus or malware.	Check if something is blocking the air vents. Make sure that air can flow freely around your computer.
	Check for viruses on your computer. Update your antivirus software and scan your computer.

Problem 10: The printer does not print or is not working properly.

Problem 10 is that the printer is not printing or working correctly. Table 1.12 shows some causes for why a printer may not print or work, and a few possible solutions.

Table 1.12 Some causes and possible solutions for a printer not printing or working correctly

Causes	Possible solutions
• The printer cables are not connected properly. • Paper is jammed. • The printer is out of paper, ink or toner. • The printer is not connected to the network or wirelessly to your computer. • There is a printer error (orange or blinking light). After your printer has completed its initial start-up, you should see a solid-coloured light. If the indicator light is blinking or is orange, this often means that there is a printer error, such as a paper jam or an issue with the ink or toner cartridge.	Check that you are sending your print instruction to the correct printer.
	Check to make sure that the printer is turned on and that the power light is on.
	Check that the power cord and the printer cable are securely attached. If the printer is connected wirelessly, check if wireless light is on.
	Check if the printer has a paper jam. The printer will display a message on the LCD screen or an indicator light to show that there is a paper jam. Note: Check the printer's manual on how to remove a paper jam.
	Check if the printer is out of paper, ink or toner. Load the printer paper tray with paper. Install new ink cartridges or toner cartridges. Note: Check the printer's manual on how to install new ink or toner cartridges.
	Turn off the printer, wait 15–20 seconds and turn the printer back on. Unplug the printer, wait 15–20 seconds and plug it back in. Restart the printer.
	Check the printer's print queue by looking for the printer icon in the system tray and double-clicking it. The print queue shows the status of each job, as well as the general status of your printer. Delete any jobs sent to the printer and resend.

> **Note!**
> The toner in cartridges is carcinogenic (cancer causing), so empty toner cartridges need to be disposed of carefully and responsibly. Check the printer's manual on the correct disposal procedures for ink and toner cartridges.

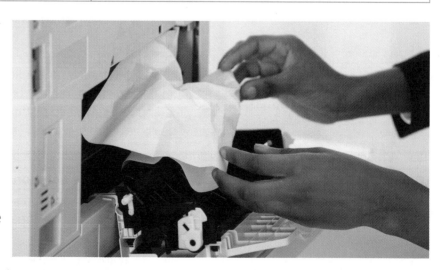

Figure 1.7 Always follow the instructions in the manual for removing paper jams.

Problem 11

Problem 11 is that the internet (WiFi) is slow or not working. Table 1.13 shows some causes for why the internet (WiFi) may be slow or not working, and a few possible solutions.

Table 1.13 Some causes and possible solutions for the internet (WiFi) being slow or not working

Causes	Possible solutions
• The computer's WiFi is not turned on. • The modem is not plugged in. • The internet connection is down (not working).	Check if the WiFi on your computer is turned on. Many laptops have a light, usually green or blue, to show that the WiFi is turned on. Some laptops may have either a WiFi button or function key. If neither a button nor function key is present, then you can find the WiFi icon in the Notification area of the taskbar. Double-clicking on the icon with your mouse will give you the option to enable (turn on) or disable (turn off) the WiFi on your device.
	Make sure that the internet is working. Check that you are connecting to the internet using another device such as your tablet or smartphone.
	Reset the modem. Unplug or disconnect the modem power cord, wait 15–20 seconds and then reconnect the power. Wait a few minutes to reconnect to the internet. Test your connection.
	Reboot your computer.
	Note: If these solutions do not work to solve the problem, then you will need to contact your technician.

Problem 12

Problem 12 is that the computer is not seeing the flash drive or external drive, or cannot access files on the drive or save to the drive. Table 1.14 shows some causes for these problems, and a few possible solutions.

Table 1.14 Some causes and possible solutions for a computer not seeing the flash or external drive, or being able to access files on the drive, or save to the drive

Causes	Possible solutions
• The computer's USB port is not working. • The drive has a virus. • The drive is locked. • The drive is corrupt. • The drive is physically damaged.	Try another USB port. The problem may not be that your flash drive is not working but that the port to which it is connected is not.
	Use your computer's antivirus to scan and clean any viruses.
	Check to see if your flash drive or external drive is locked. Some drives have a physical lock on the drive, which prevents persons from deleting files or saving to the drive.
	LAST RESORT (Only attempt this if the other options all fail): Your flash drive or external drive may be corrupt and you may have no other choice but to format your drive. Remember that formatting your drive deletes all information on the drive. To format your drive, right-click on the **Drive icon** in the Explorer folder and select **Format**.

Scenario

Work through this scenario to practise your problem-solving skills.

You have just completed your assignment that is due for tomorrow. You clicked on Print, but the document has not printed. Use the process of elimination to determine what is wrong and try to resolve the issue. Use the troubleshooting form. Figure 1.8 shows an example of a completed troubleshooting form to resolve the problem.

Computer Troubleshooting Form
Device name: Printer
Date: 4 February 2020
Owner of device: My own
Model #: HP Officejet 8610　　　　Serial #: 1459826
Possible problem type: Software ✓　　　　Hardware ✓
Problem description: Sent document to print, but printer is not printing.
What were you doing when the problem occurred? What software was open when the problem occurred?
Finished working on my assignment in Microsoft Word and sent it to print.
Was there an error message?　Yes ☐ No ✓
If Yes, what was it?
Has the problem occurred before? Yes ☐　No ✓
Option 1: Power is on.
Did it work? Yes ☐ No ✓
Option 2: Cables are secure.
Did it work? Yes ☐ No ✓
Option 3: Printer is out of paper.
Did it work? Yes ✓ No ☐
Resolved:　Yes ✓ No ☐　　　　If Yes, date resolved: 4 February 2020
If No, need to call a technician:

Figure 1.8 Completed troubleshooting form for resolving the issue of a printer not printing

Health and safety legislation

No Occupational Safety and Health (OSH) Standards are provided for the use of computers. However, many Occupational Safety and Health Acts (OSHA) legislated in various countries have guidelines for injuries that occur while working on the job.

The Jamaican Occupational Safety and Health Act (JOSHA) and the Occupational Safety and Health (OSH) Management Policy of Trinidad and Tobago, as well as the OSHAs in many other countries, require the following to prevent injuries in the workplace:

* employers to take reasonable precautions to ensure the safe operation of equipment
* employees to follow all safety procedures to operate equipment safely.

Many companies also write and implement their own acceptable-use policies or guidelines to reduce the problems that can happen through extended and improper computer use. These policies refer to general computer use, **email**, the internet and other online computer use, hardware, security, copyright, cyberbullying and the physical impact of increased computer (computer health-related injuries) use in the workplace.

Figure 1.9 Many companies have their own safety procedures and guidelines for working safely with computers.

Note!

Not all printers can use refills and refilling ink cartridges can damage your printer. Refilling ink cartridges also void (cancel) the warranty on the printer.

Green computing

The term 'green computing' is an emerging field in information technology and computer science. Also called green information technology or green IT, green computing is the use of computers and computer resources in an environmentally-friendly and responsible manner. It involves the using and disposing of computers and their devices in a way that reduces the impact on the environment. It also means designing, engineering and manufacturing computers and devices in an eco-friendly way.

Green computing involves reducing the impact on computers and devices on the environment by using fewer resources to build the devices. This can involve the following:

* **Green design**, where computers and devices are designed to be energy efficient
* **Green manufacturing**, where computers and devices are built with minimal wastage of resources
* **Green use**, where the amount of electricity used by computers and devices is the least possible
* **Green disposal**, where computer equipment is recycled and re-purposed to make other devices, or is disposed of correctly.

As computer users, we can also play our part in green computing by using some green approaches, including the following:

* Place the computer in sleep or hibernation mode if you are away from it for a long time.
* Purchase energy-efficient laptops and notebooks instead of desktops.
* Use the power management system on your computer to reduce the amount of energy your computer uses.
* Shut down your computer and devices at the end of the day.
* Refill printer cartridges instead of purchasing new ones.
* Refurbish your computer or devices instead of buying new ones.

Summary 1

1 'Troubleshooting' means finding the source of the problem and fixing it.

2 Hardware malfunctions can be caused by wear and tear of parts and circuitry, poor assembly by the manufacturer, dust, extreme heat, humidity, power fluctuations and vermin.

3 A fragmented disk has files that are divided into several segments and stored in different locations.

4 Defragmentation puts the files back as one single file in a single location.

5 Many computer problems can be caused either by hardware or software, or both.

6 Driver corruption errors are caused when software (drivers) that allow the hardware device to communicate with the computer's operating system are not working properly.

7 Green computing involves using computers and devices in a way that reduces their impact on the environment.

Questions 1

Copy and fill in the blanks questions

1 A _____ disk is one in which the files on the disk are divided into several segments and stored in different locations.

2 _____ are a type of software that allows the hardware device to communicate with the computer's operating system.

True or false questions

1 The print queue shows the status of each job, as well as the general status of your printer.

2 If the speakers are plugged into the wrong port, you will not hear sound.

3 A keyboard may not work if its wireless adaptor is connected to the computer.

4 Defragmenting your hard drive will destroy all the information on it.

Multiple-choice questions

1 Which of the following is NOT a cause for the computer not starting up when the power button is pressed?

   a A loose cable

   b A bad power strip

   c The speaker not plugged in

   d A flat battery

2 All are causes for a frozen computer except for:

   a an infection by a virus or malware.

   b driver corruption.

   c an overheating system.

   d a keyboard that is not working.

Short-answer questions

1 Explain the term 'troubleshooting'.

2 List two situations for which you need to contact a technician.

3 Give two reasons why you should record the steps you take in troubleshooting a problem with your computer system.

Scenarios

Use the troubleshooting form to identify and suggest possible solutions for problems:

1 Jason is using his mother's computer. He plugs in his flash drive, but it does not appear in the Explorer window. Suggest what Jason can do to try and resolve the problem.

2 The computer shows a blue screen when you start it. How can you solve this problem?

3 Your sister uses her computer on the bed. She complains that her computer continually shuts down and restarts.

Research question

Determine if your school has any guidelines or policies based on the Occupational Safety and Health Act to protect employees and students when using ICTs in the school.

Hint: Ask your school's health and safety officer or guidance councillor, teachers or principal. Your school may have a representative for the school board or teacher's union from whom you can get information.

Project

Produce a campaign to promote health and safety practices when using the computer system. You can use promotional flyers and charts, audio podcasts, speeches, debates, and demonstrations. At the end of your campaign, create and distribute a survey to find out if students learned anything from your campaign.

Crossword

Across

4 The 'blue screen of death' can be caused by corrupt _____.

5 The process of finding the source of a problem and fixing it

8 The process of putting files back in a single location as one single file

Down

1 Files that are divided into several segments and stored in different locations on the hard disk

2 A reason for a computer to randomly restart

3 When driver software that lets hardware communicate with a computer's operating system has errors, it is said to be _____.

6 The Act that contains regulations to safeguard employees in the workplace

7 A computer being asleep or in hibernation mode can be a reason for _____ screen.

STEM project

Kevin, your friend who is not doing IT at school, is working on a computerised presentation for his mid-term English Language assignment and is having problems. Firstly, he successfully downloaded a video from a website without a secured sign. Then he realised that he was not getting sound during the video playback and now his computer screen has frozen. He has asked for your help to get his presentation back on track.

1 What do you suspect are the major causes of the problems that Kevin is experiencing?

2 Outline the steps you would take in troubleshooting the problems.

3 Write brief notes to explain the most likely problems and corresponding solutions in language that Kevin can understand.

4 Develop a checklist for Kevin if he has such problems again. Share it with a classmate.

5 What feedback did you receive from your classmate? How can you use this feedback to improve your checklist?

Hints

1 Write down any assumptions you are making in suggesting the most likely problems.

2 Create a glossary of the IT terms that Kevin will not understand.

✳ Objectives

At the end of the chapter, you will be able to:

- ❏ identify the basic components of the Windows 10 desktop

- ❏ store a file to both online and offline storage

- ❏ define the terms 'file' and 'file management'

- ❏ use the conventions for naming a file correctly

- ❏ categorise files based on their file extensions

- ❏ solve the path to a file, with the tree directory structure

- ❏ perform file management tasks in a directory folder

- ❏ discuss the role of drivers in device management.

In Chapter 2, we will look at the four categories of system software, which are the programs that manage and support the resources and operations of a computer system:

- ✳ operating system
- ✳ utility programs
- ✳ device drivers
- ✳ language translators.

We will discuss the Windows 10 operating system. Then we will look at the utility programs, device drivers and language translators built into this operating system.

Windows 10 operating system

Windows 10 is Microsoft's newest operating system for personal computers, tablets, embedded devices and Internet of Things (IoT) devices. Windows 10, which is an upgrade of Windows 8, was released with several new features such as Continuum, Microsoft Edge and integrated search.

- ✳ Microsoft Windows 10 Continuum allows users to toggle between the touchscreen and keyboard interfaces on devices that offer both. Continuum automatically detects the presence of a keyboard and orients the interface to match.
- ✳ Microsoft Edge replaced Internet Explorer as the default web browser. Edge contains various tools including the following:
  - The Web Notes tool allows users to markup websites.
  - The Reading View tool allows users to view certain websites without advertisements.
  - The Markup tools allow users to write, draw and make notes on webpages, screenshots, PDFs and ebooks, using highlights, sticky notes and comments, among others (see Figure 2.1).
- ✳ Integrated search allows users to search all local locations within their PC, as well as on the Web, at the same time, using Bing as the default search engine.

Figure 2.1 Markup tools in Microsoft Edge

If you use an Apple® (Mac®) computer, the operating system is probably Mac® OS X®. If you use a personal computer (PC), your operating system is probably Windows. Many versions of these operating systems remain in use as they continue to change and develop.

In this chapter, we will look at the following aspects of the Windows 10 operating system, as it is almost certain to be the starting place for your use of computers:

* The Windows 10 desktop
* File management operations using Windows 10
* Firmware.

The Windows 10 desktop

In this section, we will look at the Windows 10 desktop and how to perform tasks and functions such as:

* interacting with the CPU and the hard drive
* opening software programs
* managing files, folders and directories
* creating documents, printing photos and listening to music.

After booting up a modern PC that runs Windows 10, the desktop appears on the screen, as shown in Figure 2.2. You can think of the Windows desktop as being like the traditional office desk. Just as you can move objects around on a real desk and put away items in drawers, as well as add and remove items, you can do the same on your Windows desktop. The Windows desktop contains shortcuts that allow you to access various processes available in the Windows operating system. Some of the components on the Windows 10 desktop are shown in Figure 2.2 and described on the next page.

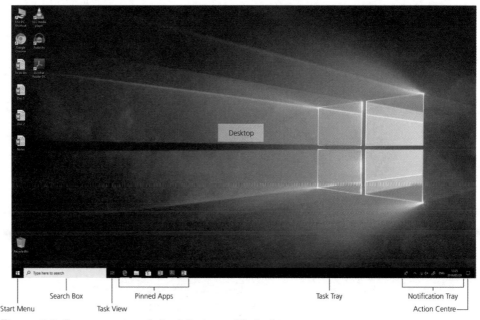

Figure 2.2 Components of the Windows 10 desktop

Components of the Windows 10 desktop

The Windows 10 desktop has these components as shown in Table 2.1.

Table 2.1 The Windows 10 desktop components

Start menu	The Start menu lets you launch applications, shut down your computer and access system settings, as well as much more.
Search box	The Search box allows you to quickly search your computer and the Internet from a location on the taskbar.
Task View / Timeline	The Task View button allows you to manage your virtual desktops and move application windows between them.
Pinned apps	Applications that you use commonly can be pinned to your taskbar. By default, Windows has a couple that it pins for you.
Task tray	If an application is open, and has not been pinned to the taskbar, it will show in the Task tray.
Notification tray and Clock	The Notification tray shows icons of applications that are running in the background and provides access to the internet and to sound settings. The clock displays the current time and date.
Action Center	The Action Center is Windows' main notification system. Any slide-out notifications that you receive are stored in this panel until you clear them. The Action Center also provides quick access to system features such as WiFi, Bluetooth, tablet mode and All settings.
Desktop	The desktop contains your desktop icons and has a customisable background image.
File Explorer	File Explorer is the utility used for file management functions in the Windows 10 operating system. It can be used to move, copy, rename, duplicate and delete files, as well as to browse through the directory.
Quick Access Toolbar	The Quick Access toolbar allows you to save (pin) the commands that you use most often. Quick Access also automatically pins your most frequently accessed folders.

File management operations using Windows 10

A **file** is a storage unit in a computer for storing data, information or commands. **File management** is the process of creating, sharing and manipulating files in a computer system. A **file manager** is software on a computer with a graphical interface, where electronic files and documents are organised into folders. Files can be saved inside the folders, and each folder can contain subfolders with more files. The top-level folder is called a directory.

A directory is used to store, organise and separate files and directories on a computer. For example, you could have a directory to store pictures and another directory to store all your documents. Storing specific types of files in a folder lets you quickly locate the type of file you want to view. Directories are also used as locations for storing programs. For example, when you install a program on a computer, all its files are stored in a directory that could contain dozens or hundreds of files related to that program.

The file manager for Windows is called Windows Explorer, and on a Mac® OS, it is called the Finder®.

You can use File Explorer for various tasks. In addition to management and organisation of files and folders, it is also used to view and manage the resources of your computer such as internal storage and external storage. You can carry out these file management operations using Windows File Explorer:

* Creating new files
* Locating files in the computer system
* Sharing files among different users
* Storing files in separate folders known as directories
* Solving the path to a file, with the tree directory structure.

Did you know?

When you install a program on a computer, all its files are stored in a directory that could contain dozens or hundreds of files related to that program.

We will examine the following file management operations more closely in this section:

* Naming files
* Saving files
* Working with directories or folders.

Naming files

Each file on your computer has to be given a name to identify it. File-naming conventions are important for maintaining a well-organised electronic directory. A file-naming convention (FNC) can make it easy to identify the file that contains the information that you are looking for just from its title and by grouping files that contain similar information close together. A good FNC can also help others better understand and navigate through your stored files.

Here are some tips to follow when naming files:

* Name the files so that they can be easily identified and distinguished from one another.
* Make sure the names are logical and reflect the content of the file. Do not use names that only you understand.
* Use title case, which means making the first letter of every word a capital letter.
* Keep file names short and relevant. Although filenames can be up to 255 characters long, in practice you will not use file names that long. In addition, the following symbols cannot be used in a filename: \ / : * ? " , .
* Use the format Year-Month-Day (four-digit year, two-digit month, two-digit day) for dates: YYYY-MM-DD. This will keep the files in chronological order, for example: 2019-03-04 Agenda, 2019-03-24 Minutes of Meeting.
* Use version numbers if files have multiple changes. This will keep the files in numerical order in the file directory, for example: Project v01, Project v02, Project v03.
* State the name of the person who created the file.

Another aspect to consider when naming files is the use of the file, which can be archive, backup or current. A file that is archived is not actively used and is usually the original version of a file. This file will need to have a more detailed name to make it easier to find later. A backup is a copy of the file currently being worked on, which can be used if the current file is lost or damaged. It is usually stored in another location or device. For example, here are three versions of the same file, one labelled for current use, one for backup and one for archive.

* **File name for current use:** 20190615_Tower1_ProjectReportv03.xls
* **Backup file name:** 20190610_Tower1_ProjectReportv02.xls
* **Archived file:** The archive file name has more information added: 20191025_Contract231_Negril_Tower1_ProjectReportv01_Brown.xls

Table 2.2 File name extensions and their associations

Extension	Association
BAT	**BAT**ch files containing a series of DOS commands
COM	Executable **COM**mand files
EXE	**EXE**cutable command files
SYS	Various types of **SYS**tem files – usually drivers to control devices
DOC	**DOC**ument files created by, for example Microsoft Word, the word-processing program
XLS	A spreadsheet file created by, for example Microsoft Excel, a spreadsheet program
WPD	**W**ord **P**erfect **D**ocuments (WordPerfect is another word-processing program)
TXT	**T**e**XT** files associated with the Notepad program
JPG or JPEG	A graphics file commonly used for photos and illustrations
BMP	**B**it**MaP**ped graphics, such as photos and illustrations
PDF	**P**ortable **D**ocument **F**ormat – a file type that displays finished text and graphics in an application such as Acrobat® Reader®.

Parts of a file name

The descriptive name usually consists of two parts – the descriptive name and the file extension, which are separated by a period (.). The file extension is made up of the three or four letters that follow the period. When renaming a file, do not delete or change the file extension as this may cause problems with opening the file.

For example, the file name RESUME.DOC has RESUME as the descriptive name and DOC as the file extension. The extension tells you and the computer which type of file it is, in this case, a DOCument. When you click on the file to open it, the computer then knows which application is needed. The RESUME.DOC file is opened by Microsoft Word (or another word-processing package you have installed), as DOC is a common file extension for Word documents. Table 2.2 gives some extensions and their associations.

The tree directory structure

You can solve the path to a file using the tree directory structure. The root directory in Figure 2.3 is 'C:'. The root directory has several folders, which can have subfolders, and so on.

The location of a file is often specified by listing the folders and subfolders that lead to the file. This list is called a path. For example, Figure 2.4 shows the path for the file 'Sample Project'. This file is located in the sub-folder 'Powerpoint Example 2', which is stored in the older 'Camtasia Example' subfolder located in the 'Documents' folder, which is stored in the Root Directory 'This PC'.

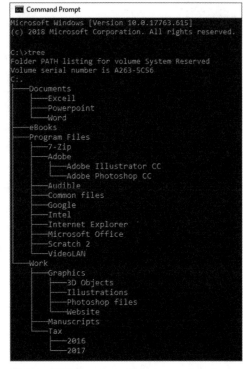

Figure 2.3 The tree directory structure

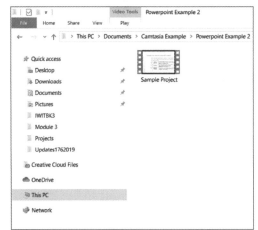

Figure 2.4 The path for the file 'Sample Project'

Saving files

You can save files or documents:

* offline
* online
* to OneDrive.

Saving files offline

Saving documents offline refers to storing them on the hard drive or on other storage devices such as flash drives, external hard disks, optical disks, and so on. Follow these steps to save documents offline:

1   Open the document. Click **File / Save As / Select storage option** (hard disk, flash drive, and so on).

2   Input the name of the document.

3   Click **Save**.

Saving files online

The technology industry has been steadily moving away from local storage to remote, server-based storage and processing, which is known as 'the cloud'. Some examples of cloud storage services are iCloud®, Google Drive™ and Microsoft OneDrive. Saving your files to the cloud provides seamless access to all your important data, such as Word docs, PDFs, spreadsheets, photos and any other digital assets, from anywhere in the world, and makes it easy to share them with family and friends.

Your files are saved online and also to your cloud provider's folder on your computer. Storing files in your cloud provider's folder on your computer allows you to work offline, in addition to online, and your changes are synchronised when you reconnect to the internet. Some cloud services such as Dropbox, Google Drive™ and Microsoft OneDrive are free, while others such as SugarSync and SpiderOak One Backup require the user to pay a fee. In order to use the free cloud storage services, you need to register for the service online.

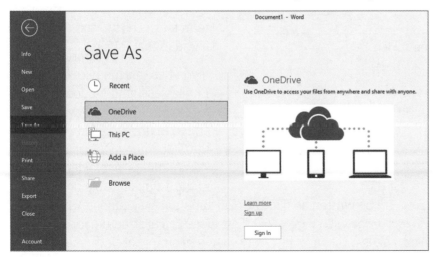

Saving files to OneDrive

Follow these steps to save a file to OneDrive:

1   Open the document. Click **File / Save As / OneDrive** (see Figure 2.5).

2   If you have not signed in, do so now by clicking **Sign In**.

3   After you sign in, name your document and save to OneDrive.

Figure 2.5 Saving a file to OneDrive

Working with directories or folders

At first, a new disk will not have any folders on it: there is just the disk itself with a single base position called the **root drive** of the disk. The root drive will be C:\ for the hard disk, D:\ for CD-ROM or CD-RW, E:\ for an external hard drive, F:\ for a flash drive, and so on. It is possible to store your documents, programs, music files and others directly onto one of these devices, with no arrangement into sections for the different types of files you are adding. However, after continuously adding files for some time, it will become very difficult to find specific files stored on the disk. You would need to look through all the individual files, in a long list, to find the one that you want. A logical system for storing documents would enable you to quickly locate and retrieve the documents when you need them.

One way of keeping all files of a certain type together, so that you can easily view and access them, is to store them in a **directory** or **folder**. Directories or folders are used to hold documents, programs, files and even subdirectories and subfolders. There is no limit to the sub-levels you could add.

Directories allow you to group related files and place them in one location. For example, in your computer you may have assignment documents for the different subjects you are doing at school. These might be stored in drive C (referred to as 'This PC' in Windows 10), in the 'Documents' folder. You may have English documents, Social Studies documents, and so on. Each type of document can be stored in an individual folder corresponding to a particular subject, as shown in Figure 2.6. For even easier reference, all the folders for the different subjects could be placed in the one folder called 'Assignments' (see Figure 2.6). The name chosen by the user – 'Assignments' – is an 'umbrella' term for the all the subfolders found in that folder.

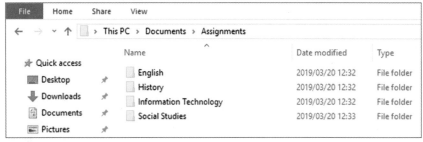

Figure 2.6 Several folders stored in one folder

Figure 2.7 Hierarchical structure for storing files

If you use this method, an English assignment document, for example Project 1, will be stored in drive C (This PC) in the 'Documents' folder, in the 'Assignments' subfolder and in the 'English' subfolder.

This can be written as 'This PC:\Documents\Assignments\English\ Project 1.doc' (see Figure 2.7). This hierarchical structure for storing files makes retrieval of files very easy: you simply click through the hierarchy of folders to find the file that you want.

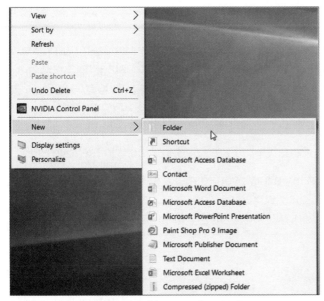

Figure 2.8 Creating a folder on the desktop

Creating a folder

Follow these steps to create a folder on the desktop, (for example Windows 10):

1. Right-click on any clear area on the desktop.
2. When the pop-up menu appears, select **New**.
3. Select **Folder** from the menu that appears, as shown in Figure 2.8.
4. A folder icon appears on the desktop and you can give it a name.

Folders can be created in a hard drive or flash drive by selecting the relevant drive, opening it and following the procedure outlined above, or by clicking the **File menu** and selecting **New** and **Folder**. Folders can also be created and stored within other folders.

Copying a folder

Follow these steps to copy a file or folder:

1. Highlight the file or folder that you want to copy.
2. Right-click and select **Copy**.
3. Navigate to the desired location, such as a flash drive, and click the icon.
4. Then click **Paste**.

Deleting a folder

Follow these steps to delete a file or folder:

1. Highlight the file or folder that you want to delete.
2. Then click **Delete**.
3. The Delete Folder dialog box displays to confirm the Delete request. Click **Yes**.

> **Note!**
> Deleting a file removes it from its current location and sends it to the Recycle Bin. The file remains in the Recycle Bin until the bin is emptied.

Firmware

Firmware is programming added to a computer's non-volatile memory during manufacturing to run user programs on the device. Think of it as software that allows hardware to run. Hardware manufacturers use embedded firmware to control the functions of various hardware devices and systems, in a similar way to how a computer's operating system (**OS**) controls the function of software applications.

Firmware may be written into read-only memory (ROM), erasable programmable read-only memory (EPROM) or flash memory. Firmware is 'semi-permanent' because it remains the same unless it is updated by a firmware updater. Firmware that is embedded in flash memory chips can be updated more easily than firmware written to ROM or EPROM, which makes it more adaptable.

Utilities

Utilities are system software programs that provide useful services, such as performing common tasks and 'housekeeping' routines. Some utility programs are included with the operating system (for example, disk repair programs), while others are purchased separately by the user (for example, Glary Utilities Pro 5).

Some functions that utility programs perform include the following:

* **Backup:** This utility allows you to make a duplicate copy of every file on your hard disk, which can be stored on an external hard drive. Figure 2.9 shows the Backup option in Windows 10.

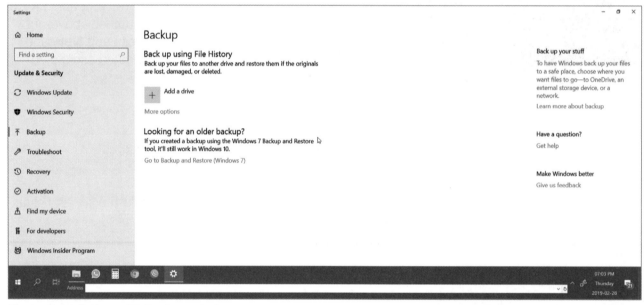

Figure 2.9 Windows 10 Backup window

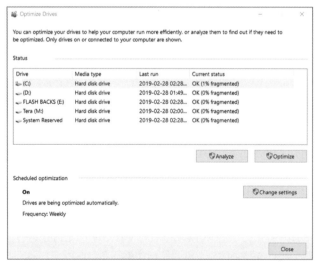

Figure 2.10 The Windows disk defragmenter in Drive Tools

* **File defragmentation:** Files stored in a new computer or hard disk are stored next to one another (contiguously). After using your computer for some time, you will probably have deleted old files and added new ones. The computer fills free gaps with new files, including parts of files. After a while, the constituent (component) parts of a typical file are scattered all over your hard disk – the files are fragmented. Fragmented files can slow down your computer considerably, as the operating system must first find all the parts of a file before they can be put back together and loaded. A defragmenter utility program finds these fragmented files and organises them back into a contiguous format. Figure 2.10 shows the defragmenter option in Windows 10.

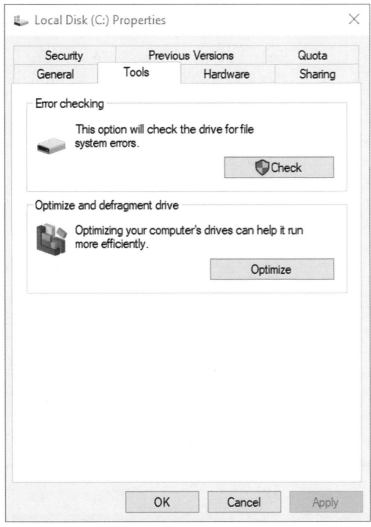

Figure 2.11 Windows Optimize Drives window

* **Disk repair:** A Disk repair utility scans a hard disk for bad sectors (defective areas) and then either repairs these sectors or marks the defective area so that the operating system will not store any data in that location. Figure 2.11 shows the Disk repair option in Windows 10.
* **Virus protection:** Antivirus software programs are also utility programs. These programs are covered in Chapter 3.

Device drivers

A **device driver** is a computer program that enables a computer to interact with hardware devices that are attached to it. A device driver acts as a translator between the hardware device and the programs or operating systems that use it. Device drivers help with device management by telling a computer how to communicate with each input/output (I/O) device through translating the operating system's I/O instructions to a software language that the hardware device understands. When you install an operating system, many device drivers are built into the product. There are device drivers for printers, displays, cameras, CD-ROM readers, and so on. Without the required device driver, the corresponding hardware device will not work. Drivers are separate from the operating system, so that new functions can be added to the driver without requiring updates to the operating system.

Language translators

Language translators (assemblers, compilers and interpreters) are programs that translate programs written in a particular programming language into another programming language without losing the functional or logical structure of the original code. In most cases, the program is translated into machine language (the language the computer can understand).

Summary 2

1 Windows 10 is Microsoft's latest operating system for PCs, tablets, embedded devices and Internet of Things (IoT) devices.

2 The Windows desktop contains shortcuts that allow you to access various processes available in the Windows operating system.

3 File Explorer is the utility used for file management functions in the Windows 10 operating system. It can be used to move, copy, rename, duplicate and delete files, as well as to browse through the directory.

4 The descriptive name of a document usually consists of two parts – the descriptive name and the file extension, which are separated by a period (.).

5 Files can be saved online using cloud services and offline using the secondary storage devices that you have available.

6 Saving your files to the cloud can provide continuous access to all your important data.

7 Some examples of cloud storage services are iCloud®, Google Drive™ and Microsoft OneDrive.

8 Directories or folders are used to hold documents, programs, files and even further subdirectories and subfolders.

9 Utility programs are system software programs that provide useful services by performing common tasks and 'housekeeping' routines, such as backup, disk fragmentation, disk repair, virus protection and language translation.

10 Device drivers are programs that enable a computer to interact with the hardware devices that are attached to it.

11 A language translator is a program that translates a program written in a particular programming language into another programming language without losing the functional or logical structure of the original code.

Questions 2

Copy and fill in the blanks questions

1 _____ is Microsoft's newest operating system for PCs, tablets, embedded devices and Internet of Things devices.

2 File _____ is the utility used for file management functions in the Windows 10 operating system.

3 _____ programs are system software programs that provide useful services by performing common tasks and 'housekeeping' routines.

4 Device _____ are programs that enable a computer to interact with hardware devices that are attached to it.

True or false questions

1 Firmware consists of RAM chips.

2 Microsoft Windows 10 Continuum allows users to toggle between touchscreen and keyboard interfaces on devices that offer both.

3 The Windows 10 Search box allows you to quickly search your computer and the internet from a location on the taskbar.

4 The Action Center is the main notification system for Windows.

5 Saving your files to the cloud means that you can only access them from one location.

6 A folder can only hold one file.

Multiple-choice questions

1 An example of a graphic file extension is:

   a DOC   **b** TXT

   c SYS   **d** JPEG

2 Which of the following is a service performed by a utility program?

   a Protecting against viruses

   b Booting up the computer

   c Interacting with hardware devices

   d Translating computer languages

3 The 'Assignment' file is stored in drive C in a folder named 'Homework', which is stored in a folder named 'ICT'. Which of the following represents the hierarchical structure of how the 'Assignment' file is stored?

   a C:\Homework\Assignment\ICT

   b ICT\Homework\:C\Assignment

   c C:\Assignment\Homework

   d C:\ICT\Homework\Assignment

4 Which of the following best describes the function of a device driver?

   a Translating programs written in one programming language into another

   b Acting as a translator between the hardware device and the operating system or programs that use it

   c Scanning a hard disk for bad sectors and either repairing these sectors, or marking them so that the operating system will not store any data in that location

   d Making a duplicate copy of every file on the hard disk, which can be stored on an external hard drive.

5 Utility programs are an example of:

   a system software programs.

   b application software programs.

   c graphic programs.

   d productivity software.

Short-answer questions

1 Name the type of software that can perform each of these tasks:

   a Back up data files and software

   b Translate programs from one programming language to another.

2 Mary wants to organise her notes and assignments for her four subjects: mathematics, physics, chemistry and communications. She wants a folder for each subject. However, she also wants her assignments in one folder and her notes for that subject in another folder. All the information must be stored in the Documents folder in the C:\ drive.

   a Draw a hierarchical chart to show how Mary's notes and assignments would be stored.

   b The file 'Quiz 1' is stored in the mathematics folder. Write out the location of the file 'Quiz 1'.

Research questions

You are an analyst for a small manufacturing company in Jamaica. The company has 200 desktop computers that run the Windows 7 operating system. This year, the company plans to upgrade the operating system of all the desktop computers to Windows 10. You are asked to do research on the internet and provide the following information:

1 How much would it cost to upgrade one computer?

2 What are the memory and storage requirements of Windows 10?

3 Will the existing system be able to run the operating system or will new systems be required?

4 Which of the two operating systems provides better protection against malware?

5 Which new features included in Windows 10 are not available in Windows 7?

Crossword

Down

1   The extension of a graphics file commonly used for photos and illustrations

2   A structure for storing files that makes retrieval of files very easy

Across

3   The term for constituent parts of a typical file being scattered all over the hard disk

4   Programming that is added to a computer's non-volatile memory at manufacturing

5   Used to hold documents, programs, files and folders

6   System software programs that provide useful services such as performing common tasks and 'housekeeping' routines

7   The extension of a spreadsheet file created by Microsoft Excel

STEM project

Mr David works for the Government Statistical Office where Windows 10 has just been installed. He previously used Windows 7 for about five years. He is currently working on a national survey of the spending habits of individuals whose income exceeds $6 000 per month.

The categories of spending are food, transportation, utilities, entertainment and savings. Mr David had previously compiled separate electronic Word tables of persons employed in the public and private sectors. He is now setting up his system for sending out the survey and collecting and storing the responses. His system will allow for hard copies of the survey forms to be sent via post and for soft copies to be emailed. His supervisor is urging him to have the system up and running as quickly as possible so that the data collected can be sent for analysis by the Consumer Affairs Office.

You and a group of your classmates who are very knowledgeable about Windows 10 have been asked to help Mr David in any way possible. His report on the usefulness of your help will provide you and your classmate with points towards winning the National Youth IT Awards.

1   Write a paragraph stating three positive comments you would like to see in Mr David's report on your contributions to his survey.

2   What are six critical pieces of information about Windows 10 that you can share with Mr David to help make his survey both speedy and successful?

3   How do you plan to present your information to Mr David so that he can easily refer to it as needed?

4   Draw a hierarchical chart to show how survey questionnaires sent and received can be stored in a useful manner for export to the Consumer Affairs Department.

Hints

1   Research how data and information are handled at your Government Statistical Office. How can this help you assist with the current survey?

2   Why do you think the Consumer Affairs Office wants to analyse the data? How can this guide you in assisting Mr David?

3 Data communications, networks and the internet (3)

Objectives

At the end of the chapter, you will be able to:

❑ describe communication software that is used in computer networks

❑ compare uses of communication technologies in different types of computer networks

❑ describe the purpose of each component within a web address

❑ explain how a web browser retrieves a desired web page

❑ identify some characteristics of distinct types of websites

❑ describe threats to a computer network

❑ explain the terms 'data integrity' and 'security'.

In Chapter 3, we will take a closer look at these aspects of data communications, networks and the internet:

* Networks
* Communication software
* System security
* Finding information on the internet.

Networks

In Book 1 of this series, you learned that a network is formed when two or more computers are connected together. You also learned that there are several different types of networks, such as personal area networks (PANs), local area networks (LANs), metropolitan area networks (MANs) and wide area networks (WANs).

The computers in these networks can be connected wirelessly or with cables, as well as with networking devices that have different functions. Some network devices discussed in Book 2 included routers, switches, modems, gateways and bridges. We will start this chapter by looking at some uses of the different types of networks.

Figure 3.1 Networking devices such as routers connect computers in a network.

Note!

Some disadvantages of PANs:

- Some PANs interact badly with other wireless networking technologies using the same radio frequencies.
- PANs have slow data rates.
- PANs using Bluetooth are not suitable for wireless connections over larger distances.

Personal area networks (PANs)

A personal area network (PAN) is a computer network set up for personal use. A PAN usually involves the interconnection of devices such as laptops, personal digital assistants (PDAs), cellphones, printers, PCs or other wearable computer devices organised around an individual person's workspace. PANs have the following uses:

* **Multiple device connections:** Many devices can be connected to one device at the same time in a PAN. You can connect one mobile device to many other mobile devices or tablets to share files.
* **Cost effective:** No extra wires are needed in this type of network. There are also no extra data charges, so a PAN is an inexpensive way to communicate.
* **Data security:** This network is secure because all devices are authorised before data sharing takes place. All information stored on the devices is only shared on the network by authorised people.
* **Data synchronised between different devices:** One person can synchronise several devices, which means that they can **download**, **upload** and exchange data among devices.
* **Portable:** A person can move many devices without affecting the exchange of data. For example, you can move from one place to another with portable devices, such as a laptop, cell phone and PDA, and set up a PAN in the new location without the need for wires, using wireless technology.

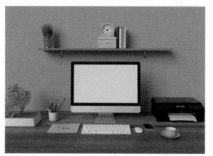

Figure 3.2 A PAN is a network set up for use in a personal workspace.

Local area networks (LANs)

A local area network (LAN) is a computer network that interconnects computers and other associated devices within a small geographical area such as a home, a school, a laboratory, a university campus or an office building. This network allows its users to share library programs, databases, languages and special facilities such as an expensive supercomputer. LANs also have the following uses:

* **Shared resources:** LANs allow computer resources such as printers, modems, DVD-ROM drives and hard disks to be shared. This reduces costs and the need to buy additional computer hardware.
* **Shared software applications:** Using the same software over a network is cheaper than buying separate licensed software for each user.
* **Centralised data:** The data of all network users can be saved on the hard disk of the server computer. This allows users to access their data from any workstation in the network.
* **Data security:** Storing the data in one location makes it easier to manage and more secure.
* **Shared internet connection:** LANs allow all the network users to share a single internet connection.
* **Easy communication:** Messages can be sent very quickly to anyone else on the network.

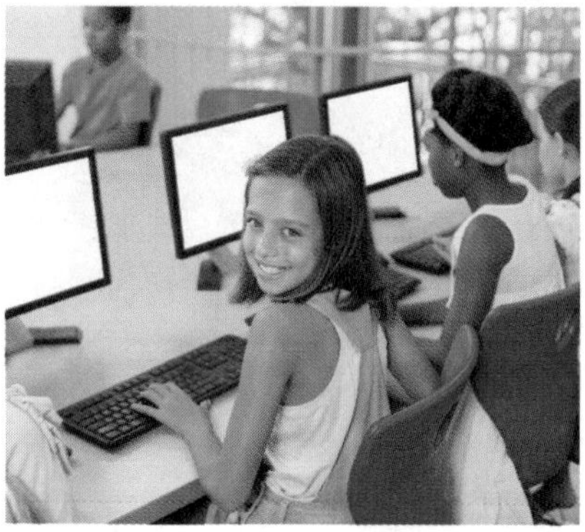

Figure 3.3 A LAN connects the computers in this school computer room.

Figure 3.4 A MAN connects users in a city to computer resources.

Figure 3.5 A WAN connects many LANs across a country or around the world.

LAN topologies

The way in which the computers on a network are connected together determines the network's topology (configuration). The most common LAN topologies are star, line or bus and ring. These LAN topologies can be modified easily to expand the network without affecting its performance:

* **Star topology:** Easy to add new devices.
* **Line or bus topology:** Easy to connect new equipment by accessing the main cable.
* **Ring topology:** Easy to add new nodes (workstations and other devices).

Metropolitan area networks (MANs)

A metropolitan area network (MAN) is a computer network that interconnects users with computer resources in a geographic area that covers an entire city or very large campus. A MAN is formed by multiple LANs connected together. MANs have the following uses:

* **Fast and easy communication:** Messages can be sent very quickly to anyone else on the network via high-speed carriers, such as fibre optic cables. These messages can include pictures, sounds or data as attachments.
* **City-wide coverage:** MANs cover a large geographical area, so businesses with many branches in the same city can connect them all on one network.
* **Shared software:** MANs allow all computers on the network to share software and resources.
* **Shared devices:** All computers on the network can share expensive devices, such as printers, plotters, and so on. This saves having to buy a different peripheral for each computer.
* **Shared data:** Everyone on the network can use the same data. This avoids problems where some users may have older information than others.

Wide area networks (WANs)

A wide area network (WAN) is a computer network that interconnects multiple local area networks over a very large geographical area. The main objective of this type of network is to allow users to access specialised library programs, databases, and so on available at any of the computers in the network. WANs have the following uses:

* **Centralised files and data:** All office branches share files and data through the head office server. The company's head office provides users with back up, support, useful files and data. The files and data are also updated among all office branches.
* **Multiple communication resources:** Many web applications, such as Messenger, WhatsApp and Skype, allow users to communicate using text, voice and video chat.
* **Shared software and resources:** As with a LAN, users on the network can share software applications and other resources such as a hard drive, printers, plotters and application software.
* **Distributed workload and reduced travel costs:** WANs allow companies to distribute work to teams in other places. For example, a company with an office in one parish in Jamaica can hire people from any other parish to work, as the WAN makes communicating and transferring data very easy. Companies can also monitor the activities of various teams online, which reduces travel expenses.
* **Large geographical area coverage:** WANs provide services to businesses and other organisations with many branches in locations over a large geographical area, such as one or many countries, or even throughout the world.

Communications software

Communications software is a set of web applications that make it possible for users to exchange data and communicate in real time. You can use this software to:

* transmit information from one system to another
* exchange files in various formats
* hold face to face or audio meetings.

Some popular types of communication software discussed in Book 2 were Voice-over Internet Protocol (VoIP), messaging services and email services. In this section, we look at other types of communication software available on the internet.

Figure 3.6 Video conferencing software allows these colleagues to call each other from different offices.

Web conferencing and video software

Web conferencing and video software provides desktop computers and cell phones with video connections to allow users to conduct online meetings and webinars, as well as share documents and screens.

Traditionally, video conferencing was used in boardroom meetings. The new trend is the use of video-enabled tablets and smartphones that allow users to call from any location and at any time. The latest video conferencing systems offer features such as screen sharing, text chat and document sharing, which allow users to work as a team.

Live chat software

Live chat software is installed on websites so that businesses can provide personalised support to their customers. This software also provides reports on the browsing behaviour of website visitors, which businesses can use to create customised chat and support experiences. The data can also be used for advertising campaigns.

Podcast software

Podcasting is online audio content delivered over the internet. The name 'podcast' comes from iPod®. However, you do not need to own an iPod® or any portable music player to create or listen to a podcast.

A **podcast** provides more options in terms of content and programming than traditional radio. You can create your own syndicated online talk show or radio programme, with content of your choosing. In addition, with a podcast, listeners can decide what programming they want to receive and when they want to listen to it. Listeners can also keep audio archives to listen to at their leisure.

Figure 3.7 Popular podcasts are talk shows and storytelling.

Podcasts have the following uses:

* Self-guided walking tours – informational content
* Music – band promotional clips and interviews
* Talk shows – industrial or organisational news, investor news, sportscasts, news coverage and commentaries
* Training – instructional informational materials
* Stories – storytelling for children or people who are visually impaired.

Webcast software

The delivery of live or delayed sound or video broadcasts over the World Wide Web (WWW) is called **webcasting**. Conventional video or audio systems capture the sound or video, which is then digitised and 'streamed' on a web server. Live webcasting is commonly used to transmit radio broadcasts. For example, if you are a student from St Lucia studying a long way from home in the United States, it might still be possible for you to listen live to your favourite radio station in Castries, using your computer's speakers and internet connection. With delayed webcasting, individual web users can usually connect to the server via a website to view or listen to the webcast at a time of their choosing. In both cases, the transmission is one way, with no interaction taking place between the presenter and the audience.

Figure 3.8 Many radio stations use webcasting software to digitally stream their broadcasts on the WWW.

Webinar software

The term **webinar** is short for **web**-based sem**inar** and refers to conducting a seminar or lecture over the WWW, using graphics (often slides), text and even live voice. Unlike webcasting, the audience is able to interact with the presenter, for example by 'asking' questions sent as instant messages. This interactive element allows the presenter and the audience to give, receive and discuss information.

System security

The increasing use of computers, along with the expansion of the internet and the many services that it offers, has resulted in new types of crime and new ways to commit old crimes. To reduce the level of computer crime, governments, companies and organisations have to find ways to manage system security. System security involves the protection of hardware, software and data.

Access control to the server room is a physical form of security.

Antivirus software installed on computers protects against viruses and malware.

Figure 3.9 Many companies use both physical and software forms of security to protect their hardware, software and data.

Data integrity and security

The protection of **data integrity** and **data security** is a very important part of system security:

* **Data integrity** means the consistency, accuracy and reliability of data. Data has integrity if it is accurate and complete when it enters a system and does not become inaccurate after further processing. The goal of maintaining data integrity is to protect data from being corrupted, which means being changed, deleted or replaced without permission. Data integrity can be affected by threats to a network.
* **Data security** involves protecting data from unauthorised access and is one of the methods of maintaining data integrity. Data can be secured using both physical and software protection.

Network threats and appropriate security measures

Network monitoring software is used by network administrators and security staff to continuously monitor and manage the traffic flow over a network. The software regularly reviews the network and generates an alarm and a report when an issue is identified. Some examples of issues that are reported are active devices, response time, slow or failing components such as a router or server, or when a suspicious packet is detected.

Did you know?

Turnkey solutions

A turnkey solution is a system, such as network security, billing or website design, which can be easily incorporated into a company's existing operations and processes. A turnkey security product is completely set up for immediate use. For example, companies can keep their network more secure by installing a turnkey identity solution to protect and guard the network against identity theft, malware and viruses.

Network security is a broad term that covers many technologies, devices and processes used to prevent and monitor unauthorised access, misuse, modification or denial of a computer network and network-accessible resources. Typically, it consists of physical and logical security controls.

* Physical security controls are designed to prevent unauthorised personnel from gaining physical access to network components such as routers, cabling cupboards, and so on. Controlled access, such as locks, biometric authentication and other devices, is essential in any organisation.
* Logical network security consists of software safeguards for an organisation's systems, including user identification and password access, authenticating, access rights and authority levels. These measures ensure that only authorised users are able to perform actions or access information in a network or a workstation.

Most threats to a network can be divided into two types:

* Internal threats
* External threats.

Internal threats

An internal threat is one that comes from inside the organisation and commonly occurs due to employee actions or weak access control.

Employee actions

Employee actions include:

* deliberately modifying, deleting or stealing confidential information for personal gain
* sabotaging (damaging) a company's data, systems or network.

Weak access controls

Weak access controls include the following:

* **No suitable authentication procedures:** Unauthorised people may gain physical access to the computer room if authentication processes such as biometric scans or doors that require a personal identification number (PIN) to enter are missing.
* **No suitable authorisation procedures:** Authorisation means that only people who have permission can access the data and information stored in the computer. Authorisation to access the network should only be given to people who have a password for the system and passwords for individual files or folders.
* **No suitable accounting processes:** Accounting processes mean the ability of the system to produce a list of the actions carried out on the network and the individuals who may have carried out these actions. The ways in which the system does this is through audit trails or access logs.

Security methods to protect against internal threats

Companies can protect their systems against internal threats by using one or more of these security methods or operating procedures to allow only authorised personnel to access the computer facilities:

✷ Install locks, grills, burglar alarms, video surveillance cameras and motion detectors.

✷ Post (place) security guards.

✷ Install electronic doors with keypads that can only be opened using passwords or magnetic cards such as identification badges, magnetic stripe cards and smart cards with a PIN.

✷ Use biometric devices to confirm a person's identity. These devices convert a personal characteristic, such as a fingerprint, into a digital code. This digital characteristic code is then compared to the digital characteristic code stored in the computer, to confirm that the characteristic is correct. Examples of biometric devices and systems include fingerprint readers, face recognition systems, hand geometry systems, voice recognition systems, signature verification (confirmation) systems, iris recognition system and retinal scanners.

Figure 3.10 This security system uses both a PIN and a fingerprint reader for access control.

✷ Use passwords to access the computer system. A password system means that users must enter a password and/or PIN to access the system.

✷ Create network access control policies (NAC) for both users and devices. For example, you can create passwords for individual files or folders. Multiple levels of passwords allow users to access only specific levels of information in a database or other computer storage system. You could also grant administrators full access to the network, but prevent their personal devices from joining the network.

✷ Use multiple levels of passwords for individual files or folders.

✷ Generate audit trails or access logs. Security software programs can audit computer use by providing a comprehensive record of all network or system activity, including who is accessing what data, when, and how often.

External threats

An external threat is one that comes from outside an organisation or institution, and which aims to corrupt or steal that organisation's confidential information. Examples of external threats include:

✷ malware
✷ eavesdropping
✷ data breaches

✷ DoS attacks
✷ industrial espionage
✷ phishing and pharming.

Malware

Malware is software that specifically intends to corrupt, steal, disrupt or erase data or information on a network. It includes computer viruses such as the Trojan horse, worm and logic bomb viruses, as well as spyware and key loggers.

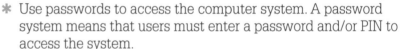

Did you know?

A worm known as 'Code Red' replicated itself over 250 000 times in about nine hours on 19 July 2001, causing traffic on the internet to slow down considerably.

Viruses

A **virus** is a program that someone writes deliberately, which activates without the victim knowing and destroys or corrupts data. A virus must attach itself to another program or document in order to start up. Viruses are one of the main threats to a computer system and have caused many businesses to lose millions of dollars due to corrupted data and lost data.

Worms

A **worm** is a program that uses computer networks and security holes (weaknesses in a security system) to repeatedly copy itself into a computer's memory or onto a magnetic disk, until no more space is left. A copy of the worm scans the network looking for another machine that has a specific security hole, and then starts to replicate itself again.

Trojan horses

A Trojan horse is a computer program that places destructive code in programs such as games. When the user runs the game, the hidden code runs in the background usually unknown to the user. The code can erase either an entire hard disk or just some programs on the disk. Trojans can create backdoors to give malicious users access to the system, so they can steal personal or embarrassing information from a person's computer, or perhaps sensitive information from an organisation's or a government's network. Unlike viruses and worms, Trojans do not reproduce by infecting other files nor do they self-replicate. Trojans must spread through user interaction such as opening an email attachment or downloading and running a file from the internet.

Logic bombs

A logic bomb is a malicious programming code that is inserted into an operating system of a single computer or network system where it lies dormant until a specific event occurs, such as a specified date or time or a command from the programmer. When the bomb finally releases the code, it can delete files, send confidential information to unauthorised parties, wipe out databases and disable a network for a period of days.

Botnets

A botnet is a string of connected computers coordinated together to perform a task, such as maintaining a chatroom, or taking control of a computer. These types of botnets are entirely legal and help to maintain a smooth user experience on the internet. However, there are the illegal and malicious botnets. These botnets gain access to a user's machine through a piece of malicious coding. In some cases, the machine is hacked directly, while in others, a 'spider' (a program that crawls the internet looking for holes in security to exploit) does the hacking automatically. Most botnets want to add your computer to their web. Then, once the botnet's owner is in control of the computer, they use it to carry out cybercrimes.

Common crimes that botnets carry out include:

* using the machine's power to help in distributed denial-of-service (DDoS) attacks to shut down websites
* emailing spam to millions of internet users
* generating fake internet traffic on a third-party website for financial gain
* designing pop-up advertisements to get users to pay for the removal of the botnet through a fake anti-spyware package.

Spyware

Spyware is a type of software secretly installed on a computer to monitor the user's actions without their knowledge. It may save its findings locally or transmit them to someone else. Spyware can be legal or illegal. For example, law enforcement officials can use spyware legally after obtaining the relevant legal permission. However, it is illegal for someone to install spyware on another person's computer without that person's specific permission. One method of detecting and removing spyware is the use of anti-spyware software. This type of software is designed to detect and remove spyware software from your system.

Keyloggers

A keylogger is a really small program that runs in background of the computer without the user's knowledge, and saves all keystrokes by the keyboard. It sends a log file of the keystrokes to a certain email address or server. The hacker then uses a 'master key' to access the keylogger.

Security methods to protect against malware

Antivirus and anti-malware software protect organisations from a range of malicious software. The best software scans files on entry to the network, and also continuously scans and tracks them. Implement these security methods to protect against malware:

* Install a **firewall**. This is software or firmware that monitors or controls all incoming and outgoing information through the internet connection into a computer system or network. The software or firmware is programmed with specific security rules to prevent unauthorised users from accessing the system or network.
* Install an antivirus software package on your computer system.
* Do not use storage media from other computers on your computer. If you have to use them, make sure you run a virus scan first to remove any viruses.
* Do not open any email attachments that contain an executable file. These attachments have file extensions such as '.exe', '.com' and '.vbs'.
* Use an operating system such as Unix or Windows 10, which has security features that protect computers from many types of malware.

Denial-of-service (DoS) attacks

A denial-of-service (DoS) attack is one that floods a computer or website with data, which overloads and stops it from functioning properly.

Security measures to protect against DoS attacks

Implement these security methods to protect against DoS attacks:

* Install an antivirus program and firewall in the network, so that only authenticated users can access the bandwidth.
* Set up the firewall policies to block unauthenticated users from accessing the server's resources.

Figure 3.11 A device for tapping a telephone system to access conversations or data transmissions

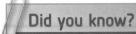
Eavesdropping

Eavesdropping means to tap into (connect to) a telephone or data transmission line and secretly listen to conversations or access data being transmitted. It can be carried out on ordinary telephone systems, emails, instant messaging or other internet services.

Security measures to protect against eavesdropping

Implement these security methods to protect against eavesdropping:

* Carry out an electronic search of the radio frequency (RF) spectrum to detect any unauthorised signals from the area being examined.
* Use software to **encrypt (encode) data** transmissions or conversations.

Industrial espionage

Spying on competitors in order to steal confidential information about their products, formulae, systems, plans or processes is called **industrial espionage**. Companies that carry out industrial espionage want to steal a competitor's **trade secrets** in order to gain an advantage over that company. Industrial espionage is illegal in most countries. Examples of confidential information include new product designs, unpublished prices of new products, formulae for new medicines, business plans for expansion into new markets, and new technology or systems. The spying can be done by employees working for the company or by using surveillance technology such as hidden cameras or microphones.

Security measures to protect against industrial espionage include:

* implementing an effective security policy such as no password sharing and no personal devices allowed at work
* doing detailed background checks on all employees.

Data breaches

A data breach is a situation in which sensitive, protected or confidential data has potentially been seen, stolen or used by unauthorised personnel. This situation may involve stealing personal information and intellectual property.

Security measures to protect against data breaches

Implement these security methods to protect against data breaches:

* Encrypt all sensitive information and shred documents containing this information before throwing it away.
* Use of levels of passwords to ensure that only authorised users can access the system and data.

Phishing and pharming

Phishing refers to attempts by cybercriminals and hackers to trick you into giving them your personal information so that they can access your account numbers or infect your computer or device with malware. Phishing attempts can happen in different ways, including through email, social media or text messages, and can affect security, as well as lead to the theft of personal and financial data.

Pharming involves installing malicious code on a personal computer or server, to misdirect users to fraudulent websites without their knowledge or consent.

Figure 3.12 A website with HTTPS (Hyper Text Transfer Protocol Secure) in its URL shows that all data between users and the site are encrypted.

Security methods to protect against phishing and pharming

Implement these security methods to protect against phishing:

* Keep website certificates up to date so that users can be sure that the websites are legitimate.
* Educate users about the best practices that they should follow when using internet services. For example, users should think carefully about clicking a link or opening a document that seems suspicious and should double-check that every URL that requires a password looks legitimate.

Finding information on the internet

You need signs or pointers to help you find information on the internet. Internet protocol (IP) addresses and uniform resource locators (URLs) are identifiers that you can use to find information. The main difference between an IP address and a URL is what they point to.

An IP address points to a computer – either a computer's physical hardware or a virtual computer as in the case of shared hosting.

In comparison, a URL is a distinct address on the internet for a web page, a PDF file or any other file format available. A typical URL contains the:

* protocol to be used, for example, HTTP and FTP
* domain name or IP address
* path
* optional fragment identifier (typically used to identify a portion of a document).

Internet protocol (IP) addresses

Each computer on the internet has a unique address that identifies it as a **node** on the internet, so that information can be sent to it. This unique address, which is similar to your home address, is really a number called the internet protocol (IP) address.

* An IP address has two parts. The first part of an IP address is used as a network address and the second part is the host address. For example, the IP address 192.168.1.34 can be divided into two parts (see Figure 3.13):
  – 192.168.1. refers to the network
  – 34 refers to the host.
* The network part of the address is similar to a house address, number or postcode. The host part of the address is similar to the name of the person on the mail who lives at that address. In essence, an IP address is a unique number used to identify a device or machine on the internet.

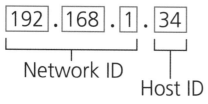

Figure 3.13 Parts of an IP address

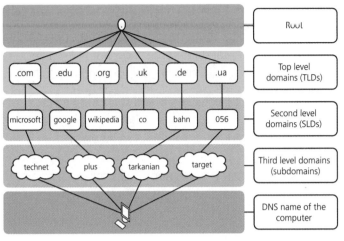

Figure 3.14 Domain name system (tree structure)

Figure 3.15 DNS hierarchical naming structure

The **domain name system (DNS)** was developed to allow users to refer to hosts by names. This system divides the internet into a series of domains. It uses a hierarchical naming system or tree structure to represent a host (see Figure 3.14).

A domain is divided into second-level domains, which further subdivide into third-level domains, and so on. A host is therefore named for the largest domain to which it belongs, then for any subdomains within the largest domain, and finally for the unique host name. Domain names are easier to remember because they are alphabetic.

The Internet operates with IP addresses. Therefore, every time you use a domain name, a DNS service must translate the name into the corresponding IP address to allow the internet host to find another internet host. For example, the domain name 'www.example.com' might translate to 198.103.232.4.

At the top level, there are domains corresponding to educational institutions (edu), commercial entities (com), public organisations (org), governmental bodies (gov) and the military (mil). Individual organisations each get their name at the second level of the naming hierarchy. For example, Microsoft has 'Microsoft.com' and the Association of Curriculum Developers has 'ASCD.org'.

Departments within an organisation will be at the third level of the hierarchy, for example, 'shop.ASCD.org' (see Figure 3.15). Sometimes a fourth level, which includes the unique host name, is included. For example, if your domain is 'fun.com' which points to your website, you can create 'holiday.fun.com', which points to the holiday section of your website. You may also have a 'Caribbean.holiday.fun.com' which now gives the name of the computer in the holiday section of the website. The complete name of a host therefore includes: the unique host name, all sub-organisation units, the organisational name and the top level domain.

Table 3.1 shows the current top-level domains in the United States.

Table 3.1 The current top-level domains in the United States

Domain name	Purpose
.com	Commercial
.edu	Educational institutions
.gov	Government bodies
.mil	US military institutions
.net	Computer networks
.org	Other organisations, for example, non-profit
.rec	Recreational organisations
.store	Retailers
.info	Distributors of information
.int	International bodies

Finding information on the World Wide Web (WWW)

You learned in Book 1 and Book 2 that you can find information on the Internet by clicking on a direct link using your browser, or by using one of the many **search engines**. Users can access web pages by:

* searching through subject directories linked to organised collections of web pages
* browsing through pages and selecting links to move from one page to another
* entering a key word or a search statement in a search engine to retrieve pages on the topic of your choice.

In the next section, we focus on retrieving information on the internet via its web address or URL.

Finding information using a uniform resource locator (URL)

You can find information by typing in a website's direct address or **uniform resource locator (URL)** into the Address field, located at the top of the browser window, just below the menu bar. A URL is the address of an internet file, and is usually in this format, made up of four parts:

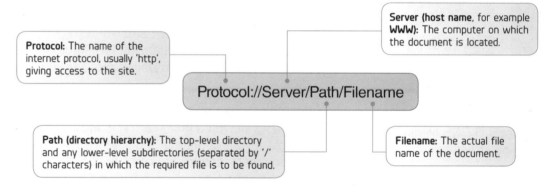

Server (host name, for example **WWW):** The computer on which the document is located.

Protocol: The name of the internet protocol, usually 'http', giving access to the site.

Protocol://Server/Path/Filename

Path (directory hierarchy): The top-level directory and any lower-level subdirectories (separated by '/' characters) in which the required file is to be found.

Filename: The actual file name of the document.

An example is: **http://WWW.ascd.org/publications/books/study-guides.aspx**

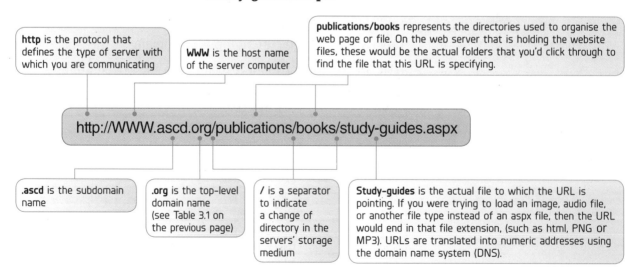

http is the protocol that defines the type of server with which you are communicating

WWW is the host name of the server computer

publications/books represents the directories used to organise the web page or file. On the web server that is holding the website files, these would be the actual folders that you'd click through to find the file that this URL is specifying.

http://WWW.ascd.org/publications/books/study-guides.aspx

.ascd is the subdomain name

.org is the top-level domain name (see Table 3.1 on the previous page)

/ is a separator to indicate a change of directory in the servers' storage medium

Study-guides is the actual file to which the URL is pointing. If you were trying to load an image, audio file, or another file type instead of an aspx file, then the URL would end in that file extension, (such as html, PNG or MP3). URLs are translated into numeric addresses using the domain name system (DNS).

Other services offered by the World Wide Web (WWW)

Some services that the internet offers include the following:

* email, **chat rooms**/IRC, FTP, VoIP, message boards and instant messaging
* newsgroups
* websites.

In Books 1 and 2, we looked at internet services that included email, chat rooms/IRC, **File Transfer Protocol (FTP)**, VoIP, newsgroups, message boards, and instant messaging. In Book 3, we will look at newsgroups and different types of websites.

Newsgroups

A **newsgroup** is an online discussion forum that allows a group of people with common interests to communicate with one another. There are thousands of newsgroups on the internet that cover virtually every topic imaginable. A subscriber to a newsgroup posts a message, which can vary from a few lines to whole articles. The other subscribers read the message and may or may not choose to reply. You can only read and **post** messages to newsgroups if your computer has newsreader software. For example, Microsoft's Outlook Express has a built-in newsreader.

Types of websites

The first websites on the internet were used for informational purposes. However, with the development of the World Wide Web (WWW), several other types of websites were created. We will look at some examples of different types of websites in this section.

Personal websites

You can create a personal website to show family photos, an online diary or information that you would like to share. You can create a personal website from scratch using HTML or by using free website-building sites such as Weebly, Wix.com, GoDaddy® and WordPress.

Educational websites

Educational websites are mainly used to distribute information between teachers and students. These websites contain **web resources**, such as course material, grades, games, videos or topic-related resources, which act as tools to enhance learning and supplement classroom teaching. These websites help to make the process of learning entertaining and attractive to students, and can also guide teachers by providing feedback from students. Many companies also use educational websites to provide online training for employees.

News, weather and sports websites

News, weather and sports websites contain both current and past news material on a wide range of topics. Many sites are linked to television networks and may provide a live stream. These websites provide an avenue for individuals to access the news and other related stories at their convenience.

Examples of educational websites:

* AppInventor: www. appinventor.org. This site offers tutorials and an online book to help beginners program mobile apps for android.
* Discovery Education: www.discoveryeducation. com/parents. This site provides resources that contain high quality, relevant material for parents and children.

These are popular international news websites:

* BBC News available at: https://www.bbc.com/ news
* CNN Breaking News available at: https:// edition.cnn.com/

Here are some news websites from the Caribbean:

* https://www. jamaicaobserver.com/
* https://www.cnc3.co.tt/ livestream
* https://www. caribbeannewsnow.com/

Business websites

A business website is an important part of any business in this technological age. It showcases the business and provides information about the company and its products and services. Most private, corporate and government businesses have a business website. For example, 'The Gateway to Government Information and Services' website provides a number of government services to residents and non-residents of Jamaica. Similarly, the 'ttconnect' website provides similar services for Trinidad and Tobago residents.

Web portals

A web portal provides links to a wide variety of internet services (information, data and resources) from a single location. A portal provides services such as:

* search engine(s),
* email and other communication services
* links to other related sites
* news, sports and weather
* yellow pages
* stock quotes.

Photo-sharing websites

Websites such as Flickr.com offer free photo-sharing and hosting services. Also, many digital cameras, photo printers and smartphones come with software to create digital photo slide shows that can be uploaded to the web.

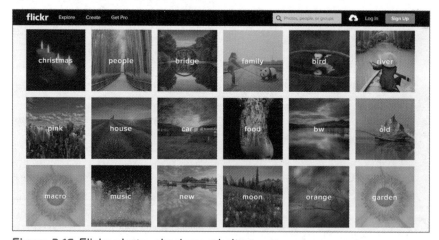

Figure 3.16 Flickr photo-sharing website

Blogs

A **blog**, short for 'web log', is a website that allows people or groups to post items on the internet. It features a diary or journal type commentary and links to articles on other websites, usually as a list of entries in reverse chronological order. Blogs contain the interests and opinions of the author, called a blogger. Typical blog items consist of text, hypertext, images and links (to other web pages, as well as to video, audio and other files). A person needs to register on a blogging site to become a blogger and set up a blog.

Blogs can be used as online journals, personal diaries or places to put forward personal views on interests such as sports, politics or gardening – the possibilities are endless. Blogs can be used in education as a way of getting students' views on various topics. For example, teachers can use blogs to collaborate with students by facilitating online group discussions and activities. An example of one of the most popular Caribbean blogs is the Caribbean Beat Magazine. This blogs deals with Caribbean people, places, culture and lifestyles. Many individuals use this blog to put forward their views on different cultural issues in the Caribbean.

Wikis

A wiki is a website where users can organise, add, remove and update content on the site using their own web browser. The term 'wiki' comes from the Hawaiian phrase, 'wiki wiki', which means 'super-fast'. A wiki allows a group of people to collaboratively develop a website with no knowledge of HTML or other markup languages. Anyone can edit pages in a wiki or create new wiki pages simply by creating a new link with the name of the page. Pages are connected with hyperlinks.

Wikis can contain articles, videos, photos and various types of documents. Many companies setup wikis for employees to collaborate on projects or access company information. Teachers allow students to use a wiki to work collaboratively on assignments. One of the best known wikis is Wikipedia, a free encyclopaedia in many languages that anyone can edit. Popular software that can be used to create wikis are Tiki Wiki CMS Groupware, MediaWiki and DokuWiki.

Figure 3.17 About LinkedIn page

Community-building websites (social websites, forum websites and sharing websites)

Community-building websites build online communities of people who want to interact with other people socially or meet people who share their interests. Some of the best-known websites of this type are facebook.com, LinkedIn.com (see Figure 3.17) and Myspace.com. For sharing and discussing mutual interests, there are online forums for almost any subject you can think of. These forum websites can be a great source of information.

Figure 3.18 A mobile-friendly website

Mobile device websites

Mobile devices (smartphones, tablets, watches and so on) are used world-wide. However, one problem is that standard websites are difficult to view and sometimes take a long time to download on these devices with their small screens and wireless connections. Websites that have pages narrower in width and that take up less bandwidth work much better for mobile devices. A new domain designation '.mobi', which has been available since 2006, was created to identify websites that are 'mobile-friendly'.

Directory websites

Directory websites are the modern version of the printed Yellow Pages in phone books. These websites allow you to find services and businesses. Directories can be specific to a certain topic or industry, or they can cover a geographical area. Some examples of general website directories are real estate, jobs, hotels and restaurants.

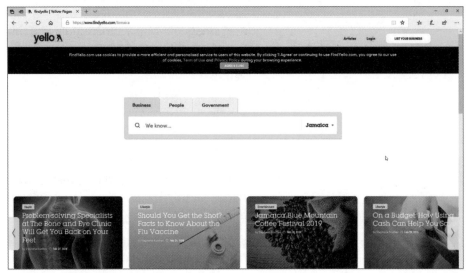

Figure 3.19 A directory website

E-commerce websites

Millions of small businesses worldwide use their e-commerce websites to sell their products over the Internet. Almost anything that can be sold in a built store can be sold online – with fewer overheads. Some popular e-commerce sites are Amazon and eBay.

Figure 3.20 An Amazon e-commerce website

Informational websites

Informational websites are those that provide information on a wide range of topics. Newspaper companies, television companies, governments and business organisations all have websites that provide information to the public. One of the main informational sites available is wikipedia.org, the online encyclopaedia. This site allows members to contribute and edit articles.

Figure 3.21 An informational website

Business owners also create websites to provide information about the products they sell. These websites can be made into hybrid sites by adding an e-commerce feature, which allows the business to provide services and sell products.

Intranets

An intranet is similar to a micro version of the internet within a company or organisation. It offers the same features as the global internet, but in a localised environment such as a factory site or an office. Many companies handle large volumes of information such as training manuals, company reports, job openings and descriptions, and newsletters.

Authorised users within a company can use the company's intranet to find information stored on it easily and quickly. The documents in an intranet contain tags that provide links to other documents found in the company's network (or outside on the wider internet). This is handled using the same browsers, other software and TCP/IP as used for the internet.

Extranets

A company's intranet that allows limited access by people from outside the company is called an extranet. A company may set up an extranet, for example, to provide technical support information to its customers based on products it sells or services it provides.

Summary 3

1 A PAN is a portable, cost-effective and secure network that lets users connect to many devices and synchronise data between devices.

2 LANs, WANs and MANs can be used for sharing resources, application software and for connecting to the internet.

3 Communications software is a set of web applications that make it possible for users to exchange data and communicate in real time.

4 Web conferencing and video software on desktop computers and cell phones lets users conduct online meetings and webinars, as well as share documents and screens.

5 Live chat software on websites lets businesses provide personalised customer support.

6 Podcasting is online audio content that is delivered over the internet.

7 Webcasting is the delivery of live or delayed sound or video broadcasts over the WWW.

8 A webinar (web-based seminar) involves conducting a seminar or lecture over the WWW.

9 Data integrity means the consistency, accuracy and reliability of data.

10 Data security involves protecting data from unauthorised access and is one of the methods of maintaining data integrity.

11 Internal threats come from inside the organisation, and are caused by employee actions or weak access control.

12 An external threat comes from outside the organisation and aims to corrupt or steal confidential information.

13 Types of external threats include malware attacks, denial-of-service (DoS) attacks, eavesdropping, data breaches and phishing.

14 Malware is software that specifically intends to corrupt, steal, disrupt or erase data or information on a network.

15 A denial-of-service (DoS) attack floods a computer or website with data, which overloads it and stops it from functioning properly.

16 Eavesdropping means to tap into a telephone or data transmission line and secretly listen to conversations or access data being transmitted.

17 A data breach is where sensitive, protected or confidential data has potentially been seen, stolen or used by unauthorised personnel.

18 Phishing refers to attempts by cybercriminals and hackers to trick you into giving them your personal information so that they can access your account numbers or infect your computer or device with malware.

19 The internet protocol (IP) address is a unique address that identifies your computer as a node on the internet, so that information can be sent to it.

20 An IP address has two parts. The first part of an IP address is used as a network address and the second part is the host address.

21 A uniform resource locator (URL) is the address of an internet file, and usually is in this format, made up of four parts: Protocol:// Server/Path/Filename

22 Several types of websites exist on the internet.

Questions 3

Copy and fill in the blanks questions

1 _____ chat software installed on websites allows businesses to provide personalised customer support.

2 _____ is online audio content that is delivered over the internet.

3 _____ refers to conducting a seminar or lecture via the World Wide Web.

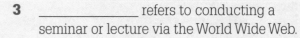

48

4 Data _____ means the consistency, accuracy and reliability of data.

5 _____ is software that specifically intends to corrupt, steal, disrupt or erase data or information on a network.

6 _____ means to tap into a telephone or data transmission line and secretly listen to conversations or access data being transmitted.

True or false questions

1 Local area networks can be used for sharing computer resources such as printers, modems, DVD-ROM drives and hard disks.

2 The exchange of data is affected when devices are moved to another location in a personal area network.

3 Wide area networks do not allow organisations to distribute work to other locations.

4 Many devices can be connected to one device at the same time in a personal area network.

5 Podcasting allows listeners to decide what programming they want to receive and when they want to listen to it.

6 A webinar is short for 'web-based seminar'.

7 Data security relates to the consistency, accuracy and reliability of data.

8 A malware threat refers to software that specifically intends to corrupt, steal, disrupt or erase data or information on a network.

Multiple-choice questions

1 All are security methods used to protect a network from internal threats, except for:

a biometric devices.

b antivirus software.

c passwords to access the system.

d passwords to access files.

2 Which of the following is an example of an external threat to an organisation's network?

a Malware threats

b An employee who intentionally deletes confidential information for personal gain

c No suitable authentication procedures

d No suitable accounting processes

3 Which of the following provides more content and programming options than traditional radio?

a A podcast

b A webinar

c A webcast

d A live chat

Short-answer questions

1 An internal threat comes from from inside the organisation and commonly occurs due to employee actions or weak access control.

a Give two examples of employee actions that may result in an internal threat to an organisation's network.

b Describe three weak access-control procedures or processes that can cause an internal threat to a network.

c Describe three security methods that can protect a network from internal threats.

2 An external threat comes from outside the organisation and intends to corrupt or steal confidential information.

a Describe three external threats to an organisation's network.

b For each external threat described in (a) above, state two security measures that can be used to protect the network.

3 The domain name system (DNS) allows users to refer to hosts by names.

a What is the domain name system?

b Using the web address 'Caribbean.holiday. fun.com', explain how the DNS system works to locate information on the internet.

4 Explain what each of the following types of websites may be used for:

a Personal websites

b Photo-sharing websites

c Community-building websites

d Informational websites

Research questions

Do research on the internet to find information to answer these questions.

1 What internet access plans are available in your country?

2 Prepare a table to compare internet access plans in your area. Include the name of the provider, the type of access (cable or wireless), access speeds and cost.

Crossword

Across

2 Conducting a seminar or lecture via the WWW

4 The delivery of a live or delayed sound or video broadcast over the World Wide Web

6 To tap into a data transmission line to access data being transmitted

Down

1 A device that authenticates a person's identity by converting a personal characteristic, such as a fingerprint, into a digital code, which is then compared to the digital characteristic code stored in a computer

3 An attack that floods a computer or website with data, causing it to overload and prevent it from functioning properly

5 A computer network that interconnects users with computer resources in a geographic area that spans an entire city or very large campus

STEM project

While using her personal computer at work, Maxine realised that files had appeared on it that she had not put there herself, after she had downloaded other files from the company's WAN. Based on her knowledge of IT, she realised that she had malware on her computer and immediately informed the IT Department in her company. You and your classmates are members of the IT Department. (*Note to teacher: Divide the class into even numbers of groups.*)

1 What is the most immediate action the IT Department should take?

2 List the steps that the IT Department should take to prevent the malware from spreading.

3 Prepare an advisory to all staff members on the appropriate actions that they need to take, in order of the most urgent first. What is the safest way to share this advisory?

4 Share your advisory with another group and obtain feedback.

5 Use feedback to improve your advisory notice.

Hints

1 Revise the two main groups of malware and how they act on a computer system.
2 What are the features of an effective advisory for this situation?

Objectives

At the end of the chapter, you will be able to:

❑ explain the terms 'software piracy', 'counterfeiting', 'softlifting', 'hard disk loading' and 'peer-to-peer sharing'

❑ explain terms related to and methods of dealing with unethical behaviours such as trolling, cyberbullying, phishing, hacking, internet fraud and prohibited, offensive and illegal content

❑ explain the term 'malware' and ways of dealing with malware

❑ describe the possible results of unethical practices using online resources

❑ define the terms 'upstander', 'escalate', 'de-escalate', 'target', 'offender' and 'bystander'

❑ find information on the internet using advanced search techniques.

In Chapter 4, we will discuss the following aspects of computer ethics and research:

* Software piracy
* The importance of data privacy
* Unethical behaviour on the internet
* Advanced internet search techniques.

Figure 4.1 Ethical online behaviour and internet practices show that we respect ourselves and others.

Software piracy

In Book 2, you learned about netiquette, copyright and the laws relating to copyright. A common copyright infringement is software piracy. Software piracy is the unauthorised copying, use or selling of copyrighted software. The following are some of the main types of software piracy:

* **Softlifting (softloading or end-user piracy):** The price of a new computer from a reputable company, usually also includes the cost of the copyrighted software present on that specific machine. Therefore, a private purchaser of a computer buys both the computer and a single-user licence for the software on that machine. Softlifting occurs when this licensed end-user makes copies of the machine's software and distributes or sells it to other individuals or companies.

Figure 4.2 Copying software from a computer that you have bought and selling to other people is illegal.

* **Hard disk loading:** Software piracy can also occur when, for example, a computer store copies a software package that was licensed for use on one computer and installs it in many computers. This form of commercial software piracy occurs when system builders purchase a legal copy of software and then copy or install the software onto other computer hard disks. These hard disks containing the pre-installed illegally copied software are then installed in computers and sold.
* **Peer-to-peer (P2P) file sharing:** This is a method of file sharing that allows normal users ('peers') to connect directly to other users to share files. Software piracy occurs when users share copyrighted works that they do not have the right to share. However, it is important to remember that peer-to-peer is not anonymous, not secret and can be unsafe.
* **Internet piracy:** Some websites allow individuals to download unauthorised copies of software.
* **Counterfeiting:** This occurs when individuals or companies make illegal copies of software and package it to look like the original packaging from the manufacturer.

Figure 4.3 Sharing copyrighted software with your friends is illegal and can be unsafe.

You may wonder what is wrong with software piracy. The main answer is that it is an infringement of ownership rights. It is the theft of the work and effort of another individual or company. The owner loses potential revenue as a result of piracy. Pirated software is therefore simply theft, and using it is morally wrong.

Other reasons for not using pirated software include the following:

* Pirated software may not contain all the elements and documentation of the original program, causing problems for the user.
* Pirated software may not have the upgrade options often provided as an add-on (for example, with an encryption key) in legitimate software.
* Pirated software may have viruses that can be harmful to your hard drive or network.

Pirated software is simply illegal – most countries have laws against software piracy. Individuals convicted of this crime can pay hefty fines or even be jailed.

All software is copyrighted, as the person or company who wrote it always retains the right to decide whether or not it can be copied. However, it is not always illegal to copy and distribute this software. For example, open-source software (OSS) is software that is distributed with source code that is released under a licence in which the copyright holder grants users the rights to modify and distribute the software to anyone and for any purpose. The modified versions may also be redistributed. For example, **public domain software** can be copied as many times as you like. Software is in the public domain when it is put on websites for free distribution, with the consent of the copyright owner. One popular public domain program is Adobe® Reader®, available from www.adobe.com.

Figure 4.4 Skype is free public-domain software for making video chats and voice calls over the internet.

There is also **freeware** software available at specialist websites such as Ninite.WOT and softpedia.WOT. Once again, this software is copyrighted, but you are allowed to copy it for personal use. In this case, the owners distribute it for free out of a spirit of cooperation, or perhaps to promote themselves as software writers.

The importance of data privacy

Many businesses, government bodies and other organisations hold information on individuals. Information given to these bodies is given for a specific purpose. In many cases, the information is personal to the individual (for example, their name, address, age, gender and telephone number) and can be valuable to any number of organisations, not least commercial organisations that want to approach you directly to offer a product or service. The ease with which data stored on databases can be accessed, cross-referenced and transmitted from one computer to the next in a local area network (LAN), wide area network (WAN) or over the internet, emphasises the need for data privacy laws. In many countries where there are no data protection laws, companies may be inclined to sell copies of their databases to other companies. The result is that personal or private information can now be used for purposes for which it was not intended.

Figure 4.5 Data privacy laws are important for protecting peoples' personal information.

Unethical behaviour on the internet

Unethical behaviour on the internet includes many types of cybercrime.

Cybercrimes

Cybercrime is an issue that has an impact on the lives of many people, businesses and organisations around the world. **Cybercrimes** are crimes directed at computers or other devices, (for example, hacking), and where computers or other devices are integral to the offence. **Cybercriminals** are individuals or teams of people who use technology to commit malicious activities on digital systems or networks in order to steal sensitive company information or personal data, and make a profit.

Common types of cybercrime include:

* hacking
* cyberbullying, cyberstalking and online cruelty
* online scams and fraud
* identity theft
* attacks on computer systems
* illegal or prohibited online content.

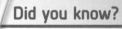

Did you know?

Jamaica lost USD$100 million or about JMD$12.6 billion to cybercrimes in 2016. Some of the crimes include ransomware, website defacement, email spoofing, phishing, unauthorised access, bullying, revenge porn and cyberespionage.

The effect of cybercrime can be extremely upsetting for victims, and not just for financial reasons. Victims may feel that their privacy has been violated, and that they are powerless. Unfortunately, as the reliance on technology grows worldwide, the cost and incidence of cybercrime is expected to increase. Therefore, to protect organisations and individuals, governments around the world have passed or are working on laws to deal with cybercrimes.

Figure 4.6 Reliance on technology has led to all forms of cybercrime increasing worldwide.

In Jamaica, the new Cybercrimes Act (2015), which addresses activities in cyberspace, includes an offence titled 'the use of a computer for malicious communication'. This offence specifically deals with using a computer to transmit data that is threatening, menacing or obscene, with the intention to harass or cause harm or the apprehension of harm, to any person or property. Trinidad and Tobago is working on a similar Bill called the Cybercrime Bill, 2017. These laws have become necessary due the high incidences of cybercrime in these countries and the Caribbean in general.

Cyberbullying, cyberstalking and online cruelty

Cyberbullying, **cyberstalking** and online cruelty occurs when people behave in offensive, menacing or harassing ways towards others using electronic means. Online methods may include emails, instant messages, tweets and blogs. Although these forms of cybercrime have become increasingly common among teenagers, they can happen to people of any age, at any time, and often anonymously.

The main difference between cyberbullying and cyberstalking is one of age. If adults are involved, the act is usually called cyberstalking, while among children, it is usually referred to as cyberbullying. In this chapter, we will use the term 'cyberbullying'. Examples of ways in which cyberbullying can occur include:

Figure 4.7 Sending hurtful messages or images to someone is cyberbullying.

* posting hurtful messages, images or videos online
* repeatedly sending unwanted messages online
* excluding or intimidating others online
* creating fake social networking profiles or websites that are hurtful
* posting nasty gossip and chat online
* gathering and posting personal information on an individual
* spreading false rumours about an individual and encouraging others to join in the harassment
* sending devious, threatening, vulgar or harassing emails from a variety of email accounts
* hacking into an individual's online banking or email accounts and changing that person's settings and passwords
* any other form of digital communication that is discriminatory, intimidating, or intended to cause hurt or make someone fear for their safety.

Terms associated with cyberbullying

The following terms are associated with cyberbullying:

* **Target:** A person who is the object of a deliberate action
* **Offender:** A person who wants to hurt someone in a nasty way
* **Bystander:** A person who does nothing when they witness cyberbullying happening
* **Upstander:** A person who supports and stands up for someone
* **Escalate:** To increase or make more intense
* **De-escalate:** To decrease or make less intense.

How to deal with cyberbullying

Cyberbullying can cause extreme distress for the victim. It can affect their quality of life due to the constant fear of being harassed, watched or followed. Although cyberbullying is against the law in many countries, it is difficult to combat because the bully is usually anonymous and difficult to track down. Here are some steps that you can take to prevent or deal with the problem of cyberbullying:

* Suspend social networking accounts until the cyberbullying stops.
* Adjust your privacy settings on your social networking sites if you wish to continue to use these sites.
* Always use a strong, unique password for every social networking site. For example, use two-factor authentication. When you enable this, your account will require you to provide something you know (such as a password) with something you have (such as a specific device).
* Limit how much personal information you post to your account.
* Do not accept 'friend requests' (or 'follow requests') from strangers.
* Warn your friends and acquaintances not to post personal information about you, especially your contact information and location.
* Do not post photographs of your home that might show its location.
* Avoid posting information about your locations, or providing information that a stalker may use to find out your location.

Figure 4.8 Cyberbullying hurts and distresses the victims, and is illegal in many countries.

How upstanders can de-escalate online cruelty

Upstanders can help to prevent or reduce online cruelty by standing up to offenders when appropriate. Speak up about negative actions and behaviour. Make it clear that online cruelty is wrong, and tell offenders to stop. Also provide support for the person being bullied.

Trolling

An internet troll is a person who deliberately posts abusive or derogatory online comments to social media or websites to provoke reactions from readers. Responding to the troll usually makes their abusive behaviour worse. The extent to which trolls participate in negative behaviour can range from annoyance to extreme cruelty. While the anonymity of the internet may hide many trolls, there are ways to minimise or prevent their abusive behaviour.

How to deal with trolls

Here are some tips for how to deal with trolls.

Figure 4.9 The best way to deal with a troll is to ignore their comments.

* Establish a detailed policy for user comments to specify the kind of comments that are allowed on your website and social media posts.
* Ignore comments made by trolls. Trolls seek attention. They want to make you angry, frustrated or uncomfortable. Although it may be difficult, simply ignoring a troll could be the best method to make them stop their offensive behaviour. It is similar to not responding to an annoying student in your class.
* Use humour, as responding with humour is not the reaction the troll is looking for from the users of a site.
* Reveal the troll's identity if possible, as this may make them powerless and think twice about leaving nasty comments on your website, blog, or social media account.
* Fight back with facts. If you become the target of rumors or misinformation being spread by trolls, you may want to fight back with facts. Discrediting the troll with facts may stop the attacks.

Prohibited, offensive and illegal content

Illegal and prohibited content can be found almost anywhere online. Examples of sites include newsgroups, forums, blogs, social media and peer-to-peer file sharing platforms. Many sites also show live visual and audio content.

One of the major risks of illegal and prohibited content is that it may reach children, for whom such content can be especially damaging. Keep the internet safe for all users by always reporting prohibited online content.

The following types of content may be classified as prohibited, offensive and illegal:

Figure 4.10 Always report illegal online content such as child abuse and violence.

* Child pornography or child abuse
* Sexting, which involves the sending, receiving or forwarding sexually explicit messages or photographs of oneself to others using cell phones or any device through the internet
* Content that shows sexual violence or materials that are very violent
* Content that provokes the viewer into committing crimes and carrying out violent acts
* Content that promotes terrorism or encourages terrorist acts.

Malware

'Malware' is a term used to describe different types of malicious software, which include viruses, worms, spyware, ransomware, Trojans and bots. Criminals may use malware to monitor your online activity and damage your computer.

Malware is often downloaded when someone opens an infected email attachment or clicks on a suspicious link in an email. Malware can also be used to steal your username, password or other information, which is then sent to a third party.

How malware is spread

Malware is usually spread by:

* downloading infected programs and files by mistake from the internet
* opening infected files received through emails
* opening unwanted attachments or embedded links in electronic mail
* using a storage medium such as a USB drive or CD that contains infected files
* self-propagating, which is the ability of malware to move itself from computer to computer or network to network, thereby spreading on its own.

How to prevent and protect against viruses

You need to be continually aware of the possibility of malware entering your computer system. Some of the signs that may indicate that your system has malware are:

* weird or obscene messages
* garbled information
* incorrect document contents
* missing files or folders
* applications crashing or hanging when opening documents.

The methods to prevent and protect against malware were discussed in Chapter 3.

Figure 4.11 Install antivirus software on your computer to prevent malware attacks.

Figure 4.12 Spam emails with attachments or links to websites can be phishing attempts.

Phishing

Phishing refers to attempts by cybercriminals and hackers to trick you into giving away personal information to gain access to account numbers or to infect your machine with malware. Phishing attempts can happen in different ways, including emails, social media or text messages. These attempts can affect the security of your devices and lead to the theft of your personal and financial data.

How to avoid phishing attempts

Phishing attempts can often get through spam filters and security software that you may have on your computer. Follow these guidelines to avoid phishing attempts:

* Be vigilant.
* Watch out for things such as unexpected urgency or an incorrect greeting.
* Think twice about clicking a link or opening a document that seems suspicious.
* Double-check that every URL where you need to enter your password looks legitimate. If anything makes you doubtful, then delete the communication immediately.

Hacking

Hacking is the unauthorised accessing of a computer system and the individual who does this is called a **hacker**. Hackers may gain access to your computer or device through security weaknesses, phishing or malware. Once they have compromised your email, banking or social media accounts, they can change passwords to prevent you from accessing your accounts. Scammers often send out messages impersonating you, directing people to fake websites or asking them to send money.

Hackers are usually excellent computer programmers. Many hackers are young people who hack into systems just for the challenge or as a prank. Although this may seem harmless, it can cause considerable damage and is illegal in many countries. The more criminally-minded hackers access computer systems for one or more of the following reasons:

* To steal important and highly confidential information
* To copy computer programs illegally
* To alter data
* To destroy data either by deleting it or installing a virus to destroy or corrupt it
* To transfer money from one bank account to another using **electronic funds transfer (EFT)**.

Figure 4.13 Hackers can change your passwords to stop you from accessing your accounts.

Internet fraud

The term 'internet fraud' refers to any type of fraud scheme that uses one or more components of the internet, such as chat rooms, email, message boards or websites, to present fake offers to potential victims and to carry out fraudulent transactions.

Some major types of internet fraud include the following:

* **Online trading schemes:** Online trading is the buying and selling of products over the internet. Companies or individuals set up virtual shops or malls on websites that users can access to view items on sale. These businesses claim to offer high-value items for sale at very low prices, which are likely to attract many consumers. Internet fraud occurs when the company or an individual bills the customer for the purchase, collects the money and then does not deliver the items purchased, or delivers a product that is substandard and far less valuable than what was promised. Another example includes impersonating charities and requesting donations for natural disasters.

* **Credit card fraud:** This type of fraud is a slight variation on the above online trading scheme. The fraud involves setting up temporary fake businesses on the internet. These businesses lure people into giving their credit card numbers in order to steal their money. A common method is to send emails pretending to be from a major bank. These messages direct you to a fake website that asks you to type in your banking details, thereby allowing the fraudster to steal your money.

* **Business opportunity or 'work-at-home' schemes online:** Many fraudulent schemes use the internet to advertise business opportunities that supposedly allow individuals to get rich or earn large sums of money working at home. These schemes typically require individuals to pay for information and material to start a business or get a job, but then fail to deliver the materials, information or the job.

Figure 4.14 Criminals often set up fake businesses to obtain your credit card details.

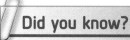

Did you know?

A leading cyber research company has predicted that, by 2021, cybercrime will cost the world more than US$6 trillion. It is the fastest-growing crime in the US and, as it grows, the attacks are becoming bigger and more sophisticated.

Other online scams and fraud schemes

The growth in online services and internet use has provided criminals with many opportunities to commit scams and fraud. These are dishonest schemes that try to take advantage of unsuspecting people to gain a benefit, such as money or access to personal details. These scams and fraud schemes are often contained in spam and phishing messages. Common types of online scams include:

* unexpected prize scams
* unexpected money scams
* threats and extortion scams
* identity theft.

Unexpected prize scams

Unexpected prize scams include lottery scams, 'scratchie' scams and travel scams. These scams can be delivered online, by telephone or by mail. They inform you that you have won a prize (for example, a large sum of money, shopping vouchers, a free holiday or travel-related products), and to claim it you are asked to send money or provide personal information.

Unexpected money scams

Unexpected money scams include inheritance scams, 'Nigerian' scams, money reclaim scams and other upfront payment or advanced fee fraud schemes. These scams ask you to:

* send money upfront for a product or reward
* provide personal information, pay lawyer fees to claim your inheritance or a large claim from a distant and or deceased relative overseas
* transfer money on someone's behalf with the promise of receiving money.

Threats and extortion scams

Threats and extortions scams involve scammers sending random death threats via SMS or email from a purported hired 'hit man'. The message contains threats to kill you unless you send the 'hit man' cash.

Identity theft

Identity theft is a widespread crime that is continually changing with the constant evolution of technology and trends. Cybercriminals have various schemes to obtain your personal information and use it to steal your money, sell your identity and commit fraud or other crimes in your name. We have already looked at phishing and hacking as two ways in which criminals can access your personal information.

Note!

Most phishing attacks are sent via spam, so it is important that you install effective anti-spam software on your computer.

How to protect yourself from identity theft

Follow these guidelines to protect yourself from identity theft:

* **Shred personal documents:** Shred any documents containing personal information before you toss them in the bin.
* **Use secure passwords:** Make sure that you password protect all of your devices, and use a different, unique and complicated password for each of your online accounts.
* **Use secure connections:** Never log in to financial accounts or shop online while using free public WiFi, and make sure to encrypt and password protect your WiFi at home.
* **Monitor accounts:** Review your credit reports and bank accounts periodically to look for suspicious activity and errors that could show identity theft.
* **Use detection products:** Use an identity theft detection product that includes identity theft restoration. If you do become a victim of identity theft, you'll be notified quickly and be able to get help from certified specialists to help restore your identity.

Figure 4.15 Always shred personal documents before you throw them away to protect your identity.

Advanced internet search techniques

In Book 1 and Book 2 of this series, you learned about several methods of finding information on the internet. In this section, you will learn other strategies for achieving better results when conducting an internet search.

Searching for a specific range

Sometimes you may want to narrow your Google™ search to find information in a specified number range, such as:

* calypso icons from the 1950s to the 1980s
* cars that get 30 to 50 kilometres per gallon
* computers priced from $600 to $800.

Google™ and many other search engines let you do this with Numrange searches. You can perform a Numrange search on any sequential set of numbers by typing two periods between the numbers without any spaces. For example, typing the following key phrases in the Google™ search field would narrow your search to the range that you indicate:

* calypso icons 1950..1980
* cars 30..50 kmpg
* computer $500..$800.

Searching for information within a specific site

Confining your search to a specific website can be done using the 'site:' operator and the following syntax:

> Site:desired website search phrase

You don't need to use the http:// or https:// portion of the URL. For example, typing 'site:bbc.com GCSE computer science' in the Google™ search box will reveal the results shown in Figure 4.17.

Including synonyms or similar words in a search

Sometimes you may want to include a word in your search, as well as results that contain similar words or synonyms. When you put a tilde (~) in front of your search term (see Figure 4.16), Google™ looks for both your chosen search term and synonyms for that term.

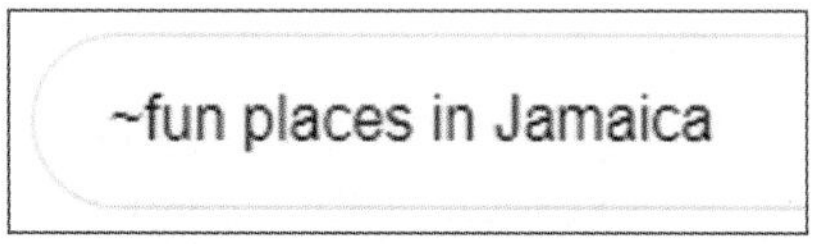

Limiting a search to specific file types

In addition to normal web pages in HTML format, Google™ also indexes .pdf (Adobe®), .doc (Word), .xls (Excel), .ppt (PowerPoint) and .jpg (Image) files. Your result list can be limited to a specific file type, with the help of the 'filetype' operator. For example, if you want to find only PowerPoint presentations related to computer ethics enter the search term as shown in Figure 4.18.

~fun places in Jamaica

Figure 4.16 Syntax for searching synonyms

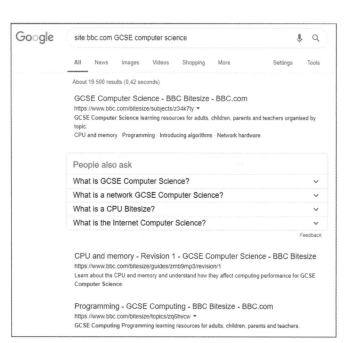

Figure 4.17 Results of a site specific search

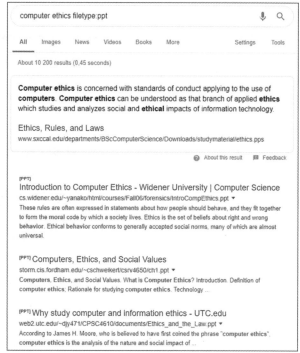

Figure 4.18 Results of a filetype search

Using different operators in a search

You can use different techniques and strategies to search for multiple types of content on the internet, such as texts, documents, images, sounds and videos.

These techniques and strategies include:

* using operators in the search box, for example: @, #,!, *, ·· , site, link, OR
* narrowing search results using: language, region, last update, exact phrase/word and a specific range).

Table 4.1 shows other operators that you can use to refine your search for text and documents.

Table 4.1 Operators to use to refine text and document searches

Operator	Purpose	Example
* (Asterisk)	Use an asterisk (*) to find every possible results of a particular keyword. For example, add the asterisk as a placeholder for an unknown word or fact.	For example: • enter Health.* in your search engine to find out everything related to health • use Bob Marley.* to find out everything about Bob Marley.
" (Quotation marks)	Look for an exact word or phrase by putting it in double quotes.	• For example, find information about "Jamaica Carnival".
- (Hyphen)	Use a hyphen before a key word or site to exclude it from your search results.	• For example, a search using Liverpool -football will display information that leaves out football.
OR	Perform two search queries at the same time by separating your search terms with OR.	• For example, pages that reference white chocolate OR dark chocolate.
@	Put @ in front of a word to search social media.	• For example: @twitter
#	Put # in front of a word to search hashtags.	• For example: #jamaicacarnival2019
AND	Search for X **and** Y. This will return only results related to both X **and** Y. Note: It doesn't really make much difference for regular searches, as Google™ defaults to 'AND' anyway, but it is very useful when paired with other operators.	• For example: Job and Gates
Group multiple terms or search operators to control how the search is executed.	Combine several search operators to narrow a search.	For example: • (iPad or iPhone) and Apple • (fitness or health) and (food or exercise).
link:	Find pages linking to a specific domain or URL.	For example: link:apple.com

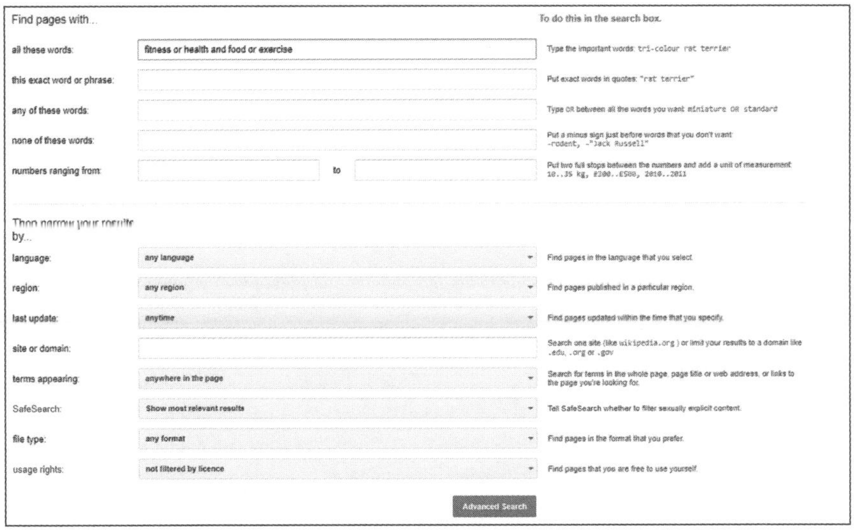

Figure 4.19 The 'Advanced search' dialog box

Using the Advanced search dialog box

You can use the 'Advanced search' dialog box to narrow your results. Fill in the appropriate boxes in the Advanced search dialog box shown in Figure 4.19.

Summary 4

1. Software piracy is the unauthorised copying, use or sale of software that is copyrighted and is not public domain software or freeware. Some of the main types of software piracy are licensed-user duplication for unlicensed users, pre-installed piracy in a store, internet piracy and counterfeiting.

2. Cybercrimes are crimes directed at computers or other devices, (for example, hacking), and where computers or other devices are integral to the offence. Common types of cybercrime include hacking, cyberbullying or cyberstalking, online scams and fraud, identity theft, attacks on computer systems and illegal or prohibited online content.

3. Cybercriminals are individuals or teams of people who use technology to commit malicious activities on digital systems or networks with the intention of stealing sensitive company information or personal data to make a profit.

4. Cyberbullying or cyberstalking occurs when someone engages in offensive, menacing or harassing behaviour towards another person using electronic means.

5. An internet troll is a person who deliberately posts abusive or derogatory online comments to social media or websites to provoke reactions from readers.

6. Illegal and prohibited content includes content that shows child pornography or child abuse, shows extreme sexual violence or materials that are overly violent, provokes the viewer into committing crimes and carrying out violent acts, and promotes terrorism or encourages terrorist acts.

7. Hacking is the unauthorised accessing of a computer system to access, copy, steal, corrupt or destroy data. The individual who does this is referred to as a hacker.

8. Internet fraud refers generally to any type of fraud scheme that uses one or more components of the internet, such as chat rooms, emails, message boards or websites, to present fake offers to potential victims, carry out fraudulent transactions or transmit the proceeds of these.

9. Phishing is an attempt by cybercriminals and hackers to lure individuals into giving away personal information in order to access their accounts or infect their computers with malware.

10. Other online scams or fraud schemes committed online include unexpected prize scams, unexpected money scams, threats and extortion scams, and identity theft.

11. Identity theft refers to the theft of someone's personal information; such as credit cards numbers and banking information, and to use it to steal the person's money, sell their identity or commit fraud or other crimes in their name.

12. Using a search engine to perform various types of searches can yield better search results. These include range, site-specific, synonyms and filetype.

Questions 4

Copy and fill in the blanks questions

1. _____ are crimes that are directed at computers or other devices (for example, hacking), and where computers or other devices are integral to the offence.

2. Individuals or teams of people who use technology to commit malicious activities on digital systems or networks with the intention of stealing sensitive company information or personal data to make a profit are known as _____.

3. The act of engaging in offensive, menacing or harassing behaviour towards other individuals using electronic means is called _____.

4. An internet _____ is a person who deliberately posts abusive or derogatory online comments to social media or websites to provoke reactions from readers.

5. The unauthorised copying, use or selling of copyrighted software is known as _____.

6. _____ is a term used to describe different types of malicious software, which include viruses, worms, spyware, ransomware, Trojans and bots.

7. The ability of malware to move itself from computer to computer or network to network, thereby spreading on its own, is known as _____.

8. _____ refers to attempts by cybercriminals and hackers to trick you into providing personal information so that they can access your accounts or infect your machine with malware.

9. The unauthorised accessing of a computer system is referred to as _____.

10. _____ means respecting other users' views and displaying common courtesy when posting your views online.

True or false questions

1. Cyberbullying is not considered a type of cybercrime.

2. Posting hurtful messages, images or videos online is a form of cyberbullying.

3. Public domain software can be copied as many times as you like.

4. Adobe® Reader®, available from www.adobe.com, is an example of public domain software.

5. Malware is often downloaded when someone opens an infected email attachment or clicks on a suspicious link in an email.

6. Using storage media from other computers in your computer does not pose any malware risk to your computer.

7. The UNIX or Windows 10 operating system can protect your computer from many types of malware.

8. Downloading of infected programs and files from the Internet by accident can spread malware.

9. Phishing attempts cannot get through spam filters and security software that you may have on your computer.

10. Hackers are usually poor computer programmers.

Multiple-choice questions

1. Which of the following is an example of cyberbullying?
   a. Sending friendly emails to a classmate
   b. Helping your friend with her homework online
   c. Gathering and posting personal information about an individual online
   d. None of the above

2. Which of the following might be the best method to deal with cyberbullying?
   a. Suspend your social networking accounts until the bullying stops.
   b. Try to meet the cyberbully to have a discussion.
   c. Ignore the cyberbully and hopes it stops.
   d. All of the above.

3 A person who deliberately posts abusive or derogatory online comments to social media or websites to provoke reactions from readers is known as a:

  a hacker.   **b** cyberbully.

  c troll.   **d** cyberstalker.

4 Malware is usually spread by all of the following except for:

  a downloading infected programs and files from the internet by accident.

  b opening infected files received through emails.

  c placing an infected storage device such as a USB drive with other storage devices in the same desk drawer.

  d self-propagation.

5 One method of avoiding phishing attempts is to:

  a try to contact the individual responsible for the phishing attempts.

  b double-check that every URL where you enter your password looks legitimate.

  c hire a hacker to hack the phisher.

  d click the links the phisher sent to see what happens.

6 Which of the following may be considered an online scam?

  a Unexpected money prizes

  b Threats and extortion from persons online

  c Identity theft

  d All of the above

Short-answer questions

1 Cybercrime is an issue that affects the lives of many people, businesses and organisations around the world.

  a Explain the terms 'cybercrime' and 'cybercriminal'.

  b List three cybercrimes.

2 Cyberbullying is becoming very common among secondary school students.

  a Explain the term 'cyberbullying'.

  b List three three software tools used for cyberbullying.

  c Explain the difference between cyberbullying and cyberstalking.

  d State three examples of some ways in which cyberbullying can happen.

  e List three steps that someone can take to deal with the problem of cyberbullying.

3 **a** Explain the term 'internet troll'.

  b Describe three methods to deal with trolls.

4 **a** Give three examples of types of content that may be classified as prohibited, offensive and illegal.

  b Explain one potential risk of prohibited, offensive and illegal content.

5 **a** Define the term 'software piracy'.

  b Describe three main types of software piracy.

  c State three reasons why pirated software should not be used.

6 **a** Explain the term 'copyright' with reference to software.

  b Explain the difference between public domain software and freeware software.

7 **a** Explain the term 'malware'.

  b List three ways in which malware can be spread.

  c List three signs that your computer has malware.

  d Describe three methods of preventing your system from becoming infected with malware.

8 **a** Explain the term 'phishing'.

  b List three methods to avoid phishing.

9 **a** Explain the term 'hacking'.

   b State three reasons for hacking.

10 **a** Explain two types of internet fraud.

   b Describe two types of online scams.

11 **a** What is meant by the term 'identity theft'?

   b State three methods to protect yourself
         from identity theft.

Research questions

1 **a** Define the term 'cybercrime'.

   b Describe phishing, identity theft, DOS
         attack and hacking. For each type of crime,
         state one way to prevent or reduce the
         chances of you or your company becoming
         a victim of such a crime.

2 Conduct research on the Internet and complete the table for three major cybercrimes committed
   over the last five years. List the type of crime, the year it was committed, a description of the crime
   and the loss incurred.

Type of cybercrime	Year	Description of crime	Loss incurred

3 Malware can cause problems for individuals and organisations. Complete the table below to show
   the names of three types of malware that have caused problems for organisations and individuals in
   the last 10 years.

Name of malware	Year	Description of attack	Effects of attack/cost to the individuals and organisations

Crossword

Down

1 A person who posts abusive comments online to provoke reactions from readers

2 This occurs when someone engages in offensive, menacing or harassing behaviour towards another person using electronic means

5 Unauthorised accessing of a computer system

6 Refers to attempts by cybercriminals to trick you into giving away personal information to gain access to account numbers or to infect your PC with malware

Across

3 A term for different types of malicious software that includes viruses, worms, spyware, ransomware, Trojans and bots

4 This means to respect other users' views and displaying courtesy when posting views online

7 Individuals or teams of people who use technology to commit malicious activities on digital systems to steal sensitive company information or personal data for profit

STEM project

Your grandmother who lives in a country outside of the Caribbean now uses her computer every day since you taught her how to use it. She sends emails to family and friends, blogs, joins in online discussions and does online banking as well. Recently she read Jamaica's new Cybercrimes Act of 2015 and is now anxious about being a perpetrator or victim of cybercrimes. She has asked you to prepare a quick reference checklist for her. You ask your classmates for help with preparing this. (*Note to teacher: Divide class into two groups, A and B.*)

1 Decide on the content and format of the checklist. What process did you and your group follow to decide on the content and format? Write a brief outline of this process.

2 Produce the checklist and ask your other group of classmates to evaluate it.

3 What feedback did you get from the evaluation? What improvements can you make in your checklist?

Hints

1 Read Jamaica's Cybercrimes Act of 2015 and summarise the main points.
2 List the major types of cybercrimes and write short notes on each one.

5 Databases

Objectives

At the end of the chapter, you will be able to:

- ❏ define the terms 'database' and 'database package'

- ❏ list situations where a database can be useful

- ❏ define the terms 'table', 'record', 'field', 'query' and 'report'

- ❏ explain and justify the need for database management systems

- ❏ compare and contrast electronic databases and manual databases

- ❏ create simple queries and reports from single tables

- ❏ create a database using Microsoft Access

- ❏ create tables in Design View

- ❏ design and populate a database table

- ❏ enter, delete and edit records in a table

- ❏ create a form using Form Wizard

- ❏ create a report using Report Wizard

- ❏ create and run simple select queries.

A **database** is a collection of related data about a particular subject (person, place or thing) that is stored together. Manual databases stored in filing cabinets were the main method of storing large volumes of information before computers became popular in offices and businesses. Many organisations in the Caribbean still use manual databases to store much of their data. This method has been in use for a long time and works well for small amounts of data. However, once the volume of data starts to increase, it can present many problems to the organisation, including the following:

- ✱ Cross-referencing data is difficult and retrieving information is slow.
- ✱ Large amounts of storage space are needed for the cabinets.
- ✱ Folders can be easily misplaced.
- ✱ Information cannot be accessed from a remote site.
- ✱ Data may be duplicated unnecessarily in more than one file.

With the introduction of computers and database packages into organisations, manual databases are becoming outdated. A **database package** is a piece of software that enables you to organise and store related data together, so that specific pieces of information can be retrieved easily and quickly.

Databases can be used for various applications, such as organising and storing information about students in a school, disc jockeys' music collections, stock in a supermarket, members in a club and employees in a company.

This chapter will focus on the Microsoft Access 2016 database package, which is another application in the Microsoft Office running on Windows.

Figure 5.1 Databases allow users to find, extract and cross-reference data quickly and easily.

Manual databases

Understanding how a manual database is set up will help you to understand how databases are set up in Access. Consider this example.

In a school without a computer system, all the information about students, teachers, furniture and equipment is stored in different drawers in filing cabinets. Let us imagine that the principal is looking for information relating to a particular Form 1 student. In the first drawer of one cabinet, she finds several folders containing information about Form 1 students in the school. One folder contains students' personal information, another folder contains information about the parents, and another folder contains information about students' performance. There are other folders that contain information about students that were extracted from the students' folder, as shown in Figure 5.2.

To find information about a student, the principal opens the drawer, selects the appropriate folder and reads through the documents in the folder one by one until she finds what she wants. If the folder contains a lot of information, this could be a time-consuming process. The principal may also find a lot of information that is duplicated.

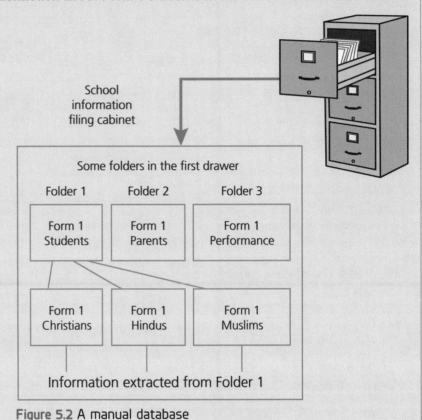

Figure 5.2 A manual database

Computerised database management system

A database management system is application software that enables the easy, efficient and reliable processing and management of data. You can use this system to:

* create a database
* retrieve information from a database
* update a database
* manage a database.

Access is a database management package that allows you to create several databases. The school just described could use Access to organise and store the school's information. Figure 5.3a shows four different databases created using Access. Each database can have a number of **objects**. An object is an option that you can select and manipulate. In this book, the objects in Access that we will look at are tables, forms, queries and reports.

A **table** is the basic unit of a database. It is a collection of related data about a specific subject. A table is divided into rows and columns. Each **row** holds a **record** and each **column** represents a unique field. A **field** is an area reserved for each piece of individual data (each data item) such as ID, Surname, Firstname and DOB (Date of Birth) as shown in Figure 5.4.

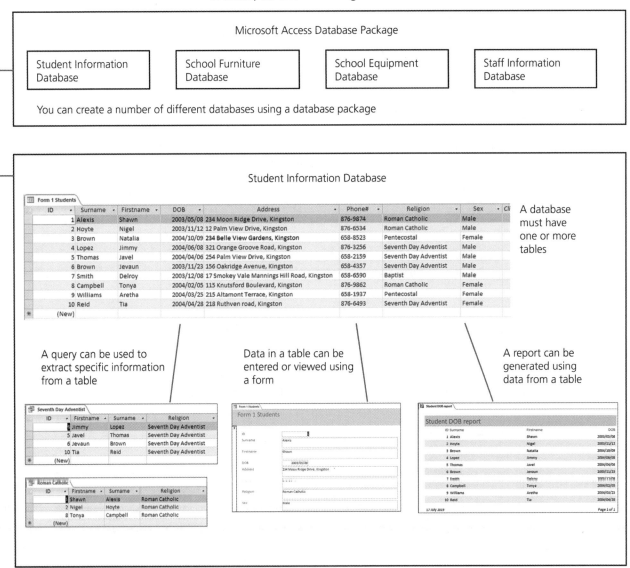

Figure 5.3a Some objects contained in a database

To extract information from tables you need to create queries. A **query** is a method of storing and answering questions (questioning) about information in a database. For example, you can create queries to extract all the Seventh Day Adventists and Roman Catholics from the Form 1 Students table, as shown in Figure 5.3a. You can also create queries that would require using two tables to get the information. For example, by linking the Form 1 Students table with the Form 1 Parents table using a common field (ID field) you could find out the names of all the students whose parents are engineers (Figure 5.3b).

The information in a table or query can be entered, viewed or printed in different formats other than rows and columns by using the **form object**. You can also generate **reports** to display the information from a table or query in a customised format. These are just a few of the many things that are possible with a database package.

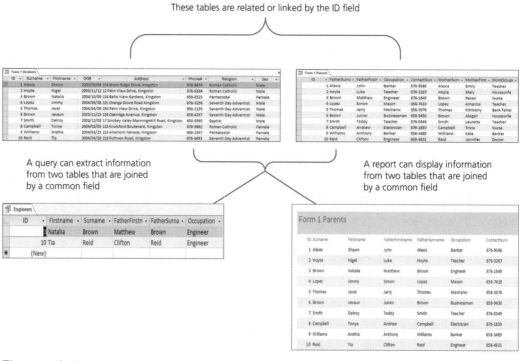

Figure 5.3b Queries can extract information from a database

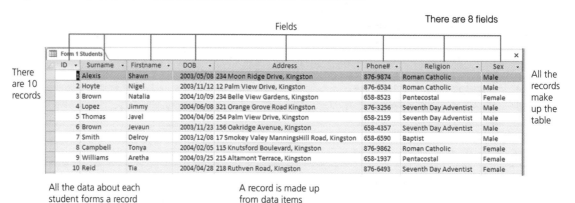

Figure 5.4 Elements of a table

Starting Access

Follow these steps to start Access.

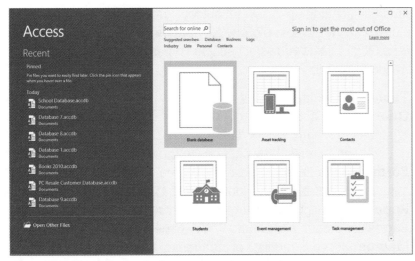

Figure 5.5 The Microsoft Access opening screen

1 Click on the **Start button**.

2 Select **Access** from the Recently used applications menu.

Or

Select **Access 2016** from the list of programs displayed.

On entering Access, you will see an opening screen showing the available templates (see Figure 5.5). This screen provides several options to help you create your own databases. You can use the templates available or search for additional ones online. These templates can be quite helpful for particular applications, but you nearly always have to tailor the database template to your own requirements. You can also either create a new blank database (without help) or open an existing one. In this chapter, you are going to learn how to create a database and about some ways it can be used.

Creating a database

1 Select the **Blank desktop database option** in the Access opening screen (see Figure 5.5).

2 The File Name dialog box appears, as shown in Figure 5.6.

3 Type an appropriate name for the new database. Database names should be meaningful so that the database can be easily accessed by users at a later date.

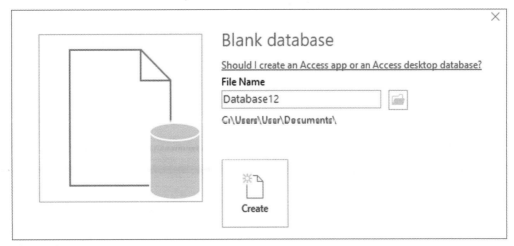

Figure 5.6 Blank desktop database File Name dialog box

In the blank database screen shown in Figure 5.7, a Navigation pane appears on the left. This pane controls the navigation within a particular database.

A database is made up of several objects, grouped into a single file. The down arrow at the top of the Navigation pane (to the right of All Access Objects) lets you select specific types of objects. The full list of objects is as follows:

* **Tables**, for holding the raw data
* **Queries**, for extracting part of the raw data to produce dynasets, which are dynamic sets of data that can change each time the query is run to reflect any changes to the data in the tables
* **Forms**, for displaying data on the screen (either in a table or from a query) in user-friendly layouts
* **Reports**, for using as output files, ready for printing
* **Pages**, for creating or editing WWW pages
* **Macros**, for providing lists of commands to perform particular functions
* **Modules**, for performing tailor-made functions not generally available, written in code by expert users in a programming language called Access Basic.

As you use the different objects, the tabs on the Ribbon change.

1   Click on the **down single arrow** on the left to show or hide the different objects available.

2   Click on the **double arrows** at the top of the Navigation pane to view the objects created.

> ### Note!
> The objects are accessed from the Navigation pane. Pages, Macros and Modules are not explained in this chapter.

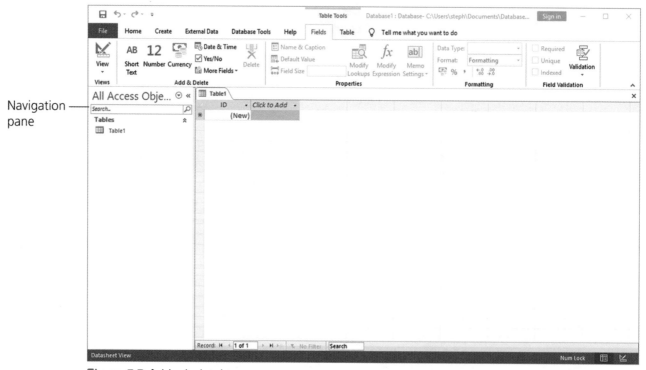

Navigation pane

Figure 5.7 A blank database

Access tables

With database management systems, you need to create your tables before you can enter data. Access makes creating tables extremely easy. In fact, when you create a database, Access creates your first table for you and calls it Table1 (see Figure 5.7).

You can create a table using either of the two methods:

* **Datasheet View:** You enter data into the datasheet grid, which consists of rows and columns labelled 'Field 1', 'Field 2', 'Field 3', and so on. Access will determine the data type based on the data you enter.
* **Design View:** This method enables you to create a table from scratch by personally identifying the characteristics of the table.

In this Student's Book, we will create a table using the Design View method.

Creating a table in Design View

Follow these steps to create a table in Design View:

1   Open the database.

2   Click on the **Create tab**.

3   Select **Table Design** from the Tables group.

The Table Design View window will appear, as shown in Figure 5.8.

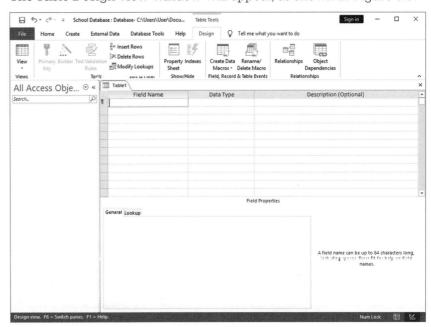

Figure 5.8 The Table Design View window

Defining fields in the table

The Table Design View window shows these four columns:

* The Row selector enables you to select the row in which you wish to enter, change or delete information, by using the mouse or the up and down arrow keys.
* The Field Name column is where you type in a field name.
* The Data Type column lets you select an appropriate data type from a drop-down list. When you have selected a data type, the Field Properties pane appears at the bottom of the window. Access provides default field properties that are suitable for many applications, but you can change these if necessary. Table 5.1 lists three data types and their descriptions.
* The Description column is to type a short description of the field.

Figure 5.9 shows the field names for the Form 1 Students table and their selected data types.

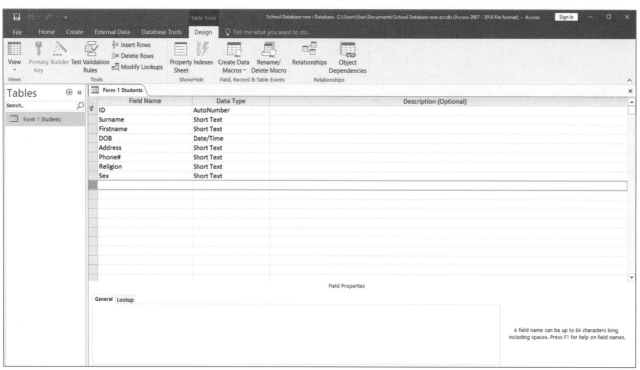

Figure 5.9 Field name and data type

If your data consists of numbers only (and no spaces, dashes or so on), then choose Number. If your data consists only of letters (Surname, First Name, Religion, Sex) or a combination of letters and numbers, or numbers and special characters (addresses, phone number, occupation) then accept the default data type, Short Text. To store dates (date of birth, date received) in different formats, select Date/Time and choose the desired format from the field properties box.

Table 5.1 Data types and their descriptions

Data type	Description
Short Text	Alphabetic, alphanumeric, numeric and special characters can be stored. A number stored in a text field cannot be used in a calculation. A Short Text field can hold up to 255 characters.
Long Text	Large amounts of alphanumeric data (sentences and paragraphs) can be stored. A Long Text field can store up to about 1 gigabyte (GB) of data, but controls to display a long text are limited to the first 64 000 characters.
Number	Only a number, a decimal point and a plus or minus sign can be contained. The Number data type can be used in calculations.
Date/Time	One of several different formats of date and/or time can be used.
AutoNumber	A unique value that Access generates for each new record.

Adding fields to a table in Design View

Follow these steps to add fields to a table in Design View:

1   Type a field name in the Field Name column.

2   Press the **Tab key** or use the mouse to move to the Data Type column.

3   Select a data type from the drop-down list.

4   Move to the Description column and type a short description of the information that will be held in the field.

5   Once you have done this for all the fields, close the table window.

6   The Save As dialog box appears, as shown in Figure 5.10.

7   Type in a name for the table and click **OK**.

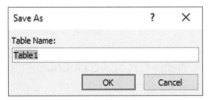

Figure 5.10 Save As dialog box

Setting a primary key

A **primary key** is a selected field in a table that uniquely identifies a record. When a primary key is set, Access creates an Index for the field, which speeds up operations. A primary-key field:

✱ speeds up data retrieval and the running of queries
✱ sorts records according to the values in the field
✱ enables you to establish relationships between tables, so that tables can be joined.

If you create a table using the Table option, Access creates a primary key with the AutoNumber data type.

Activity 1

The manager of Hitters Cricket Club wants to move away from the manual method of record-keeping to a computerised method. He decides to place the information about the members into a database. You are required to do the following:

1 Create a database called 'Club Information'.

2 Create a table called 'Members' within that database, with the structure shown in Table 5.2.

3 Define 'Memno' as the primary-key field.

Table 5.2 Members' information structure

Field name	Data type	Description
Memno	AutoNumber	The number used to identify each member
Surname	Short Text	The surname of a member
First Name	Short Text	The first name of a member
DOB	Date/Time	Date of birth of a member
Address	Short Text	Address of a member
Phone Number	Short Text	Phone contact number of a member
Religion	Short Text	The religious belief of a member

Here is how it is done.

1 Create the 'Club Information' database.

   a Open the Access program (the Access opening screen appears as shown in Figure 5.5 on page 73).
   b Check the 'Blank desktop database' icon.
   c The File Name dialog box appears as shown in Figure 5.6 on page 73.
   d Type 'Club Information' in the File Name box and click **Create**.
   e The 'Club Information' database will be created.

2 Create the 'Members' table.

   a Select the table automatically created as Table 1.
   b Select **Design View** from the Views group in the Fields tab.
   c The Save As dialog box appears.
   d Type the name 'Members'. Click on **OK**.
   e The Table Design View window appears, as shown in Figure 5.8 on page 75.

Activity 1 continued

3 Place the cursor in the Field Name column in the first row.

  a Replace the default field with 'Memno' into the column. Access automatically assigns the data type as AutoNumber.

  b Move to the 'Description' column. Type 'The number used to identify each member'.

  c Move to the second row and enter the field name, data type and description for the second field.

  d Do likewise for all the remaining fields.

  e Save the table structure.

4 Close the Design View window.

5 The Save changes box appears (see Figure 5.11). Click **Yes**.

The complete structure for the 'Members' table is displayed in Figure 5.12.

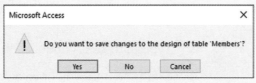

Figure 5.11 The Save Changes option box

Field Name	Data Type	Description (Optional)
Memno	AutoNumber	The number to identify each member
Surname	Short Text	Surname of a member
First Name	Short Text	First name of a member
DOB	Date/Time	Date of birth of a member
Address	Short Text	Address of a member
Phone Number	Short Text	Phone contact of a member
Religion	Short Text	Religious persuasion of a member

Figure 5.12 The structure of the 'Members' table

Deselecting a primary key

Follow these steps to deselect a primary key:

1   Display the table in Design View (Design tab/Fields/Design View).

2   Click on the 'Memno' row and then select **Primary Key** from the Tools group in the Design tab. Select the **Primary Key option** to select and deselect the primary key.

Adding a field to an existing table

Follow these steps to add a field to an existing table:

1   With the table in Design View, enter the new field name, data type and description in the appropriate columns. However, if the field has to be inserted between two existing rows, then follow Steps 2, 3 and 4.

2   Place the record selector in the row below where you want the new field to be inserted.

3   Click on the **Design tab/Tools group/Insert rows**.

4   A blank row appears. Type in the new field name, data type and description.

Deleting a field

Follow these steps to delete a field:

1   Open the table in Design View.

2   Select the desired row.

3   Click on the **Design tab/Tools group/Delete rows**.

4   The row will be deleted.

Entering records into a table

After saving the structure of the table, you can now insert data into each field of each record. Follow these steps:

1   Double-click on the 'Members' table displayed in the All Access Objects pane.

2   The table will be displayed in **Datasheet View** (a table appears, with its first row filled in with the field names at the top of the individual columns – see Figure 5.13).

3   Type in the data under each heading.

4   Continue until you have entered data for all the records.

Figure 5.13 Table in Datasheet view

Entering records from the main database window

Follow these steps to enter records from the main database window:

1   Select the **Tables tab** (all the tables in the database will be listed).

2   Select the table to which you wish to add records.

3   Double-click the desired table or select the table and right-click the mouse and select **Open** from the drop-down menu (the datasheet for the table appears).

4   Type in the data under each heading.

Activity 2

The Manager of Hitters Cricket Club looked at the structure of the table in Activity 1 and decided that the field 'Religion' should be removed and the fields 'Occupation' and 'Sex' should be added before inserting the records.

You are required to:

1 Retrieve the database 'Club Information'.

2 Remove the 'Religion' field from the structure.

3 Insert the fields 'Occupation' and 'Sex'.

4 Enter the records shown in Figure 5.14.

Here is how it is done.

Members							
Memno	Surname	First Name	DOB	Address	Phone Num	Occupation	Sex
1	Aldon	Mckewsi	1980/09/23	12 Ridge Road	435-5678	Teacher	Male
2	Banks	Jerry	1985/11/25	234 Well Road	445-5532	Unemployed	Male
3	Birbal	Varun	1988/11/12	90 Calypso Stre	487-5467	Engineer	Male
4	Brown	Tanya	1990/07/16	123 Market Str	324-4567	Doctor	Female
5	Chen	Jacky	1995/03/19	14 Alcazar Stre	213-5672	Teacher	Female
6	Dwight	Larry	1998/02/28	13 Rushworth {	543-0987	Policeman	Male
7	Phillips	Tia	2001/06/17	14 Renn Avenu	345-5678	Nurse	Female
*	(New)						

Figure 5.14 The updated table

1 Retrieve the database 'Club Information'.

   a Click the **Start button** on the taskbar.
   b Open Access.
   c Double-click on the 'Club Information' database in the Recent pane as shown in Figure 5.15.

2 Remove the 'Religion' field from the structure.

   a Select the 'Members' table.
   b Select the **Design View option** (Fields tab/Views group/Design View).
   c Click the Row-selector column for the 'Religion' field (the row becomes highlighted).
   d Press the **Delete key** and click **Yes** when the option box appears.
      Or
      Select the **Delete rows option** (Design Tab/Tools group/Delete Rows).

Figure 5.15 The Recent pane

3 Insert the field 'Occupation'.

   a Click in the next empty row in the 'Members' table in Design View.
   b Type 'Occupation' in the Field Name column ('Short Text' will be displayed in the 'Data type' column).
   c Move to the Description column and type 'Occupation of member'.
   d Enter the 'Sex' field using the same method.
   e Close the box and select **Yes** to accept the changes.

4 Enter records into the table.

   a Open the 'Members' table ('Members' table is displayed in Datasheet View).
   b Move the pointer to the second column using the mouse or press the **Tab key** and type 'Aldon'.
   c Continue to complete the record.
   d Move to the first column in the next row by pressing the **Enter** or **Tab keys** or use the mouse to click in the cell. Enter the data in the appropriate field.

Deleting a record

Follow these steps to delete a record:

1   Open the table as a datasheet.

2   Select the record to be deleted.

3   Press the **Delete key** (a message appears to inform you that a record is about to be deleted) (see Figure 5.16).

Or

Select **Delete Record** by clicking **Home tab/Records group/ Delete** (see Figure 5.17).

Figure 5.16 Using the Delete key

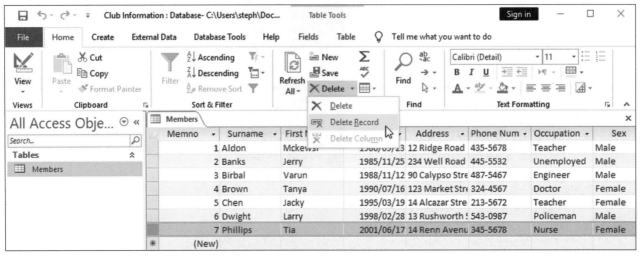

Figure 5.17 Select Delete Record in the Records group.

Editing a record

Follow these steps to edit a record:

1   Open the table as a datasheet.

2   Select the required field of the appropriate record.

3   Type in new information or edit the existing information.

Activity 3

Using the table named 'Members' created in the 'Club Information' database in Activity 1 and developed in Activity 2, perform the following tasks:

1 Delete the record with member number 4.

2 Change the surname for record number 1 from 'Aldon' to 'Aldron'.

3 Add the following record to the table:

Memno	8
Surname	Hooper
First name	Brian
DOB	03/27/77
Address	23 Golf Course Road Moka
Phone no	476-2344
Occupation	Teacher
Sex	Male

Here is how it is done:

1 Delete the record with member number 4.

   a Display the 'Members' table in Datasheet View.
   b Find the record with 'Memno' 4.
   c Select it by clicking on the Record-selector column (the row becomes highlighted).
   d Press the **Delete key** (a message appears to inform you that a record is about to be deleted).
      Or
      Select **Delete Record** by clicking **Home tab/Records group/Delete**.

2 Change the Surname for record number 1 from 'Aldon' to 'Aldron'.

   a Display the 'Members' table in Datasheet View.
   b Find record number 1.
   c Place the mouse pointer in the 'Surname' cell and make the change.

3 Add the new record to the table.

   a Display the 'Members' table in Datasheet View.
   b Move to the first empty row and fill in the data in the appropriate columns.

The updated table is shown in Figure 5.18.

Memno ▾	Surname ▾	First Name ▾	DOB ▾	Address ▾	Phone Num ▾	Occupation ▾	Sex ▾
1	Aldron	Mckewsi	1980/09/23	12 Ridge Road	435-5678	Teacher	Male
2	Banks	Jerry	1985/11/25	234 Well Road	445-5532	Unemployed	Male
3	Birbal	Varun	1988/11/12	90 Calypso Stre	487-5467	Engineer	Male
5	Chen	Jacky	1995/03/19	14 Alcazar Stre	213-5672	Teacher	Female
6	Dwight	Larry	1998/02/28	13 Rushworth S	543-0987	Policeman	Male
7	Phillips	Tia	2001/06/17	14 Renn Avenu	345-5678	Nurse	Female
8	Hooper	Brian	1977/03/27	23 Golf Course	476-2344	Teacher	Male
(New)							

Figure 5.18 The updated table

Forms

A form is a method used to enter, view or print the information in a table or query in a format other than as rows and columns. Forms allow us to perform the following tasks:

* View the data stored in tables or queries in another format.
* Add new records to a table.
* Make changes to data in any field of a record.

Creating a form using Form Wizard

Follow these steps to create a form using Form Wizard:

1   Click on the **Create tab** from the database window, as shown in Figure 5.19.

2   Select **Form Wizard** from the Forms group. The Form Wizard dialog box appears as shown in Figure 5.19.

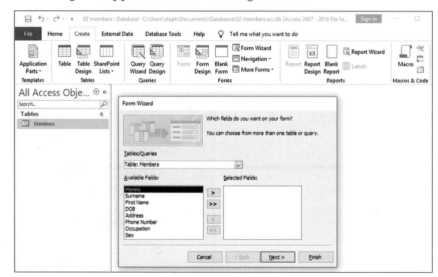

Figure 5.19 The Form Wizard dialog box

3   Select the tables or queries that contain the fields you want displayed in the form. When a table or query is selected, all the field names contained in it are displayed in the Available Fields pane.

4   Select the fields you would like displayed in the form by clicking on the single arrow to select one field at a time or on the double arrow to select all the fields displayed at once. The fields are placed in the Selected Fields pane. Click **Next** after you have made your selection.

5   The Form Layout dialog box appears as shown in Figure 5.20. You can choose any one of the following layouts: Columnar, Tabular, Datasheet and Justified. After selecting the layout, click **Next**.

6 The Form Title dialog box appears. Type a name for your form and click the **Finish button**, as shown in Figure 5.21.

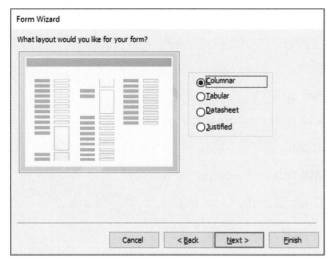

Figure 5.20 The Form Layout dialog box

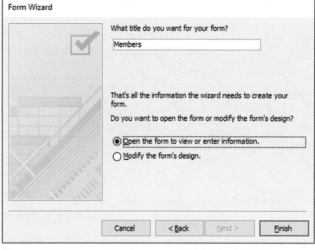

Figure 5.21 Name the form and click the Finish button.

The completed form appears as shown in Figure 5.22, displaying the contents of the first record of the table or query that was used to create the form.

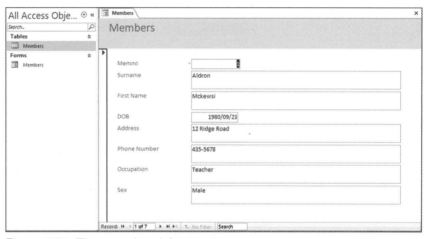

Figure 5.22 The completed form

Queries

A query is an Access object that enables you to view data from one or more tables in a specified order. You can also add columns to show the results of calculations, thus displaying data that is not explicitly stored in any table.

A query stores the questions you ask about information from one or more tables in a database. The question is developed and stated in the design grid. After you run a query, the answer (data) is displayed in a **dynaset** – a group of records that answers a query.

Types of queries

There are three main types of queries:

* Select queries
* Action (Delete, Append, Update and Make-table) queries
* Crosstab queries.

Creating a new query

Follow these steps to create a new query:

1 Open the database.

2 Click the **Create tab** in the database window.

3 Click **Query Design** in the Queries group (see Figure 5.23).

4 Click **OK**. The Show Table dialog box shown in Figure 5.24 appears, with the query grid.

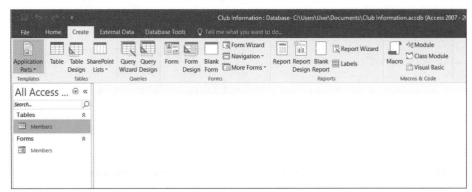

Figure 5.23 The Queries group in the Create tab

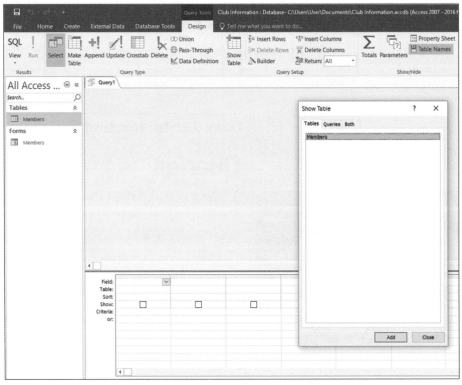

Figure 5.24 The New Query dialog box and the Show Table dialog box

Adding tables to a query

The Show Table dialog box enables you to select (add) the tables that contain the data you wish to include in the new query. Follow these steps to add tables to a query:

1 Select the table(s) from the list in the Tables tab (see Figure 5.24).

2 Click **Add** to add them to the upper part of the Query design grid.

3 Click **Close**.

Removing a table from a query

Follow these steps to remove a table from a query:

1 Select the table from the Query design grid.

2 Right-click the mouse (a drop-down menu appears).

3 Select **Remove Table**.

Working with a select query

Figure 5.25 shows a Select-query design window. The top part of the pane holds the table(s) and their relationship(s). The bottom part of the pane is the **Query by example grid (QBE)** or **Design grid**, consisting of rows and columns. Table 5.3 lists the row labels and their descriptions.

Table 5.3 What the Design grid rows mean

Row label	Explanation
Field:	Select a field name to use in your query
Text Table:	Select/Name the table that the selected field is taken from
Sort:	Select any field(s) you would like sorted in ascending or descending order in the query
Show:	Specify whether you want the field to be displayed in the dynaset
Criteria:	Specify the set of criteria used to select the dynaset
or:	Specify any additional criteria that will be used to select the dynaset

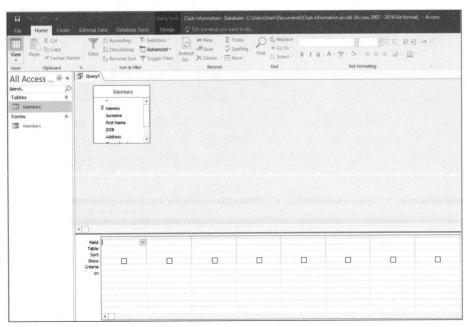

Figure 5.25 A Select-query design window

Performing a select query

Follow these steps to perform a select query:

1 Click in the first column of the row labelled 'Field' (see Figure 5.25).

2 Click on the arrow in the box. A drop-down list appears showing the name of each table, followed by all its fields. The tables and fields are listed in the order in which they were entered.

3 Select the desired field for that column. The table from which the field was taken appears in the 'Table' row.

4 Move to the other columns and select the other fields you want displayed as part of the query as shown in Figure 5.26.

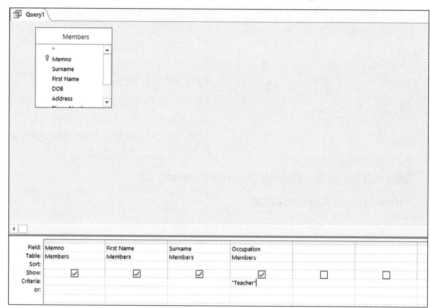

Figure 5.26 Creating a query

Sorting the results

Follow these steps to sort the results:

1 Click in the 'Sort' row in the column appropriate to the field on which you want to sort (a drop-down list appears).

2 Select the **Ascending** or **Descending option** as appropriate.

Showing fields in the results

The 'Show' row contains a check box in each column. If you would like the field in a column to be displayed, check the box.

Specifying the criteria for your query

You can use a select query to view specific data, reorganise data and calculate data. To specify selection criteria, enter a value or expression in the appropriate column or columns in the 'Criteria' row. A criterion can contain values or expressions, which can be combined with:

* the relational operators >, <, >=, <=, = and <>
* functions such as ADD, OR, NOT and BETWEEN.

You can apply these to date or number fields to find records within a designated range.

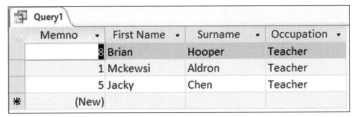

Figure 5.27 Results from the query

Running a query

The Run command is an instruction to the database to perform the operations specified in your query. Click the **Run button** [! Run] on the Design tab in the Results group. Figure 5.27 shows the result of the query.

Reports

Reports organise and group information from tables and queries, and format the data to make it suitable for online viewing or for printing from the database.

Creating a report using the Report Wizard

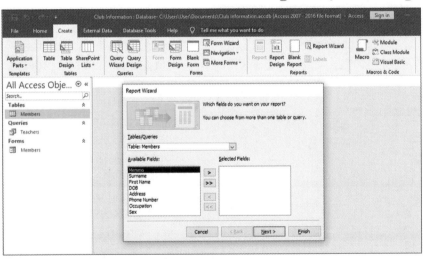

Figure 5.28 Report Wizard dialog box

The quickest and easiest method of creating a report is by using the Report Wizard. Follow these steps:

1 In the database window click the **Create tab**.

2 Select the **Report Wizard option**. The Report Wizard dialog box appears and takes you through a series of options (Figure 5.28).

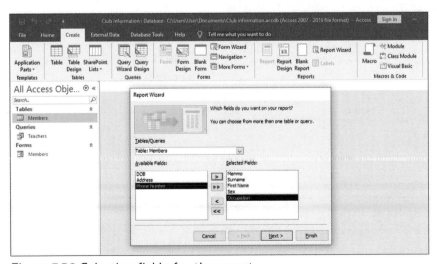

Figure 5.29 Selecting fields for the report

3 Select the tables or queries that contain the fields you want in the report by moving them from the Available Fields window to the Selected Fields window. Do this by double clicking on the **field name** or clicking on the **single right arrow button** > to move the fields across one at a time or the **double arrow** >> to move all the fields at once. When all the fields are selected (Figure 5.29), click **Next** to move to the next screen.

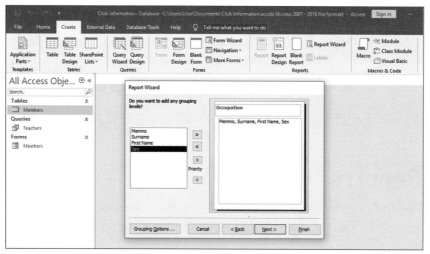

Figure 5.30 Choosing a grouping level

4 The next option in the Report Wizard (Figure 5.30) lets you group your records. For example, in the 'Members' table, you can group the records according to Occupation. You can have more than one grouping level. Use the Priority button to change the order when there is more than one grouping level. Click the **Next button** to move to the next screen.

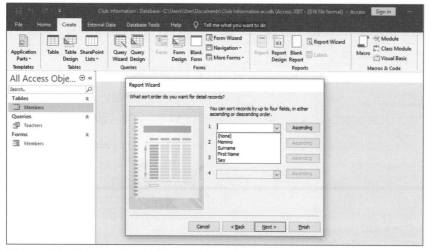

Figure 5.31 Sort option in Report Wizard

5 The Sort order dialog box appears (Figure 5.31). If the records need to be sorted, you can set the sort order here. You can sort up to four fields in either ascending or descending order. Select the field to sort and then click the **A–Z sort button** to choose the ascending or descending order. Click the **Next button** to move to the next screen.

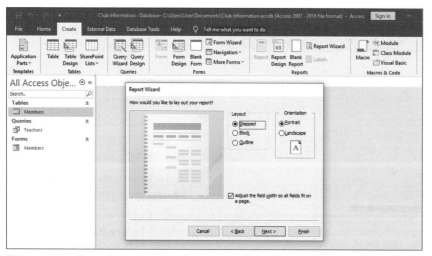

Figure 5.32 Page layout and orientation dialog box in Report Wizard

6 Select a layout and page orientation for the report (see Figure 5.32) and click **Next** to move to the next screen.

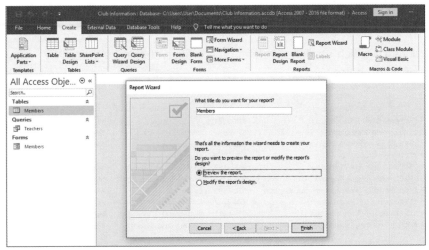

Figure 5.33 Name the report

7 This option (see Figure 5.33) allows you to give your report a name and select whether to open it in Print Preview or Design View. The default is Print Preview. Click the **Finish button** to create the final report (see Figure 5.34).

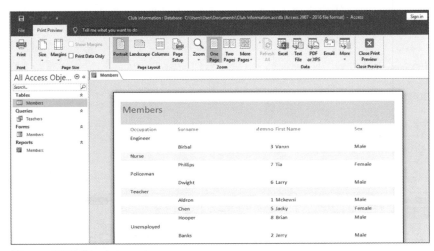

Figure 5.34 Final report

Activity 4

Create a database named 'School Database' with a table named 'Form 1 Students', as shown in Figure 5.35 on the next page.

1 Create a select query to find out which of the students are:

   a Roman Catholic.
   b Seventh Day Adventist.

2 Create a form and enter the data for the following student:

ID	11
Surname	Williams
Firstname	Shuana
DOB	5/9/2004
Address	265 Belle View Gardens Kingston
Phone #	876-4317
Religion	Pentecostal
Sex	Female

Activity 4

3 Create a report on the religious groups to which students belong. The groups should be sorted by student surname. Choose a layout of your choice.

ID	Surname	Firstname	DOB	Address	Phone#	Religion	Sex	Click to Add
1	Alexis	Shawn	5/8/2003	234 Moon Ridge Drive Kingston	876-9874	Roman Catholic	Male	
2	Hoyte	Nigel	11/12/2003	12 Plam View Drive Kingston	876-6534	Roman Catholic	Male	
3	Brown	Natalia	10/9/2004	234 Belle View Gardens Kingston	658-8523	Pentecostal	Female	
4	Lopez	Jimmy	6/8/2004	321 Orange Groove Road Kingston	876- 3256	Seventh Day Adventist	Male	
5	Thomas	Javel	4/6/2004	254 Palm View Drive Kingston	658-2159	Seventh Day Adventist	Male	
6	Brown	Jevaun	11/23/2003	156 Oakridge Avenue Kingston	658-4357	Seventh Day Adventist	Male	
7	Smith	Delroy	12/8/2003	17 Smokey Vale Mannings Hill Road, Kingston	658-6590	Baptist	Male	
8	Campbell	Tonya	2/5/2004	115 Knutsford Boulevard, Kingston	876-9862	Roman Catholic	Female	
9	Williams	Aretha	3/25/2004	215 Altamont Terrace, Kingston	658-1937	Pentecostal	Female	
10	Reid	Tia	4/28/2004	218 Ruthven road, Kingston	876-6493	Seventh Day Adventist	Female	
(New)								

Figure 5.35 The Show Table dialog box

Here is how it is done.

Create select queries

1 Open the database named 'School Database'.

2 Create the table using the field names and data shown in Figure 5.35.

3 Click the **Create tab** in the database window.

4 Click **Query Design** in the Queries group (Figure 5.23).

5 The Show Table dialog box shown in Figure 5.24 appears, with the query grid.

6 Add the 'Form 1 Students' table to the QBE box and close the Show Table dialog box.

7 Click in the first column of the row labelled 'Field'.

8 Click on the arrow in the box. A drop-down list appears showing the name of each table, followed by all its fields. Select the **ID field**.

9 Move to the second column and select **First Name**.

10 Move to the third column and select **Surname**.

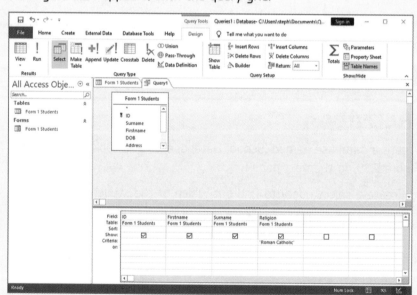

Figure 5.36 The Select query Design View

Activity 4 continued

11 Move to the fourth column and select 'Religion'.

12 Move to the Criteria row and type 'Roman Catholic' in the 'Religion column'.

13 Click the **Run button** ![Run] in the Results group of the Design tab.

Figure 5.36 shows the Design View and Figure 5.37 shows the result.

14 For listing all the students who are Seventh Day Adventist, the procedure will be the same except that the criteria will be 'Seventh Day Adventist' instead of 'Roman Catholic'. Figure 5.38 shows the Design View and Figure 5.39 shows the result of the query.

Create a form and enter data

15 Click on the **Create tab** from the database window.

16 Select **Form Wizard** from the Forms group.

17 Select the table 'Form 1 Students'.

18 Select the all the fields displayed

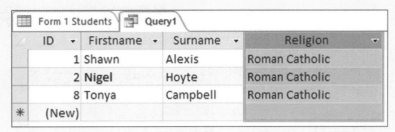

Figure 5.37 The result of the query

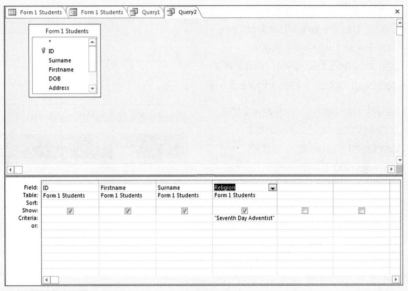

Figure 5.38 The Select query Design View

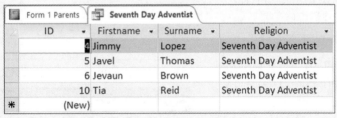

Figure 5.39 The result of the query

19 The Form Layout dialog box appears. You can choose any one of the following layouts: Columnar, Tabular, Datasheet and Justified. After selecting the layout click **Next**.

20 The Form Title dialog box appears. Type a name for your form and click the **Finish button**.

Activity 4 continued

21 The completed form appears as shown in Figure 5.40, displaying the contents of the first record of the table or query that was used to create the form.

Create a report

22 In the database window click the **Create tab**.

23 Select the **Report Wizard option**. The Report Wizard window appears and takes you through a series of options (see Figure 5.41).

24 Select the tables or queries that contain the fields you want displayed in the report by transferring them from the Available Fields window to the Selected Fields window. This can be done by double clicking on the **field name** or clicking on the **single right arrow button** > to move the fields across one at a time or the **double arrow** >> to move all the fields at once. After you have selected all the fields, click **Next** to move to the next screen.

25 The next option in the Report Wizard (see Figure 5.42) allows you to group your records. For example, in the 'Members' table, you can group the records according to the members' Occupation. You can have more than one grouping level. Use the Priority button to change the order of the grouping when there is more than one grouping level. Click the **Next button** to move to the next screen.

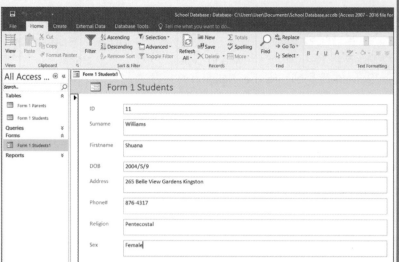

Figure 5.40 Student information entered on form

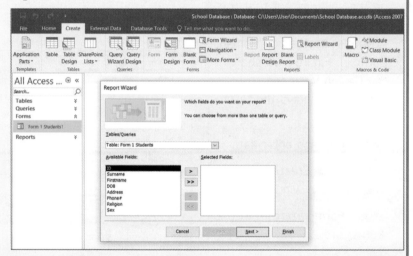

Figure 5.41 Report Wizard dialog box

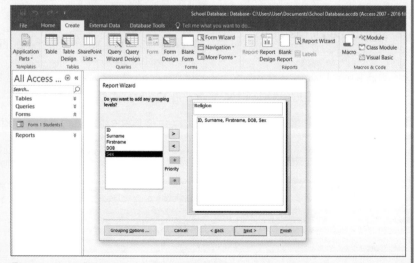

Figure 5.42 Choosing a grouping level

Activity 4 continued

26 The Sort order dialog box appears (see Figure 5.43). If the records are to be sorted, you can set the sort order here. You can sort up to four fields in either ascending or descending order. Select the field to sort and click the **A–Z sort button** to choose the ascending or descending order. Click the **Next button** to move to the next screen.

27 Select a layout and page orientation for the report (see Figure 5.44) and click **Next** to move to the next screen.

28 This option allows you to give your report a name and select whether to open it in Print Preview or Design View. The default is Print Preview. Click the **Finish button** to create the final report (see Figure 5.45).

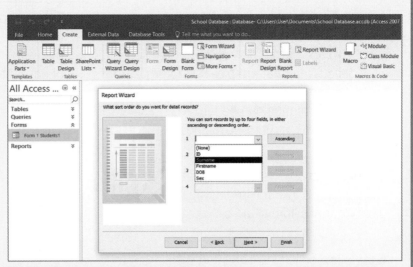

Figure 5.43 Sort option in Report Wizard

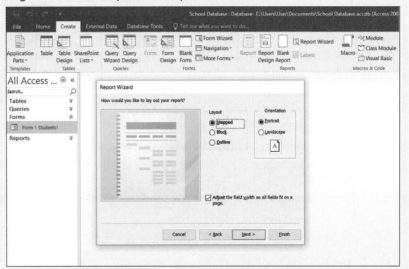

Figure 5.44 Page layout and orientation dialog box in Report Wizard

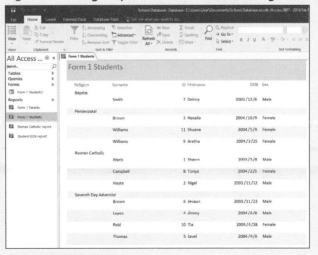

Figure 5.45 Final report

Summary 5

1 A database is an organised collection of structured data about a particular subject (person, place or thing). A database package is a set of software that enables you to organise and store data files (tables) so that specific items of information can be retrieved easily and quickly in a structured fashion.

2 A Microsoft Access database is made up of the following objects: tables, queries, forms, reports, pages, macros and modules. Only tables, queries, forms and reports are covered in this chapter.

3 A table is a collection of related data about a subject (person, place or thing) and is divided into rows and columns. Each row holds a record and each column has a unique field. A record is a group of related fields. A field is an area reserved for each piece of individual data (data item). Each record has a key field (primary field) that uniquely identifies it. A primary-key field speeds up operations such as data retrieval, sorting and the running of queries. It also allows users to establish the relationships between tables so that tables can be joined. Joining tables enables Access to create queries to cross-reference and retrieve data from different tables in the database simultaneously.

4 Each field is automatically assigned default field properties depending on the data type.

The field properties, which can be changed, determine how a field is stored, works and is displayed. The data type determines the type of data that will be stored in a field and how it will be treated. Some data types available in the Access package are: Number, Text, Date/Time and AutoNumber.

5 A query enables you to view data from one or more tables in a specified order. It is used for storing and answering questions about information in a database. When you run a query, the answer is displayed in a dynaset, which is a group of records that answers a query. There are three main types of queries: Select, Action and Crosstab queries.

6 A select query is the most common type. It is used to search table(s) to retrieve data that satisfies the query.

7 A form is a method used to enter, view and print information other than simply through rows and columns.

8 A report is an attractive display of the data or information in a table or query. It is a method used to display details as well as summary information about the contents of a database. Reports can be displayed in either a columnar or a tabular format. A columnar report displays each record in a single column. A tabular report displays all the data under the respective field names.

Questions 5

Copy and fill in the blanks questions

1 A _____ is a collection of related data about a particular subject stored together.

2 A database _____ is a piece of software that enables you to organise and store related data together, so that specific pieces of information can be retrieved easily and quickly.

3 A _____ is the basic unit of a database.

4 A _____ is an area reserved for each piece of individual data.

5 A _____ is a group of related fields relating to one person, place or thing.

6 A _____ is a method of storing and answering questions about information in a database.

7 The _____ method lets you create a table from scratch.

8 A _____ key is a selected field in a table that uniquely identifies a record.

9 A _____ is a method used to enter, view or print the information in a table or query other than as rows and columns.

10 After you run a query, the answer (data) is displayed in a _____.

11 A _____ is used to display details and summary information about the contents of a database.

12 A _____ query is the most common type of query.

True or false questions

1 You can only have one table in a database.

2 You can generate a report if you want to display information from a table or query.

3 You can build a query to extract information from only one table to answer a specific question.

4 A primary key is a unique record identifier.

5 A primary key can allow you to run a query faster.

6 Accessing information from a manual database is faster than a database created in Access.

7 A field is an area reserved for each piece of individual data.

8 A database can have a number of objects which you can select and manipulate.

9 The information in a table or query can be entered, viewed or printed other than as rows and columns by using the form object.

10 You can also generate reports to display the information from a table or query in a customised format.

Multiple-choice questions

1 Which of the following types of information can be stored in an electronic database?

  a Text   **b** Alphanumeric

  c Date   **d** All of the above

2 All of the following are problems associated with manual databases, except for:

  a easy and fast retrieval of information.

  b easily misplaced folders.

  c large amounts of space for data storage.

  d difficulty with accessing information from another location.

3 Which of the following is not an object found in a computerised database?

  a Form   **b** Table

  c Spreadsheet   **d** Report

4 An organised collection of related records is a:

  a cell.   **b** field.

  c table.   **d** record.

5 A group of related fields relating to a single person is a:

  a record.   **b** query.

  c table.   **d** report.

6 In a record containing these fields, FIRSTNAME, SURNAME, DOB, PHONENO, which of the following would be the data type of DOB?

  a Number   **b** Text

  c Date/Time   **d** None of the above

7 A primary key can:

  a speed up data retrieval.

  b sort records according to values in fields.

  c enable you to establish relationships between tables.

  d do all of the above.

8 Which field can be used as a primary key?

  a Surname   **b** First name

  c Phone number   **d** Student number

9 Which database object allows you to enter, view and print information in a table or query in a format other than rows and columns?

  a Report   **b** Form

  c Table   **d** Query

10 Which database feature can be used to list the names of the female students from a table holding information about a particular class?

a Table   **b** Form

c Query   **d** Report

11 Which is the most appropriate database data type storing the heights of students in a class?

a Text   **b** Numeric

c Currency   **d** Date/Time

Short-answer questions

1 Explain how an electronic database can help you to find information.

2 The database table 'Dental patients' has the following fields:

Field Name	Data Type	Field Sizes
PatientNo		
FirstName		
Surname		
DateofLastVisit		
DOB		
Address		
PhoneNo		
NoofFillings		
NoofExtractions		

a Copy and fill in the table with suitable data types and field sizes for the fields listed.

b Describe two queries that you may want to perform on the above database.

c List two additional fields that you could add to the above database table.

d Which field in this database table would you use as the primary key?

3 A Jamaican computer store keeps the details of its stock in a computer database. Some of the records are shown in the table below.

You are required to complete the following questions.

a Create a database named 'Computer Stock'.

b Create a table called 'Laptop Inventory' using suitable field names and datatypes to store the information.

c Enter all the data shown in the table.

d Create a form.

e Enter three (3) records of your own using the form.

f Sort the table in ascending order of quantity.

g List all the information about computers that contain a 512 GB hard disk.

h List those computers that have a 39.6 cm monitor and 512 GB hard disk.

Brand	Quantity	Processor	Monitor size	RAM	Hard disk	Price
Super	12	5.0 GHz	39.6 cm	4 GB	256 GB	60 500
Powermax	20	5.6 GHz	39.6 cm	8 GB	512 GB	95 000
Professional	23	5.3 GHz	35.6 cm	4 GB	128 GB	45 000
Kuta	30	5.3 GHz	39.6	4 GB	512 GB	75 000
Maxima	10	5.0 GHz	35.6	4 GB	256 GB	55 000
Eagle	15	1.66 GHz	39.6	4 GB	256 GB	43 000
Apex	11	1.66 GHz	35.6	4 GB	512 GB	48 900

Crossword

Down

1. An area reserved for each piece of individual data or data item

2. A collection of related data about a particular subject (person, place or thing)

6. A group of related fields pertaining to one person, place or thing

Across

3. A group of records that answers a query

4. The basic unit of a database

5. A means of storing and answering questions about information in a database

7. An option you can select and manipulate in a database

STEM project

In an effort to reduce driving infringements on the roads of a large Caribbean country, the issuing of driving tickets is to be monitored in order to efficiently and effectively target motorists who break the law.

The Transport Authority is holding a competition for all schools to help design an appropriate database for the capture and easy access of this information. The idea will then be developed further by the IT Department of the Transport Authority. The winning school will be given a cash prize and on-the-job training for a maximum of six students when they reach employment age.

You and a group of your classmates under the guidance of your IT teacher are entering this competition.

1. Write a statement on what your database will provide to the Transport Authority.

2. In a step-by-step approach, explain how you and your classmates plan to design this database. Did you decide to appoint a lead person? Give a reason for your answer.

3. Set up your database and enter some data. Run a query to see how well it works.

4. What challenges did you face in designing and creating the database? How did you overcome these challenges?

Hints

1. What are key items that you must have in your database? Ensure that you include all key items, for example, name, driver's permit number, date, type of offense, and so on.

2. Ensure that all class members contribute to the design and creation of the database.

Objectives

At the end of the chapter, you will be able to:

❑ create mail-merged documents using an Access or Excel table as the data source

❑ integrate data and graphs from an Excel spreadsheet into a Word document

❑ integrate reports and tables from an Access database into a Word document

❑ export an Access database object to an Excel spreadsheet

❑ import a spreadsheet to a database.

In the *Interact with IT* Books 1 and 2 of this series, you learned about creating documents using Microsoft Word and Excel. In Chapter 5 of this book, you learned how to create and perform operations on an Access database. As discussed previously, these three application packages (Word, Excel and Access) form part of the Microsoft Office 2016 integrated package.

An integrated software package usually has a similar graphic user interface for each application, which makes switching between applications and moving data from one application to the other seamless and simple. For example, we looked at creating a mail merge in Microsoft Word in Book 2, using a data table created in Word to perform the mail merge. With an integrated package like Office 2016, we can also perform a mail merge using tables created in Microsoft Excel or Microsoft Access. Other examples of integration include moving an Access table to Excel to analyse or produce charts, or publishing an Access report in Word to enhance a report.

Did you know?

Microsoft Office 2016 is an integrated package that makes it easier for teams to communicate, edit the same documents and plan projects together.

Figure 6.1 A table created in Excel can be used as a data source for a mail merge in Word.

Performing a mail merge in Word (using an Access or Excel table)

We have already looked at creating a mail merge using a data source that was created in Word. In this chapter, we will perform a mail merge in Word using a table created in Access or Excel as the data source. The steps to perform a mail merge using tables from other applications are the same as outlined previously in Chapter 8 of Book 2, with the exception of selecting the data file.

Follow these steps to start the mail merge:

1   Select the **Mailings tab**.

2   Click on **Start Mail Merge**.

3   Select **Step By Step Mail Merge Wizard**.

4   The Mail Merge Wizard dialog box shown in Figure 6.2 appears on the right side of the Word document you are working on.

5   Follow the six steps as shown in the Wizard, which are detailed below and on the pages that follow.

Figure 6.2 Select document type pane of the Mail merge dialog box

Mail Merge Wizard Step 1: Selecting the document type

The first step in performing a mail merge is to select the document type. You can perform a mail merge using any of the document types shown in Figure 6.2.

1   For our purposes, check the **Letters** radio button.

2   Click on **Next: Starting document** at the bottom of the dialog box to move to the next step.

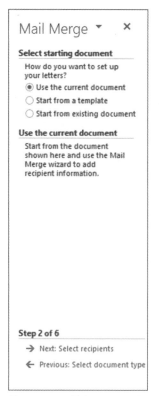

Figure 6.3 Select starting document pane of the Mail merge dialog box

Figure 6.4 Select recipients pane of the Mail merge dialog box

Mail Merge Wizard Step 2: Selecting the starting document

The Select starting document pane gives you three options to choose from for selecting the main document. You can:

* use the current document
* start from a template
* start from an existing document.

Follow these steps to select the starting document:

1 Select the starting document by checking the appropriate radio button. Figure 6.3 shows the **Use the current document option** selected.

2 Click on **Next: Select recipients** at the bottom of the dialog box to move to the next step.

Mail Merge Wizard Step 3: Selecting recipients

In the Select recipients pane, you have to indicate the location of the recipients (the data source). Follow these steps to select the data source:

1 Since the data file is coming from Access or Excel, you need to check the radio button for the option **Use an existing list**, and then select **Browse** as shown in Figure 6.4.

2 The **Select Data Source** dialog box appears as shown in Figure 6.5. Select the location of the data source from the Organize pane. Select the data source and click **Open**.

If the data source is from Access, follow the instructions in Step 3. If the data source is from Excel, follow the instructions in Step 4.

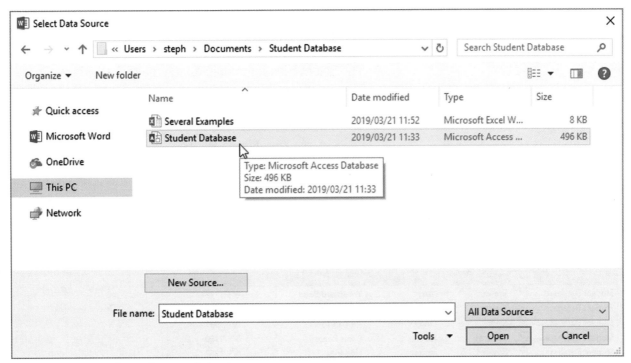

Figure 6.5 Select Data Source dialog box

3 **Using an Access table as the data source:** When the data source file is opened, the Select Table dialog box is displayed as shown in Figure 6.6.

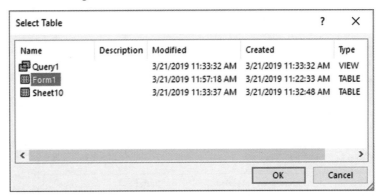

Figure 6.6 Select Table dialog box

✳ Select the table that will be used as the data source and click **OK**.

* The Mail Merge Recipients dialog box displaying all the records in the table will be displayed as shown in Figure 6.7.
* Click **OK** to accept the records.
* The Select recipients mail merge dialog box, shown in Figure 6.8, appears again, displaying the name of the table and the name of the database from which it is being taken.
* To continue the mail merge process, click on **Next: Write your letter** to go to Mail Merge Wizard Step 4.

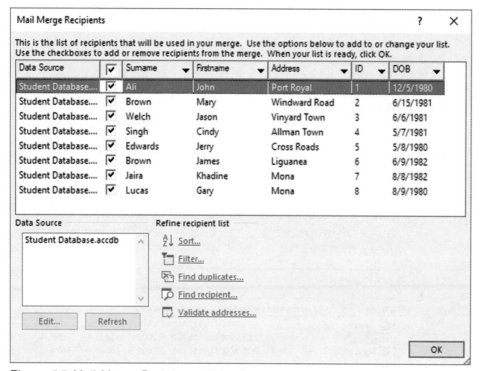

Figure 6.7 Mail Merge Recipients dialog box

Figure 6.8 Select recipients pane of the Mail merge dialog box showing the named access file

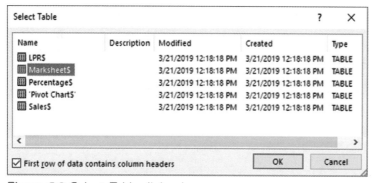

Figure 6.9 Select Table dialog box

4 **Using an Excel table as the data source:** When the data source file is opened, the Select Table dialog box is displayed, as shown in Figure 6.9.

* This dialog box displays all the sheets from the workbook selected.
* Select the sheet containing the data source and click **OK**.
* As in Step 3, the Mail Merge Recipients dialog box displaying all the records in the table is displayed as shown in Figure 6.10.
* Click **OK** to accept the data.

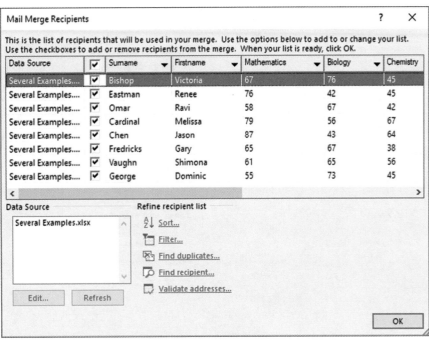

Figure 6.10 Mail Merge Recipients dialog box

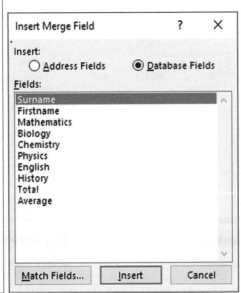

* The Select recipients mail merge dialog box displaying the name of the worksheet and workbook is displayed again.
* To continue the mail merge process, click on **Next: Write your letter** to go to Mail Merge Wizard Step 4.

Mail Merge Wizard Step 4: Write your letter

The Write your letter mail merge pane is displayed, as shown in Figure 6.11. This option allows you to view the fields for the document. Follow these steps to write your letter:

1   Open your Word document and click a location in the document where you would like to place a particular field. Then click **More items** (see Figure 6.11).

2   The Insert Merge Field dialog box as shown in Figure 6.12 appears.

3   Select the field from the Fields combo box and click **Insert**. The field will be inserted in the position selected. Repeat the process for each field.

4   When all the fields you require have been inserted, click **Next: Preview your letters**.

Figure 6.11 Write your letter pane of the Mail merge dialog box

Figure 6.12 Insert Merge Field dialog box

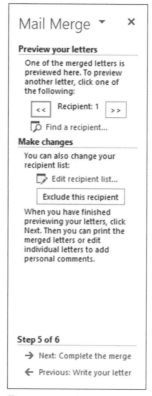

Figure 6.13 Preview your letters pane of the Mail merge dialog box

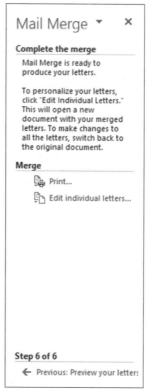

Figure 6.14 Complete the merge pane of the Mail merge dialog box

Mail Merge Wizard Step 5: Preview your letters

The Preview your letters pane appears as shown in Figure 6.13. Follow these steps to preview your letters:

1   The Preview your letters dialog box allows you to preview the merged letters. At this point, you can still make changes to the recipient list if you wish.

2   If you agree with the contents of the merged letters, then click **Next: Complete the merge** to move to the Mail Merge Wizard Step 6.

Mail Merge Wizard Step 6: Complete the merge

The Complete the merge pane now appears, as shown in Figure 6.14.

1   To display all the merged letters, click on **Edit individual letters**. The Merge to New Document dialog box appears, as shown in Figure 6.15.

2   If you want to select all the records, check the **All** radio button; otherwise input the appropriate range and click **OK**.

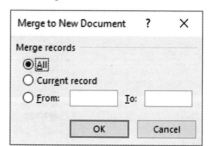

Figure 6.15 Merge to New Document dialog box

Exercise 1

1 a Type the following document and save it as 'Customers'.

> 12 Juniper Lane
> St James
> 12/05/18
>
> Dear <<Title>><<FName>><<LName>>
>
> We would like to inform you that the item you purchased with order number <<Order Number>> has arrived and will be delivered to you on <<Supply Date>> at the following address: <<Delivery Address>>. We will contact you at <<Customer Phone>> when the delivery person arrives.
>
> Yours truly,
> Adam King
> Sales Supervisor

b i Create an Access database named 'Stocks'.
  ii Create a table named 'Customer orders' using the field names and data types shown in Figure 6.16.
  iii Enter the records for 10 customers.

Field Name	Data Type
Order Number	Number
Order Date	Date/Time
Supply Date	Date/Time
Title	Short Text
Customer FName	Short Text
Customer LName	Short Text
Customer Phone	Short Text
Delivery Address	Short Text

Figure 6.16 Fields for Customer orders table

c Perform a mail merge using the Word document named 'Customers' as the source document and the Access table named 'Customer orders' as the data file.

▶ Exercise 1 continued

2 a Type the following document and save it as 'Report card'.

Report for Term 2 (January to March 2019)

Student : <<Firstname>> <<Surname>>

Subjects	Marks
Mathematics	<<Maths>>
Biology	<<Biology>>
Chemistry	<<Chemistry>>
Physics	<<Physics>>
English	<<English>>
History	<<History>>
Total	<<Total>>
Average	<<Average>>

Ann Maingot

Class Teacher

---

b i Create the Excel spreadsheet shown in Figure 6.17 and name it 'Mark sheet'.

	A	B	C	D	E	F	G	H	I	J
1	Surname	Firstname	Mathematics	Biology	Chemistry	Physics	English	History	Total	Average
2	Charles	Yvonne	75	67	78	68	75	85		
3	Dennis	Hally	45	40	60	65	65	76		
4	Estrada	Jean	85	89	69	72	75	88		
5	Eversley	Nadine	49	52	56	46	64	74		
6	Fung	Collin	68	65	72	65	84	81		
7	Govia	Leslie	79	68	56	45	77	88		
8	Gower	John	85	79	67	65	69	67		
9										

Figure 6.17 Mark sheet spreadsheet

    ii Calculate the total marks for each student.
    iii Calculate the average mark for each student.
  c Perform a mail merge using the Word document named 'Report card' as the source document and the Excel table named 'Mark sheet' as the data file.

Integrating data and graphs from a spreadsheet into a word-processing document

Many people have to write reports. For example, a teacher may have to write a report to the principal to show students' performance in her class. The principal may then have to write a report to show overall students' performances in the CSEC examinations. To make such a report more meaningful, it may be necessary to include data and charts from a spreadsheet. Moving data and graphs from an Excel spreadsheet to a Word document involves copying, cutting and pasting.

Copying data and charts or graphs from Excel to Word

Follow these steps to copy data and charts or graphs from an Excel spreadsheet to a Word document:

1. Open the Word document.

2. Open the Excel workbook.

3. Click the appropriate worksheet and select the data/chart required.

4. Select **Copy**.

5. Click the Word document on the taskbar to make it active.

6. Position the cursor in the Word document where you would like to begin to insert the data or chart.

7. Click on the **Paste icon**.

Exercise 2

1. Type the following document and save it as 'Class report'.

2. Use the spreadsheet 'Mark sheet' to create a column graph showing the average mark of each student.

3. Import the chart to the location specified in the letter to the principal.

4. Save all changes made to the document.

> The principal
> Happy Hill High School
> 26 April 2020
>
> Dear Mr John Bobb
>
> The following table shows the performance of students in my class for the different subject areas:
>
> <<Paste spreadsheet table here>>
>
> The average mark obtained by each student is represented as a chart for your convenience.
>
> <<Paste chart here>>
>
> Yours truly,
> Ann Maingot
> Class Teacher

Integrating objects from a database into a word-processing document

You can export a table, query, form or report to Microsoft Word. When you export an object by using the Export – RTF File Wizard, Access creates a copy of the object's data in a Microsoft Word Rich Text Format file (*.rtf). For tables, queries and forms, the visible fields and records appear as a table in the Word document. When you export a report, the Wizard exports the report data and layout – it tries to make the Word document look as similar to the report as possible.

Exporting an Access object to a Word document

Follow these steps to export an Access object to a Word document:

1 Open the source Access database.

2 In the Navigation pane, select the object that contains the data you want to export. You can export a table, query, form or report.

3 Select the **External data tab**.

4 Go to the Export group and select **More**.

5 Select **Word** from the dropdown menu (see Figure 6.18).

6 The Export – RTF File Export Wizard opens (Figure 6.19).

   a In the Export – RTF File Wizard, specify the name of the destination file.

   b The Wizard always exports formatted data. If you want to view the Word document after the export operation is complete, select the **Open the destination file after the export operation is complete check box**.

7 If you selected the records that you want to export before you started the export operation, you can select the **Export only the selected records check box**. However, if you want to export all the records in the view, leave the check box cleared. (Note: This check box appears unavailable (dimmed) if no records are selected.)

8 Click **OK**.

9 If the destination document exists, you are prompted to click **Yes** to overwrite the file. Click **No** to change the name of the destination file, and then click **OK** again.

The object will be published in a new Word document. To move the object to the document you are working on, you can copy or cut it, and paste it. Figure 6.18 shows the selections involved in publishing the Form1 Table from the Student database.

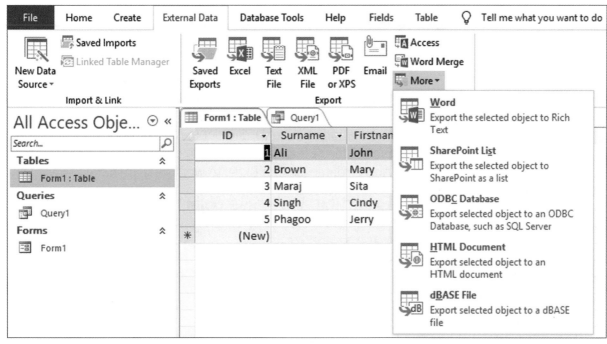

Figure 6.18 Inserting a database table into a Word document

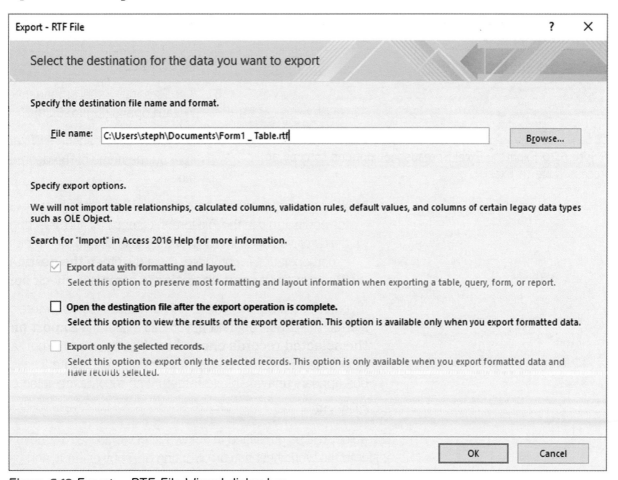

Figure 6.19 Export – RTF File Wizard dialog box

Exporting a database object to a spreadsheet

Data stored in tables in Access can be easily queried to extract information or produce reports. Sometimes, however, you may need to perform calculations on the data or represent the data graphically. Calculations can be carried out in Access, but the process is much more difficult than in Excel. Therefore, you can copy tables from an Access database into Excel to work on them more easily.

Exporting an Access object to an Excel spreadsheet

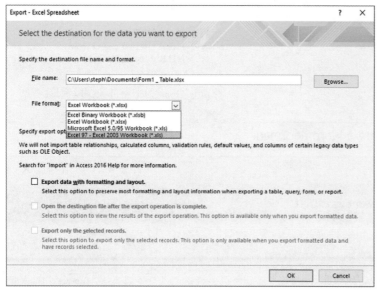

Figure 6.20 Export – Excel Spreadsheet options to copy an Access table to Excel

Follow these steps to export an Access object to an Excel spreadsheet:

1   Open the database file.

2   Click on the object.

3   Select the table, query, report, and so on.

4   Select the **External data tab**.

5   Go to the Export group and select **Excel**.

6   The Export – Excel spreadsheet Wizard opens (Figure 6.20).

a   In the Excel spreadsheet Wizard, specify the name of the destination file.

b   You can change the file format of the Excel worksheet by clicking the down arrow in the File format combo box and selecting from the displayed options. To view the Excel document after the export operation is complete, select the **Open the destination file after the export operation is complete check box**.

7   If you selected the records that you want to export before you started the export operation, you can select the **Export only the selected records check box**. If you want to export all the records in the view, leave the check box clear. (Note: This check box appears unavailable (dimmed) if no records are selected.

8   Click **OK**.

The object will be published in a new Excel worksheet. To move the object to the worksheet you are working on, copy or cut it, and paste it.

If you only want part of the table moved to the worksheet, select the contents and follow the steps outlined above.

Importing data from Excel to Access

Importing an Excel spreadsheet into Access can take place more smoothly if you take some time to prepare and clean your data.

How to clean your Excel data before importing it

Follow these steps to clean Excel data before importing it into Access:

1   Convert cells that contain multiple values in one **cell** to multiple columns. For example, a cell in Excel may contain an individual's first name, middle name and surname. The name should be separated out into individual columns that each contain only one name (First name, Middle name and Surname.).

2   Remove non-printing characters.

3   Find and fix spelling and punctuation errors.

4   Remove duplicate rows or duplicate fields.

5   Ensure that columns of data do not contain mixed formats, especially numbers formatted as text or dates as numbers.

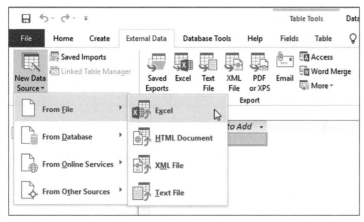

Figure 6.21 Excel option from the Import & Link group

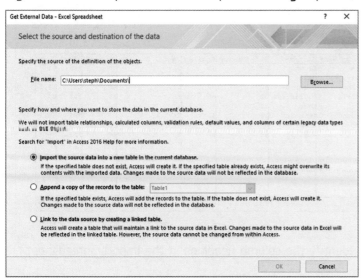

Figure 6.22 The Get External Data dialog box

Using the Access Wizard to import a spreadsheet into Access

Follow these steps to use the Access Wizard to import a spreadsheet into Access:

1   Open the Access program on your computer.

2   Open a new blank Access database to import the Excel sheet into it.

3   Choose 'Blank desktop database' to create a new database within the Access program. (Give it a new name.)

4   Click **Create**.

5   Select the **Excel option** from the Import & Link group in the External Data tab (see Figure 6.21).

6   The Get External Data — Excel Spreadsheet dialog box appears, as shown in Figure 6.22.

7   Click **Browse** to find your Excel sheet on your computer. Leave the box checked that says 'Import the source data into a new table in the current database'. It will be checked by default.

8   When you find the Excel spreadsheet you want to import on your computer, click on it. Click **OK**. This will take you into the Import Spreadsheet Wizard (see Figure 6.23).

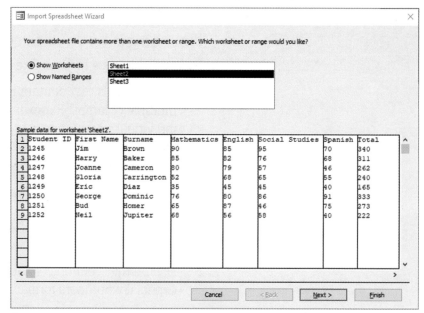

Figure 6.23 Import Spreadsheet Wizard

9   Choose the worksheet within the Excel spreadsheet that you want to import. If there are multiple pages within a single Excel spreadsheet, you need to tell the Access Wizard which spreadsheet you are choosing. Click **Next** (see Figure 6.23).

10   Figure 6.24 has a box asking if the first row in the Excel sheet has column headings, such as First name, Surname, and so on. Check 'Yes' that the first row contains column headings. Click **Next**.

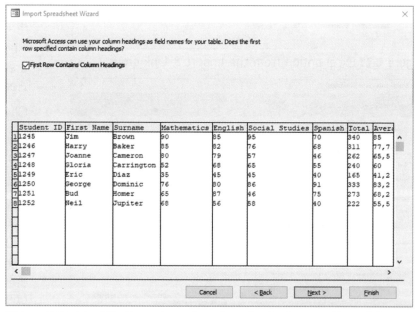

Figure 6.24 Identify the column headings in the Import Spreadsheet Wizard

11 The next page in the Wizard will ask if you want to identify a primary key. (You do not have to do this, but you can.)

12 The final screen in the Wizard has a space providing a default name. You can change the name of the Excel sheet you are importing (it will become a 'table' in Access on the left side of the page when you finish importing it). (See Figure 6.25.)

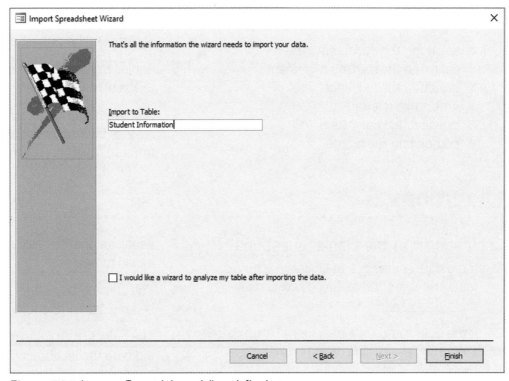

Figure 6.25 Import Spreadsheet Wizard final step

13 Click **Finish**.

14 Click **Close**. You will see your table on the left side of the screen. It is now imported within Access (see Figure 6.26).

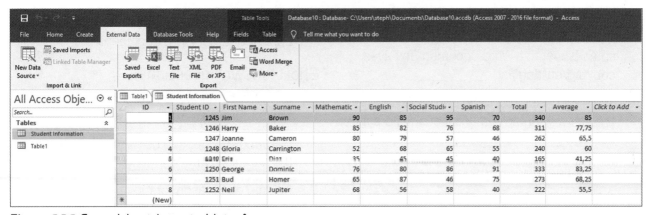

Figure 6.26 Spreadsheet imported into Access

Summary 6

1. A mail merge can be performed using an Access table or Excel table as the data source.

2. The steps involved in performing a mail merge using an Access or Excel table as the data source are:

   * selecting the document type
   * selecting the starting document
   * selecting the recipients
   * writing your letter
   * previewing your letters
   * completing the merge.

3. Data and graphs from an Excel spreadsheet can be moved to a Word document by selecting the required data or graph and cutting/copying and pasting into the Word document.

4. Access objects such as tables, queries and reports can be published in a Word document.

5. Tables from an Access database can be copied to Excel to be worked on.

6. A spreadsheet table can be imported into an Access table, if you would like to perform more in-depth queries on your data.

Questions 6

Copy and fill in the blanks questions

1. If the data source of a mail merge is an Access table, the Select Table dialog box displays the _____.

2. If the data source of a mail merge is an Excel table, the Select Table dialog box displays the _____.

3. The Mail Merge Recipients dialog box displays all the _____ in the table.

4. The Write your letter mail merge dialog box allows you to view the _____ for the document.

5. Moving data and graphs from an Excel spreadsheet to a Word document involves copying/cutting and _____.

6. To convert an Excel table into an Access table, the first row of the spreadsheet should contain the _____ or _____.

True or false questions

1. A mail merge can be performed with a table created in Access as the data source.

2. The first step in performing a mail merge is selecting the document type.

3. Labels cannot be used as a document type in a mail merge.

4. The starting document in a mail merge must be an existing document only.

5. The Select Recipients dialog box allows you to indicate the location of the recipients.

6. The Write your letter mail merge dialogue box allows you to view the fields for the document.

7. Moving data and graphs from an Excel spreadsheet to a Word document involves copying, cutting and pasting.

8. An Access object such as a table cannot be imported into a Word document.

Short-answer questions

1. Describe the steps to perform a mail merge if the datafile is an Access table.

2. Describe the steps to perform a mail merge if the datafile is an Excel table.

3. Explain one reason for moving data and charts from an Excel spreadsheet to a Word document.

4 Explain the steps involved in importing a spreadsheet table or chart into a word processing document.

5 Describe the steps involved in publishing an Access object to a Word document.

6 a State one reason why you might want to export an Access table into Excel.

   b Describe the steps involved in importing an Access table into Excel.

7 a Describe the process of importing an Excel table into an Access database.

   b State one advantage of importing an Excel table into a database.

Crossword

Down

1 An application that performs calculations to which tables from Access can be exported

2 The operation that moves an object such as a table, query, form or report from Access to Word

3 Select this tab to access the mail merge option

Across

4 This option in the mail merge allows you to see the merged letters before they are printed

5 The format to which an object has to be converted when it is exported from Access to Word

STEM project

Mr David of the Government Statistical Office has collected data in a national survey of the spending habits of individuals whose income exceeds $6 000 per month. The categories of spending were food, transportation, utilities, entertainment and savings.

You and a group of classmates helped him to set up the system to collect the survey feedback (see Chapter 2). This data is now saved in several Excel Spreadsheets, Word Tables and an Access database. Mr David wants to merge all data into an Access database before sending to the Consumer Affairs Office for analysis.

You and a group of your classmates have been asked by Mr David to help with this merging. As a reward, he will allow you to use select parts of the data in your IT SBA project when you reach Grade 10 (Form 4).

1 Consult with your classmates and write a statement on exactly how you intend to approach the merging process.

2 Draw up an action plan in which you explain each step.

3 Share your action plan with a CSEC level IT student in your school.

4 What feedback did you receive? What can you do to your action plan to make it even better?

Hints

1 What are the advantages of having all the data in an Access database?

2 Are your steps logical and easy to follow?

3 You may find it useful to create graphs to see if there are any visible trends.

Objectives

At the end of the chapter, you will be able to:

- ❏ explain the terms 'website' and 'web page'

- ❏ describe the steps in designing a website

- ❏ list the components of a website

- ❏ create a simple webpage using HTML code and Notepad

- ❏ create a simple webpage using Microsoft Word

- ❏ create a simple website using a website builder

- ❏ evaluate and test a website for accuracy, user friendliness and effective display

- ❏ explain the term 'web hosting'

- ❏ list steps for maintaining a site.

Did you know?

The first website was created on 6 August 1991 by a team of CERN engineers led by Sir Tim Berners-Lee. An updated version can be found at 'http://info.cern.ch/hypertext/WWW/TheProject.html'.

Many people interact with websites on a daily basis. A recent survey found that there are now over 1.8 billion websites on the internet. Websites are created by individuals, organisations, companies, governments or simply anyone who would like to display some type of information or conduct business.

Websites can provide a convenient way of purchasing items, paying bills, performing banking transactions, applying for jobs and much more. For example, suppose you want to make plans for a family vacation to Walt Disney World in Orlando Florida via the internet. You can book and pay for all your travel requirements over the internet from home. You can book your tickets on the Caribbean Airline website, rent a vehicle via a website from a car rental company in Miami, pay for hotel accommodation in Orlando through the hotel's website and buy tickets for all the theme parks from Walt Disney's website.

However, even with the many uses of websites and the large number of people using the World Wide Web (WWW) every day, very few of us know how websites are actually built and how they can be used.

This chapter, therefore, looks at some basic ideas in website creation.

Figure 7.1 People around the world visit the more than 1.8 billion websites on the internet every day.

Figure 7.2 Web pages are written in a language called HTML.

What is a website?

A **website** is a collection of related web pages linked together with hyperlinks and residing in a web server. Web pages are written in **HTML** (Hyper Text Markup Language), which is a language that web browsers use to understand how to display the contents of a web page.

A web page can contain text, graphic images and multimedia effects such as sound files, video and/or animation files. Websites are accessible to users via the WWW.

Figure 7.3 A website is a collection of related web pages.

Web publishing

If you want to publish a website, you must first create the web pages that will form part of the website and link them together. Next, you need to upload these pages to a web server. The six major stages in website publishing are:

* planning
* designing
* creating
* evaluating
* testing
* hosting
* maintaining.

We will now look at each of these steps in more detail.

Planning a website

The planning stage is an important first step in ensuring the success of your website. In this stage, the web designer must identify the purpose of the website and its intended audience. This will then lead to planning the layout of the website, which involves thinking about the:

* number of pages needed
* content for those pages
* layout of the pages.

This stage is when the website designer needs to talk to the customer and the people they hope will use the website to understand what the website needs to be able to do (user requirements) and how it will do it (technical requirements).

Figure 7.4 The purpose of this website is to provide information about an education institution.

The purpose of a website

Before starting to build a website, the web designer must find out the purpose of the website. Is it to educate and inform? For example, is it for a school, training institution or community? Is it to gain publicity for a business? Is it perhaps to sell or promote products, or to promote or support a cause? Is it to provide information about a club or institution?

Intended audience

It is important that the web designer has a good idea of who the audience is for the intended website before creating it. Some questions that the web designer may ask include the following:

* Who is the website for?
* Which age range is the website aimed at?
* Is the website aimed at everyone or at a specific target group, for example, students, parents, teachers, members of an organisation, and so on?

Finding the user and technical requirements

Once the designer knows the audience and the purpose of the website, they can tailor almost every aspect of the website to satisfy those requirements – from the way the information is organised to the kinds of fonts and images used. However, in order to do this, the web designer needs to ask questions of the customer and the audience to determine the user and technical requirements necessary to meet the needs of the audience. These answers will give the web designer the information they need to create a design that organises the layout of the content into one or more pages that will meet the identified purpose and requirements.

Some of the questions that the web designer needs to ask to determine which format the website will take include the following:

✳ What information do the users want to be able to find? Examples could include contact information, details of service, instructions, shopping and entertainment.

✳ How do the users want the information on the website to be presented? Examples could include written words, pictures, sound, videos or a mix.

✳ Which other websites do they use often? This information may give some ideas about how the website should look and work.

✳ Are there any legal or good practices that the website needs to follow? Examples could include using content that does not break copyright laws or not using colours that make it difficult for someone with colour blindness to read.

Including the audience's preferences in the design will keep the target audience coming back to the site, as well as encouraging them to share it with their friends.

The answers to these questions will allow you to design the website to include all the required elements, as well as how to organise these elements across the pages of the website and on each page.

Figure 7.5 The design of a website is critical to its success.

Designing a website

Design is a critical component in the success or failure of a website. The technical and user requirements help the web designer to create the best-possible design.

To start, we are going to assume that our website is just one page. We need to make sure that all the elements that the audience want to see are easy to find on the web page. These elements also need to be well organised and look attractive. It is important to go through the web page and determine which design elements (for example, text menus, images, graphics and links) make the most sense for that page. All design elements need to be designed so that they fit together, in the same way that the colours and badge in a school uniform all work together so you can recognise several different pupils as all being at the same school.

The designer needs to work out the structure and layout of the website beforehand, so that they can make sure they meet the purpose and the user and technical requirements of the customer and target audience. One tool that we can use for planning the layout of a web page is a **wireframe**.

Wireframes and storyboards

A wireframe is a simplistic sketch and/or layout of a web page. Wireframes can provide a detailed view of the content that will appear on each page. Although they do not show any actual design elements, a wireframe provides a guide for the way the content is laid out on the page. Wireframes can be done using a pencil and paper (see Figures 7.6 and 7.7), software such as Microsoft Paint or Microsoft Word, or specialised tools such as OmniGraffle and Visual Paradigm to create a sketch of the proposed website.

For a single web page, the designer will use the sketch to plan where:

* the menus should be positioned
* the menus link to on the page
* the headings, text, video and sound elements need to be placed.

The designer can use this sketch to try out different designs and to find the best way to organise the web page so that the users can find all the information they want by navigating around the page.

The sketch may show that there is too much information for a single page and this makes navigating around the page very difficult. Therefore, it might be more practical to split the website into several pages, linked by **hyperlinks**. This is called a **hierarchical structure**.

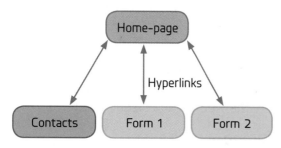

Figure 7.6 The first step in a hand-sketched wireframe

For example, a school website that tried to put information about all the classes onto one page would be really hard to use. It would be better to have a **home page**, which is the first page that you open, with menus to link to other pages where most of the information is stored. The hyperlinks in the menus then take you from the home page to a separate web page for each class.

A designer can use a simple wireframe to design the structure of a website with several pages. The diagram looks a bit like the roots of a tree going into the ground. They draw boxes to represent web pages and arrows for links to related pages of information. This process creates a basic visual outline or graphical map of the site. Figure 7.6 shows a typical example. The designer can elaborate on the design to show some of the elements on each page (see Figure 7.7). This is a critical step in the design of any website that has a lot of different elements and/or content.

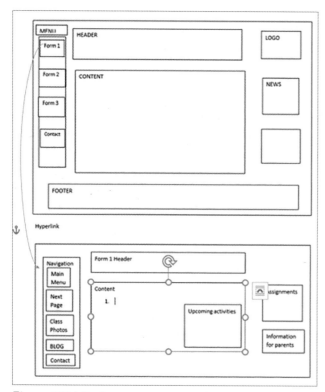

Figure 7.7 Wireframe

Moving from wireframe to storyboard

While a wireframe focuses on what the interface would look like, a storyboard focuses on what the user would experience. Storyboarding your website helps to make your website accessible and convenient for users. A storyboard can show the direction of movement through the website by laying out the different buttons and links on each page. The storyboard should give an idea of the overall organisation, structure and mood of the website. It should show how all of the pages work together, as well as which resources (videos, photos, graphics, colours, links) would be used to create the overall effect of the website. To storyboard your website, follow these simple steps.

Figure 7.8 An example of a website storyboard

* Gather information. Collect the information that you want to incorporate into your website, such as tabs, buttons, images, videos and texts.
* Create an outline. Arrange and outline the information in your website based on the wireframe.
* Link and connection. Every button, tab, and active link on your website has a function and corresponding connection with other pages. Make sure you identify the pages to pop out, once a button or link is clicked on.

Figure 7.8 shows an example of a website storyboard. Figure 7.9 shows some examples of website templates.

Figure 7.9 A sample template for a website storyboard

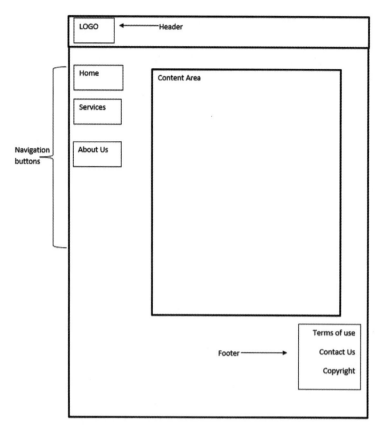

Figure 7.10 Layout of a typical web page

Figure 7.11 An example of a header

Components of a web page

Let us go back to our website made of a single web page. Figure 7.10 shows the layout of a typical web page.

The following are some basic components of a web page:

* **Header:** A website header runs across the top of the web page. It appears on every page of the website and may contain a big heading and a logo. It may also contain common information about the website such as site navigation and main contact information. Figure 7.11 shows the header for the Hodder Education website.

* **Site navigation:** You will need navigation buttons on the website. These buttons can be part of the header, as shown in Figure 7.11, or on the left or right, as shown in Figure 7.10. The navigation buttons allow you to click through to other pages if the website has more than one page. They may also take you to other parts of a single web page.

* **Body/Content area:** This is the large area in the centre that contains most of the unique content of a web page, for example the photo gallery you want to display or a feature article you want your visitors to read. This is the area that changes from page to page. Figure 7.12 shows part of the Hodder Education Caribbean Curriculum website. You can find the website at https://www.hoddereducation.co.uk/caribbean-curriculum.

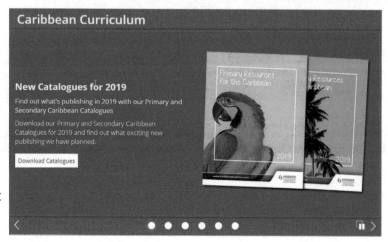

Figure 7.12 Part of the content area of the Hodder Education Caribbean Curriculum website

Figure 7.13 An example of a footer

* **Footer:** A web page footer in a website works the same way as a footer in a Word document. The footer may contain:
  – the page author details
  – the copyright statement
  – contact details
  – links to related sites.

Figure 7.13 shows the footer of the Hodder Education website.

Larger websites may also have the following elements:

* **A Back to Home Page button:** It is a good design feature for the other pages to have a link back to the home page.
* **A site map:** This map shows a list of hyperlinks to all web pages on the site that can be accessed by search engines and users.
* **Website search features:** These features allow users to search the website for what they are interested in.
* **An About us page:** This page would include:
  – a complete description of the individual/company/organisation
  – the objectives of the websites
  – the name, address, phone numbers and email addresses of the individual/company/organisation
  – a logo displayed in the left corner of each page of your website, which can take one back to the home page if clicked.

Content

The content, which includes text, graphics, animation, video, audio and links, is the most important part of your website. Well-thought-out web content will make your website design engaging, effective and popular. By taking the time to create or put together your content during the website design phase, you can make all of the necessary changes before the site actually goes live.

Here are some tips to consider when working out the content for your website. The content should:

* be engaging, easy to understand and suitable for its intended audience (for example, if it is aimed at young children, the text needs to be suitable for a lower reading age)
* contain keywords so that the site can be ranked highly on search engines, thereby allowing it to draw more visitors
* be written in a way that leads the reader through the website
* encourage readers to look at the entire website.

Figure 7.14 Website content must engage the target audience and be effective.

The appearance and layout of the content also plays an important role in overall design of the website.

Appearance and layout of content

Scale

Scale is the sizing of individual elements to create emphasis, drama and add hierarchy. You can resize your elements to make them extremely large or small to create effects and to show which parts of the design are more or less important. The scaling of elements to indicate importance is often called 'hierarchy'.

Colour and format

Figure 7.15 This travel website uses bright colours to appeal to its target audience.

Colour is a very essential aspect of any website. Colour creates specific moods and atmospheres, and channels emotions. Each shade has certain specific meanings associated with it. You should use colours that look pleasing and make the most sense for your website. You also need to consider which colours look good together and make text easy to read. Using a single colour scheme throughout is a good way to achieve consistency. Some website builders (see below) have tools to help you choose a colour scheme and use it consistently. Typically, you will need about five colours. When choosing a colour, ask yourself the following questions:

* Which colours make the most sense for the website?
* Which background colours and font colours will appeal to the target audience?
* What colours will support the theme of the site?

Font

The typeface and size of the text in the web pages should be comfortable to read and make the content easy to understand. Consider the following suggestions when using text in your website:

* Make sure that your typeface is not too big or too small for the website you are building. Using two or three different sizes will help to organise the text by making headings stand out.
* Try to avoid using too many typefaces at once. Again, two or three typefaces are probably enough.
* Left-alignment of large areas of text is the easiest to read.

Note!

Images and videos can add significantly to the appearance and experience of your website. However, they should be developed and implemented with care as they can also greatly increase the load time of a website.

Images

Images can add visual or artistic appeal to the information on a web page and also hold viewer interest and attention. They are also used to communicate or explain ideas visually. Here are some points to consider when using images in a website:

* **Use high-quality images:** Free websites or your personal photographs are good sources for high-quality images.
* **Use the right file type:** Photographs should be saved and uploaded as JPEGs. This file type can handle all of the colours in a photograph in a relatively small, efficient file size. Graphics (for example, cartoons, diagrams) should be GIF or PNG files.

* **Resize images to optimise page speed and appearance:** It is important for a web designer to find the right balance between size and resolution. The higher the resolution, the larger will be the file size, which also slows down the website's page speed. Resize images to improve page speed and appearance. Some website-building software recommends making your smaller images about 30Kb and your larger ones 60–100Kb.
* **Make images the same size and style:** Images on a web page will look better if you use a consistent style and size or proportion. Consistency will also help when lining up the text, columns and other information on your page.
* **Name the image file correctly to help your search engine optimisation (SEO):** Rename your images before you upload them to your website to give your SEO a boost. When Google™ scans your website, it can read your text but it cannot see what is in your images. The file name provides information about what is in the image, so that Google™ can interpret it correctly, (for example, bluemountain.jpg rather than DSC12345.jpg).

Figure 7.16 High-quality images at the correct resolution will not affect the website's page speed.

Web development tools

As people live more and more of their lives online, web design is going to become more important. At the moment, if you want a website, you either do it yourself or get a professional to do it for you.

In the beginning, web developers created websites using HTML code. Building websites using this method was slow, expensive and hard to maintain. This method also meant that the developer needed a high level of skill.

The introduction of web-authoring software (Web Editors) allowed developers to create websites cheaper, faster and more easily. For example, web-authoring software such as Dreamweaver®, CoffeeCup and SeaMonkey allow website developers to create websites using a familiar visual interface, by typing text and formatting it using buttons, menus and dialog boxes, similar to that in most word-processing software. Many of these programs include WYSIWYG editors ('what you see is what you get'), which means the content in the editor has the same general appearance and layout as it will have as a finished web page.

The latest tool being used to develop websites is artificial design intelligence (ADI). Artificial design intelligence is a method of building a website without hiring a professional or doing it yourself. Users state what they want and the ADI generates a personalised design. The technology is still in the early stage, but machine learning is enabling ADI to understand creative rules and apply them independently. This is done by making the programs capable of understanding design principles and then 'observing' what existing web pages are doing. ADI can produce functional, attractive sites completely independent of human expertise. Examples of platforms that have introduced ADI are Wix, GoDaddy®, Bookmark and Adobe® Sensei®.

Creating a web page

Web pages can be created using:

* application software, such as Microsoft Word, Excel and Access
* a text editor program, such as Notepad to write an HTML program
* an HTML generator, such as Aptana Studio 3
* website builders, such as Sitebuilder, Site123, Wix and Jimdo
* specialist web editor creation programs, such as Dreamweaver® and Webflow
* website writer software that allows you to write in HTML and create web pages as they appear on screen, as well as provide tools to manage a website.

In this chapter, we will briefly discuss the creation of websites using Notepad, Microsoft Word and Wix.

Figure 7.17 Notepad window

Creating a web page using Notepad

Notepad is a basic Microsoft text editor program that you can use to create simple documents – a very basic word processor. The most common use for Notepad is to view or edit text (.txt) files, but Notepad can also be used for creating web pages. Web pages can be created in Notepad by entering HTML code and saving the file as a .html or .htm file. The Notepad program can be accessed by clicking on Start/Windows/Accessories/Notepad. Figure 7.17 shows the Notepad window.

HTML

An HTML file is a text file containing **markup tags** (commands). The mark-up tag instructs the web browser how to display the page. HTML has many tags that can be used to generate exciting web pages. Learning all the different tags in HTML would require an entire book. Therefore, in this section, we will only look at some basic HTML tags. Table 7.1 explains some examples of HTML tags.

Table 7.1 HTML tags

Tag	Explanation
<HTML>	This is the first tag in your HTML document. It tells your browser that this is the start of an HTML document.
</HTML>	This is the last tag in your document. This tag tells your browser that this is the end of the HTML document.
<HEAD> and </HEAD>	The text between the <HEAD> tag and the </HEAD> tag is header information. Header information is not displayed in the browser window.
<TITLE> and </TITLE>	The text between the <TITLE> tags is the title of your document. The title is displayed in your browser's caption.
<H1> and </H1>	Headings are defined with the <H1> to <H6> tags. <H1> defines the largest heading and <H6> defines the smallest heading. HTML automatically adds an extra blank line before and after a heading.
<BODY> and </BODY>	The text between the <BODY> tags is the text that will be displayed in your browser.
<P> and </P>	<P> and </P> defines the start and end of a paragraph. HTML automatically adds an extra blank line before and after a paragraph.

All HTML tags are surrounded by the two characters (< , >) called angle brackets which normally come in pairs like <P> and </P>. The first tag in a pair is the start tag, the second tag is the end tag. The text between the start and end tags is the element content. HTML tags are not case sensitive: <b> means the same as <B>.

Activity 1

Writing a web page

Type in the following HTML code exactly as it appears on this page into Notepad. Save the file to your desktop, as an HTML file. View the page in your web browser.

```
<HTML>
<HEAD>
<TITLE>My First Web Page</TITLE>
</HEAD>
<BODY>
<H1>Building Websites</H1>
<P>THIS IS MY FIRST WEB PAGE.</P>
<P>I can start on a new paragraph by enclosing my
text within paragraph tags.</P>
</BODY>
</HTML>
```

Here is how it is done.

1 Open Notepad.
2 Type in the HTML code exactly as shown above.
3 Click **File**.
4 Click **Save As**.
5 Change the directory to your desktop.
6 Change the Save as type to 'All Files'.
7 Type in the file name, 'My First Web Page.html'
8 Click **Save**.
9 Go to your desktop and open the file 'My First Web Page.html'.
10 The web page will be displayed as shown in Figure 7.18.

Figure 7.18 Activity 1 HTML code displayed in a browser

Table 7.2 Commonly used HTML formatting tags

Tag	Explanation
<CENTER> and </CENTER>	Centres a heading, line or image <H1> <CENTER>This is my first web page.</CENTER> </H1> The sentence 'This is my first web page.' will be centred.
<I> and </I>	Used to display text in italics
<B> and </B>	Used to bold text
<U> and </U>	Used to underline text.

Editing text

To edit text in an existing web page, you must first open the web page in Notepad to view the page in HTML. You can then change text as needed. If you remove entire headings or paragraphs, you also need to delete all the tags associated with the relevant section, so in Activity 1 on page 129, you need to delete the <P> at the start and the </P> tag at the end, as well as the text, if you delete one of the paragraphs.

Some commonly used HTML formatting tags are shown in Table 7.2.

Activity 2

Formatting text

Retrieve the file 'My First Web Page.html'. Type in the new lines of code exactly as they appear on this page. Save the file to your desktop as an HTML file. View the page in your web browser.

```
<HTML>
<HEAD>
Building Websites
<TITLE>My First Web Page</TITLE>
</HEAD>
<BODY>
<H1>Building Websites</H1>
<CENTER>
<P>Italics, Bold and Underline.</P>
</CENTER>
<P><CENTER>I can centre my text within a paragraph.</CENTER></P>
<P><CENTER><B>Making text bold is very easy.</B></CENTER></P>
<P><CENTER><I>Text can also be in italics.</I></CENTER></P>
<P><CENTER><B><I>Text can be bold and in italics.</I></B></CENTER></P>
<P><CENTER><U>You can also underline text.</U></CENTER></P>
</BODY>
</HTML>
```

Activity 2 continued

Here is how it is done.

1 Open Notepad.
2 Retrieve the file 'My First Webpage.html'.
3 Type in the new HTML code exactly as shown in Activity 2.
4 Click **File**.
5 Click **Save As**.
6 Change the directory to your desktop.
7 Change the Save as type to 'All Files'.
8 Type in the file name 'Formatting.html'.
9 Click **Save**.
10 Go to your desktop and open the file 'Formatting.html'.
11 The web page is displayed in the browser as shown in Figure 7.19.

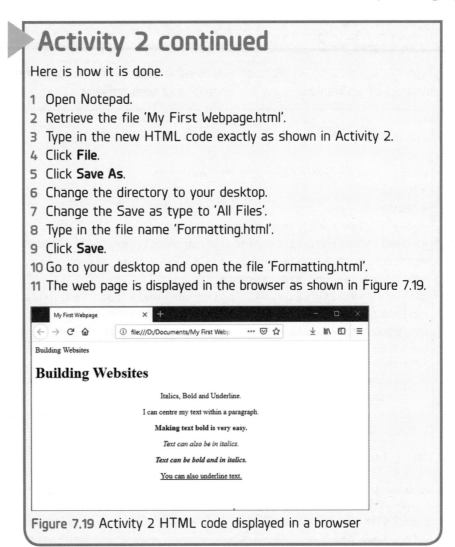

Figure 7.19 Activity 2 HTML code displayed in a browser

More formatting tags to change the text and background colour, relative size and typeface are shown in Table 7.3.

Table 7.3 Formatting tags to change the text and background colour, relative size and typeface

Tag	Explanation
Attribute background-colour	Attribute background-colour changes the background colour to the selected colour. This code changes the background colour of the web page to yellow. <body style="background-color:yellow;"> To change to another colour, replace yellow with the desired colour.
\<BIG> and \</BIG>	Used to make text bigger that the current default.
\<SMALL> and \</SMALL>	Used to make text smaller than the current default.
\<FONT> and \</FONT>	Used to select a font typeface, size and colour \<FONT SIZE=12 COLOR= "RED" FACE= "ARIAL" >\</FONT>
\<P>\<strong> and \</strong>	Used to emphasise text. Text is displayed as bold by the browser.

Activity 3

Type in the following HTML code exactly as it appears on this page into Notepad. Save the file to your desktop, as an html file. View the page in your web browser.

```
<HTML>
<HEAD>
<TITLE>
Using tags to make text big or small
</TITLE>
</HEAD>
<Body style="background-color:yellow;">
<H1><CENTER><FONT SIZE =24>Building Websites</FONT></CENTER></H1>
<CENTER><FONT SIZE=14>Using tags to make text big or small</FONT>
<P><Big>Using the BIG tag</Big></P>
<P><Small>Making text SMALL using the small tag</Small></P>
<P><FONT SIZE=1>This is font size 1.</FONT></P>
<P><FONT SIZE=2>This is font size 2.</FONT></P>
<P><FONT SIZE=12 COLOR="RED" FACE = "ARIAL">This is font size 12, colour red and font
face arial.</FONT></P>
<P><strong> Text can be emphasized </strong> using the strong tag</P>
</CENTER>
</BODY>
</HTML>
```

Here is how it is done.

1 Open Notepad.
2 Type in the HTML code exactly as shown in Activity 3.
3 Click **File**.
4 Click **Save As**.
5 Change the directory to your desktop.
6 Change the Save as type to 'All Files'.
7 Type in the file name 'Font.html'.
8 Click **Save**.
9 Go to your desktop and open the file 'Font.html'.
10 The web page is displayed in the browser as shown in Figure 7.20.

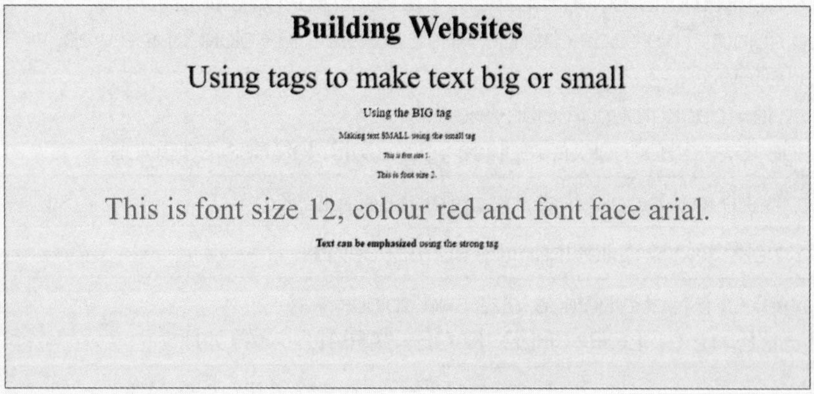

Building Websites

Using tags to make text big or small

Using the BIG tag

Making text SMALL using the small tag

This is font size 1.

This is font size 2.

This is font size 12, colour red and font face arial.

Text can be emphasized using the strong tag

Figure 7.20 Activity 3 HTML code displayed in a browser

Inserting a graphic

Graphics can be placed easily in a web page. Perhaps the most difficult part of inserting a graphic is actually obtaining it. Sometimes, depending on the design of the web page, it may be necessary to place text at different positions in relation to the graphic. Text may be aligned vertically, which means that it can be placed at the top, middle or bottom of the graphic. Text can also be aligned horizontally. This means you can place the image to the right or left of the text. If the image is aligned to the right, the text is on the left and seems to flow around the image. If the image is placed to the left, the text appears on the right.

The size of an image can also be adjusted to fit on your web page. You can make an image larger or smaller by changing the values in the "HEIGHT" and "WIDTH" attributes of the IMG tag. Adding these attributes can enhance the appearance of your web page and make it look very professional.

The format and size of an image determines the amount of storage space it requires. This has a direct impact on the time it takes a web page to load or display. To help reduce the time required to display a web page with graphics, you can use thumbnail images. A **thumbnail** is a smaller version of an actual image. When a user clicks on a thumbnail image, the actual full-sized image that is stored on another page is displayed. Table 7.4 lists some of the tags and attributes that are used to insert images into a web page.

Table 7.4 Graphic tags and attributes

Tag	Explanation
<IMG SRC= "image.jpg">	This IMG tag inserts an image into a web page. To use this element, you supply the URL of the image you want to display in the SRC attribute. SRC stands for 'source'. <IMG SRC="School.jpg">
BORDER	This places a border around the picture, for example BORDER=7. Changing the number changes the size of the border. <IMG SRC="School.jpg" BORDER=8>
ALT	The ALT attribute is used to define descriptive text that can be displayed, in case the browser is not displaying the image. <IMG SRC="School.jpg" ALT= "Premier High School" BORDER=8>
WIDTH and HEIGHT	These <IMG> attributes provide the width and height of the image in pixels. <IMG SRC="School.jpg" WIDTH="55" HEIGHT= "75" ALT= "Premier High School" BORDER=8>
ALIGN	This attribute is used to align text and images. To align vertically, you can set alignment to TOP, MIDDLE or BOTTOM. <IMG SRC="School.jpg" ALIGN=TOP> To align horizontally, you can set alignment to RIGHT or LEFT.

Activity 4 on the next page demonstrates how to insert a graphic in a web page.

Activity 4

Type in the following HTML code exactly as it appears on this page into Notepad. Save the file to your desktop, as an HTML file. View the page in your web browser.

```
<HTML>
<HEAD>
<TITLE>
Aligning Text and Images
</TITLE>
</HEAD>
<H1>
<CENTER>Aligning Text and Images</CENTER>
</H1>

<BODY>
<img src="cricket.png"  style="width:100px;height:100px;"ALIGN=RIGHT BORDER=0>


<P>[Type in text shown in Figure 7.21 – or any other text].</P>
<img src="cricket.png"  style="width:100px;height:100px;"ALIGN=LEFT BORDER=1>


<p>[Type in text shown in Figure 7.21 – or any other text]</P>
<center>
<img src="cricket.png"  style="width:100px;height:100px;"ALIGN=middle
BORDER=3>
</P>
</BODY>
</HTML>
```

Here is how it is done.

1 Open Notepad.
2 Type in the HTML code exactly as shown in Activity 4.
3 Click **File**.
4 Click **Save As**.
5 Change the directory to your desktop.
6 Change the Save as type to 'All Files'.
7 Type in the file name 'Graphics.html'.
8 Click **Save**.
9 Go to your desktop and open the file 'Graphics.html'.
10 The web page will be displayed in your browser as shown in Figure 7.21.

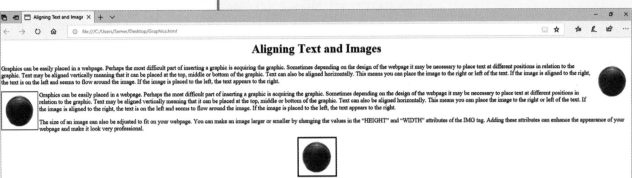

Figure 7.21 Activity 4 HTML code displayed in a browser

Exercise 1

1 List five uses of websites.

2 List three types of content that can be included in a website.

3 How can users access websites?

4 What two factors inform the structure of a website?

5 Create a website that includes a photograph of your school or a some building of interest in your community, and carry out these tasks:

   a Place a border around the photograph.
   b Include a heading.
   c Bold and centre the heading.
   d Insert a body colour of your choice.
   e Include a short description of the building.

Creating hyperlinks

A hyperlink is a reference (an address) to a resource on the Web. Hyperlinks can point to any resource on the Web: an HTML page, an image, a sound file, a movie, and so on. In HTML, the <A> tag is used to set up a hyperlink and the HREF attribute is used to set the target of the hyperlink. Hyperlinks can be either internal or external. An internal link allows you to jump from one section of your own website's page to another section in the same page or to another page in the same website, for example from your home page to an About Us page. An external link allows you to open up a new browser window from another website, for example from your home page to a Wikipedia article so someone can read more about something on the site.

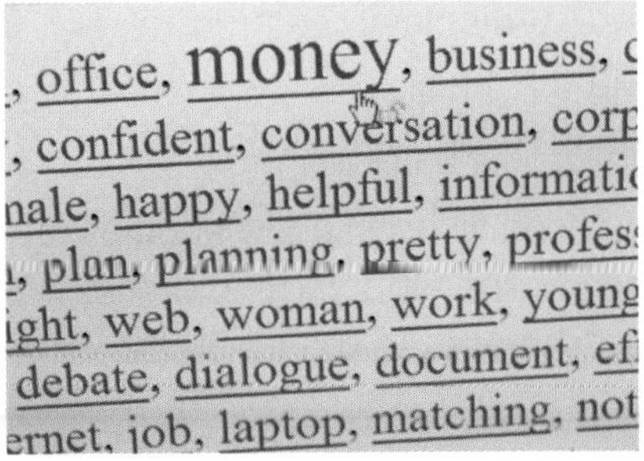

Figure 7.22 An external link lets you open up a new browser window from another website.

An internal link

In order to jump from one section to another, you first need to name the section, so that the tag can locate it when it is called. The tag <A NAME = "links"> has to be inserted in the lower section of the web page just above the position where the 'link' value is located. For example, in Activity 5, the tag <A NAME= "BOTTOM"> is inserted after the heading "End of Page".

The next step is to insert the link from which you want to jump. In the example, we want to jump from the top of the page to the bottom of the page. Therefore, we need to insert <A HREF="#BOTTOM">End of Page</A>. The hyperlinked text "Linking Tags" will appear and when clicked, will jump from the current location to the indicated section.

An external link or a file

In order to jump to another web page, you need to create text or an image that the user can click on, and then provide the address to link to. This can all be done using the <A> tags. The simplest way to do this is to use a piece of text to link to the other site. You put the <A> and </A> tags before and after the text you want to link from. Then you use the HREF attribute to specify the website address to link to. For example when this address below is opened in the browser,

<A HREF="http://www.windiescricket.com /">West Indies Cricket Board WICB Official Website</A>

the link will be displayed as 'West Indies Cricket Board WICB Official Website'. When you click on the link, the web page will be displayed.

Figure 7.23 You can use an image as an external link to a different web page.

If you want to use an image, then instead of putting the text inside the <A> and </A> tags, you put <IMG> tags. For example, <A HREF= "https://www.windiescricket.com"><IMG SRC="cricket.png" style="width:100px;height:100px;"></A> displays the picture 'cricket.png' and this links to https://www. windiescricket.com when you click on it.

This can also be used to open a file, such as an audio file. Instead of the web page address, you would insert the path to the file in the HREF Attribute.

A link to an email

You can put in a hyperlink to an email address, so that when you click on it, your email opens a new mail window, allowing you to send an email easily. Again, you use the <A> and </A> tags and put some text or an <IMG> inside them that you can click on. As with an external website, you use the HREF attribute to specify the email address, but you start the address with the word 'MAILTO'. For example:

<A HREF=mailto:someone@somewhere.com>Click to send a message</A>

This will open a new email to someone@somewhere.com when you click on the text **Click to send a message**.

Table 7.5 More HTML tags

Tag	Explanation
<A> and </A>	These tags can be used to set up a hyperlink.
NAME	The NAME attribute specifies an anchor name. It is the name of the text, image, and so on you want to use as the target of a hyperlink.
<A HREF= "http:// www.webaddress. com/">Web Address Link<A/>	This will display the "Web Address Link" as a hyperlink in your web page and when you click on the text, it will load the page www. webaddress.com<html>. For example, when <A HREF="http://www.windiescricket.com /">West Indies Cricket Board WICB Official Website</A> is opened in the browser, the link will be displayed as West Indies Cricket Board WICB Official Website. When you click the link, the web page will be displayed. The target web page will open in a new window if you use: <A HREF="http://www. windiescricket.com /" target= "-blank">West Indies Cricket Board WICB Official Website</A>
 	This tag inserts a line break into your text or allows you to move to the next line of text.

Activity 5

Type out the HTML code shown below. Save the file as 'Links.html'. Display the file in a browser.

```
1  <HTML>
2  <HEAD>
3  <BODY>
4  <h2 id="top">Top of page</h2>
5
6
7  <a href="#Bottom">Go to Bottom </a>
8
9  <H2>Local Links</H2>
10 <P><A HREF="https://www.windiescricket.com/">West Indies Cricket</A> is a link to the West Indies Cricket website on the World Wide Web.</P>
11 </P><A HREF="https://www.windiescricket.com/"><IMG SRC="Cricket Ball.jpg" STYLE="width:100px;height:100px;"></A>
12 <P> <A> The cricket ball is hyperlinked to the West Indies cricket website on the World Wide Web. Click on the cricket ball to move to the West Indies cricket website. </A></P>
13 </BODY>
14 </HTML>
15 <P>
16 <H2>West Indies Men's Cricket</H2>
17 </P>
18
19 <P><H4>The West Indies men cricket team, is a multi-national team representing several countries in the English-speaking Caribbean.
20  As of 24 June 2018, the West Indian cricket team is ranked ninth in the world in Tests, ninth in ODIs and seventh in T20s in the official ICC rankings.
21 From the mid-late 1970s to the early 1990s, the West Indies team was the strongest in the world in both Test and One Day International cricket.
22 A number of cricketers who were considered among the best in the world have hailed from the West Indies: Sir Garfield Sobers, Lance Gibbs, Gordon Greeidge,
23 George Headley, Brian Lara, Clive Lloyd, Malcolm Marshall, Sir Andy Roberts, Alvin Kallicharran, Rohan Kanhai, Sir Frank Worrell, Sir Clyde Walcott, Sir Everton Weekes,
24  Sir Curtley Ambrose, Michael Holding, Courtney Walsh, Joel Garner and Sir Viv Richards have all been inducted into the ICC Hall of Fame. </H4> </P>
25 <P>
26 </P>
27 <P>
28 <H2>West Indies Women's Cricket</H2>
29  </P>
30 <P><H4>The West Indies women's cricket team is a combined team of players from various English speaking countries in the Caribbean. The team competes in
31 the International Cricket Council (ICC) Women's Championship, Women's Cricket World Cup and Women's One Day International Cricket.</H4></P>
32
33
34 <a href="stop">Go to top</a>
35
36 <h2 id="Bottom">Bottom of page</h2>
37
```

Figure 7.24 HTML code for creating a file with hyperlinks

Here is how it is done.

1 Open Notepad.
2 Type in the HTML code exactly as shown above in Figure 7.24.
3 Click **File**.
4 Click **Save As**.
5 Change the directory to your desktop.
6 Change the Save as type to 'All Files'.
7 Type in the file name 'Links.html'.
8 Click **Save**.
9 Go to your desktop and open the file 'Links.html'. Figure 7.25 shows how the file will be displayed.
10 Clicking on the link 'West Indies cricket' will take you to the West Indies cricket website.
11 Clicking on the 'ball' will take you to the West Indies cricket website.
12 Clicking on the internal link **Go to Bottom** will take you to the bottom of the page.
13 Clicking on the internal link **Go to top** will take you to the top of the page.

Activity 5

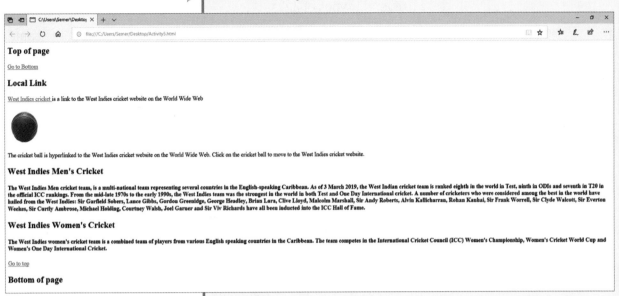

Figure 7.25 How the file with hyperlinks will be displayed

Exercise 2

Create a web page for a club. The web page should contain the following:

1 A photograph of the club building

2 A brief history of the club

3 A link to a page listing and describing all the activities of the club

4 A suitable body colour

5 Some text in bold, italics or both

6 Fonts in various sizes

7 A link to an external website of interest to the club

8 A link to send an email to an official of the club.

Creating a web page using Microsoft Word

Microsoft Word offers various options for creating new web pages. Word has a built-in HTML translator, which can automatically convert any text, graphics or hyperlinks that you insert into your Word document into a web-compatible format. Once you open a new blank document, you can start typing in text or add images, tables and hyperlinks just as you would in a normal Word document. The document can be formatted and edited using all the formatting and editing features you covered on word processing in *Interact with IT* Books 1 and 2.

Hyperlinks

Hyperlinks can be inserted into a Word document. There are two different types of links:

* An internal link is one that links to different points in the same web page.
* An external link is one that connects the page you are on to another page in the same website; to some other website on the Internet; or to an email address or to another file.

Creating a hyperlink

Follow these steps to create a hyperlink.

1 Open your Word document.

2 Place your cursor at the position at which you wish to insert your link or select the word(s) or image you will like to click on to hyperlink.

3 Click the **Insert tab**, then select **Hyperlink** from the Links group. The 'Insert Hyperlink' dialogue box appears as shown in Figure 7.26.

If you did not select a word or image, type in whatever text you want to display as the link your web page visitor will click in the 'Text to display' combo box.

Type in the full address or select from the list provided in the drop-down list in the 'Address' combo box of the website or file you want the user to access by clicking the link. Figure 7.27 shows two links. The words 'Application form' will hyperlink to the document 'Application form' in the folder 'Strikers Football Club'. Clicking the words 'Soca Warriors' will take you to the 'Soca Warriors' website http://www.socawarriors.net/ on the internet.

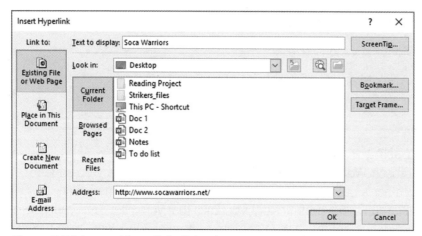

Figure 7.26 Insert Hyperlink dialog box

If you wish to create a link to another web page in the same folder as the page you are creating or to an email or a file, follow the same instructions as above but instead of typing in a web address, type or select the filename of the .htm or other file, or add the email address with 'mailto:' in front (for example, mailto:someone@somewhere.com) that you wish to access from this link.

To check to see if your links are working you need to save your Word document as a web page and publish it to the web server.

Saving Word documents as web pages

Follow these steps to save Word documents as web pages:

1   Select **File/Save As** (Save As dialog box appears).

2   Give the new web page a name that does not contain any spaces and is, preferably, eight characters or less in length.

3   Click the arrow next to 'Save as type' and change the type from Word document to Webpage (*htm,*html).

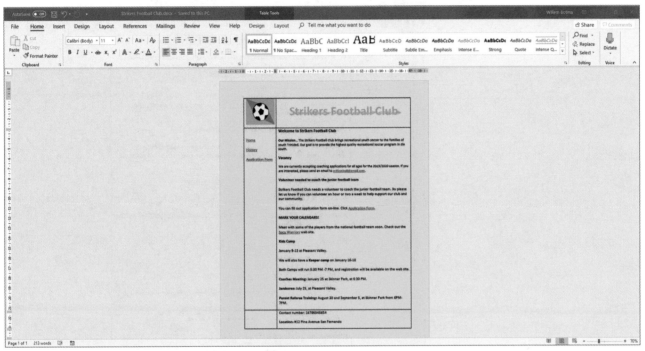

Figure 7.27 Web page created in Microsoft Word

Word will automatically save the document in an HTML format and append the file extension .htm to the file name. It will also create a folder with the same name as the file plus _files and will store an XML instruction file and all image files within this folder. In other words, if I created a Word document and saved it as a web page, giving it the name 'Strikers', Word would create a file called 'Strikers. htm' and a folder called 'Strikers_files'.

This folder contains a file with all the formatting instructions for the text and image layout on your new web page. It also contains all the image files for images you may have inserted within your web page.

Activity 6

Using the following content create a web page for the Strikers Football Club, which looks like Figure 7.28.

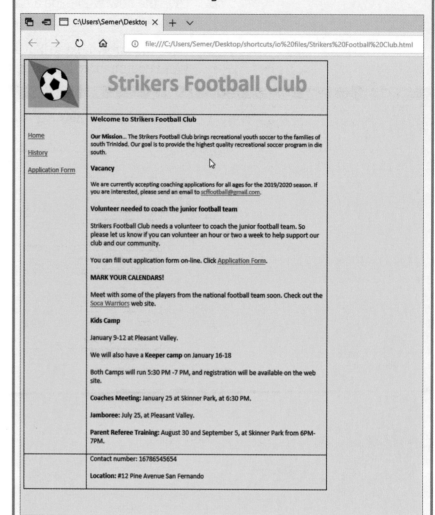

Figure 7.28 Microsoft Word document saved as a web page

Here is how it is done.

1 Create a folder in the desktop named 'Strikers Football Club'.
2 Open a blank Word document.
3 Insert a table with three rows and two columns, as shown in Figure 7.28.
4 Click the **Word art icon** and type in the heading 'Strikers Football Club'. Change the colour of the font.
5 Find an image of a ball from the internet or from your own images and insert in the appropriate location.
6 Type out the content shown in the box above.
7 Format the document as shown in Figure 7.28.

Activity 6 continued

8 Create document named 'Application form' and save it in the folder created.

9 Create another document named 'History' and save it in the folder created. The 'History' document contains information about the history of the club.

10 Create a hyperlink to the application form:
   a Select the words 'Application form'.
   b Click **Insert/Hyperlink** (Hyperlink dialog box appears).
   c The words 'Application form' will be displayed in the Text to display combo box.
   d Ensure that the **Existing file or web page** option is selected in the Link to pane.
   e Click **Desktop** in the Look in combo box.
   f Select the folder 'Strikers Football Club'.
   g Open the folder and select the document 'Application form'.
   h The name of the document is displayed in the Address box.
   i Click **OK** to confirm. (The words 'Application Form' will be displayed as shown in Figure 7.28.)

11 Create a hyperlink to the Soca Warriors website:
   a Select the words 'Soca Warriors'.
   b Follow the steps as described previously.
   c In the Address box, type 'http://www.socawarriors.net/'.

Creating a website using the Wix website builder

Wix.com is an online website builder that uses templates to help build a professional-looking website, built on good practices. Follow these steps to create a website using Wix.

Step 1: Access the Wix.com site to Sign Up

To sign up as a first time user, you just simply add your email address and set up your password to log in to your Wix account. The Let's get started screen appears (Figure 7.29). Click on **Create Your Website** and the Welcome to Wix screen shown in Figure 7.30 will appear.

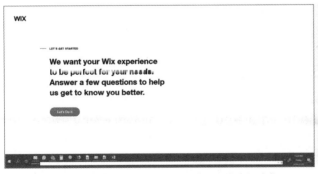

Figure 7.29 The Let's get started screen in Wix

Figure 7.30 The Welcome to Wix screen

Figure 7.31 The 'What kind of website do you want to create?' category options

Figure 7.32 The 'Choose how you want to create your website' dialog box

Step 2: Answer the questions so Wix can recommend some designs

In this step, you can choose who you are building this for, what kind of website you want to create and your level of experience, so that Wix can direct you to the right template. You can choose from the categories provided such as business, designer, blog, online store, restaurants & food, beauty & wellness, photography, accommodation, portfolio & CV, music, events or other. Figure 7.31 shows the options for the types of website.

Step 3: Choose how you want to create your website

The Choose how you want to create your website dialog box appears (Figure 7.32). Two options appear:

* Let Wix ADI create a website for you. ADI stands for Artificial Design Intelligence
* Create your website with the Wix Editor.

Step 4a: Creating a website using option 1 'Let Wix ADI Create a Website for you'

This option allows the user to develop a website by answering a few questions. Try to answer all the questions and make the selections, as your answers and choices will help Wix decide on the best template for your website. These are the questions and selection options:

1. **What type of site do you want to create?** The user is presented with several options to choose from.

2. **Does your website need any of these features?** You can apply one or more of the following options: sell online, take bookings or get subscribers.

3. **What is the name of your business or website?** Add your business name or other name relevant to your business so that people can find it online.

4. **Where is your business located?** If an address is not relevant for you, you can skip to the next page.

5. **Review and edit your info.** You can modify your website name and add additional information such as a business email, an address, a phone number and a social network, if available. Once you complete all the information, Wix processes all the data given before continuing to the next step.

6 **Pick a theme you like.** You can choose from a few designs provided in this step, but you can also still change the theme later if needed.

Next, Wix will direct you to the home page where you can actually manage your website.

Manage your home page

Once you are on the home page, there will be a quick tutorial about each navigation tool. Now you can simply change the content or even modify the layout design based on your preference. You also can always delete some sections if you find they are not relevant. Any work you do on Wix, will be saved automatically. Avoid closing your work if you see 'Saving' instead of 'Saved'.

Publish your website

Once you are done managing your website, now it is time for you to publish your website online.

Step 4b Creating a website using option 2 'Create Your Website with the Wix Editor'
Select 'Choose a Template'

You can choose from one of the preset templates. Alternatively, you can choose from a number of other templates, if the category you are looking for is not found in the preset templates by clicking on **Other**.

Find specific templates

Choose from a number of template category options.

Select a category option and expand the menu

Once you find the category you would like to use, click on it to expand the menu for the template sub-category options.

Figure 7.33 Site in Edit mode

You need to choose a category and a sub-category. The site will now be shown in edit mode in Figure 7.33. You will then be moved to the Wix editor, from where you can edit your site.

You can select your domain name by choosing to save your site by clicking on **Save** in the edit mode.

Once you click on **Save**, a pop-up appears that lets you save the site to a particular domain. The first option lets you choose a name for your site under the Wix.com domain. The second option lets you connect to your own customised domain.

Tools used to add content to your site

Wix provides the following options to create pages and add content to your chosen site:

* **Site Menu:** This displays the site map. Users can rename, duplicate, hide or delete pages. They can also choose transitions. See Figure 7.34.

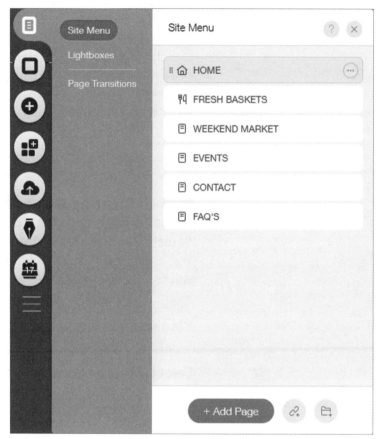

Figure 7.34 Site map in the Site Menu

* **Page Background:** The Page Background enables users to add or change the background (colour, image or video) to one or more pages of the website.
* **Add Web Elements:** Users can add web elements to the web page, such as text, images, menus, shapes, boxes, buttons and many more.
* **Wix App Market:** Wix enables users to add a number of apps and features to the site created by Wix or third-party developers. Apps enable users to add various types of functionality to their website, such as forms, calendars or stores.
* **My Uploads:** The My Upload option allows users to upload their own media files to the Media Manager, so that they are ready to use whenever they need to use them. Users can upload images, vector art, videos, fonts and documents.

Figure 7.35
Positioning and
editing tools

* **Wix Bookings**: Wix Bookings is an easy-to-use scheduling system that lets customers book services online directly on the site.
* **Blogs:** The Wix blog allows users to easily create a blog and grow an online community with people who share their passion. Readers can join a user's blog, create member profiles, like and follow posts, comment with images and videos, and even become contributing writers.

Positioning and editing tools

The Positioning and editing tools editor shown in Figure 7.35 provides several options to adjust elements on a web page.

Step 5: Publishing your WIX site

Once you preview your site by clicking on **Preview** and seeing that your site is exactly the way you want it, you can then publish it by clicking on Publish.

Evaluation and testing

Before we publish a website, we need to evaluate the website to make sure it meets the purpose, and the user and technical requirements. You also need to test the website to make sure that all the content works (for example, the videos all play); all the links and menus work; and all the content is up-to-date and formatted correctly.

Evaluation

Earlier in the chapter, we saw how the intended audience and purpose help us to generate user and technical requirements. When we evaluate a site, we are checking that these requirements and the purpose have been met.

The first step is to go through the website page by page and look for the features and content in the user and technical requirements. For example:

* If we have a requirement to use video, are there videos on the website?
* Are there clear Contact, Blog and About us sections if the users want to find addresses, read about what the writers have been up to and find out about the writers.
* Can users who want to link to sites to buy the products that your site reviews do this?
* Does your website have a map or a link to one, so users can see where the local skate parks are that you have reviewed on your site?
* How would you test that your site is 'easy to use', which is what the users want?

Figure 7.36 A test audience can give you valuable feedback on how well your website works.

The last point above is very difficult to test, as your idea of easy to use might be different to someone else's. One way to solve this is to use a **test audience**.

This is a group of people who match your intended audience who you invite to try out the website before it is published. By letting a number of people from your intended audience try it out, you will get a variety of opinions about how well it works, allowing you to improve it before it goes live (see Figure 7.36).

Testing

Testing involves making sure everything about the website works correctly. For large commercial websites, you would employ a company to do this testing, for which they would often use software. For most small websites, going through the website and carefully checking every aspect works well. Among the things to check are the following:

* Do the hyperlinks and menus work?
  - Check that the hyperlink or menu item takes you to the correct place when you click it.
  - Check that you can get back to where you came from when you check a hyperlink or menu item.
* Do the different media play?
  - Can you see all the images? Sometimes these can get saved in the wrong place and so the image does not display.
  - Do videos and sound work? Sometimes this can depend on how your web browser is set up, so it is a good idea to check these on several different computers.
* Does all the content format correctly?
  - Have all the formatting rules been applied correctly? If you want one heading to be in red text, is it red?
  - Does the text flow around the images correctly?
  - Does the site look correct on different screens? As more people use smartphones, this check is becoming increasingly important. A website builder such as Wix will often create a site that will adapt to different sizes of screen. This is much harder to do using Word or Notepad.

Web hosting

Web hosting is a service that allows organisations and individuals to post a website or web page on the internet. A web host, or web-hosting service provider, is a business that provides the technologies and services needed for the website or web page to be viewed on the internet. Websites are hosted, or stored, on special computers called servers. When internet users want to view your website, all they need to do is type your website address or domain into their browser. Their computer will then connect to the server in which your website is stored and your website will be made available to them through the browser.

Most hosting companies require that you own your domain in order to host with them. If you do not have a domain, the hosting companies will help you purchase one. Two popular web-hosting companies are Bluehost and HostGator.

Maintaining a website

To get the most from your website, you need to maintain it. Websites quickly become outdated, old-fashioned and static. When information remains static, there is little reason for people to revisit the site, and therefore the opportunity to promote new products, ideas and services is lost. Keeping your website up to date and relevant after it has been launched is important to keep people visiting and returning to your site. Here are a few things you can do to keep your website relevant and up-to-date:

1 Keep the site secure. Monitor for malware, viruses, hackers, and errors.

2 Keep a regular backup schedule to ensure that you always have the latest content stored in the event there is an attack on your server or site and everything gets deleted.

3 Keep monitoring for broken links – hyperlinks that no longer work, usually because a website has changed and the web page no longer exists. Website visitors and customers do not like broken links.

4 Keep updating your site content by posting about recent events, promotions, or news will make your site more likeable to your clients.

Figure 7.37 You need to maintain your website to keep it up to day and relevant.

Summary 7

1. A website is a collection of related web pages linked together with hyperlinks and residing in a web server.

2. Web pages are written in HTML, which is a language that web browsers use to display the contents of a web page. A web page can contain text and graphic images, as well as multimedia effects such as sound files, video and/or animation files.

3. The design of your website depends on the purpose and the intended users of the site and these help you to produce user and technical requirements that explain to the designer how the site should look and what it should do.

4. The five major steps in website publishing are planning, designing, creating, evaluating, testing, hosting and maintaining.

5. Web pages can be created using application software (Microsoft Word, Excel and Access), a text editor program (for example, Notepad), a HTML generator (for example, Aptana Studio 3), website builders (for example, Sitebuilder, Site123, Wix and Jimdo), specialist web creation programs (for example, Dreamweaver® and Webflow).

6. Notepad is a basic text editor that you can use to create simple documents. A text editor is a very basic word processor. Webpages can be created in Notepad by entering HTML (Hyper Text Markup Language) code and saving the file as an .html or .htm file.

7. An HTML file is a text file containing markup tags (commands). The markup tags instruct the web browser what the parts of the page are and how they should be displayed.

8. Microsoft Word can automatically convert any text, graphics or hyperlinks that you insert into your Word document into a web-compatible format by the built-in Word HTML translator.

9. A wireframe is a simplistic sketch and/or layout of a web page. Wireframes can provide a detailed view of the content that will appear on each page.

10. A hyperlink is a reference (an address) to a resource on the WWW. Hyperlinks can point to any resource on the Web, such as an HTML page, an image, a sound file, a movie, and so on.

11. Some of the basic components of a website are the home page, site map, website search features (navigation buttons), About us page, logo, header, footer and body/content area.

12. Evaluation and testing are important steps to carry out before publishing. They ensure that the website meets the requirements we found in the planning stage and that everything works.

13. A test audience is a good way of helping to evaluate a website.

14. Web hosting is a service that allows organisations and individuals to post a website or web page on the internet.

15. Maintaining a website involves the following: keeping the site secure, updating content, fixing broken links and regular backups.

Questions 7

Copy and fill in the blanks questions

1 A _____ is a collection of related web pages linked together with hyperlinks and residing in a web server.

2 Web pages are written in _____ code.

3 _____ is the language that web browsers use to understand how to display the contents of a web page.

4 Websites are accessible to users via the _____.

5 Notepad is a basic _____ program that you can use to create simple documents.

6 Webpages can be created in Notepad by entering HTML code and saving the file as a _____ file.

7 An HTML file is a text file containing markup _____.

8 _____ tells your browser that this is the start of an HTML document.

9 A _____ is a simplistic sketch and/or layout of a web page.

10 A service that allows organisations and individuals to post a website or web page on the internet is known as _____.

11 Wix and Jimdo are examples of _____ software.

12 Websites are hosted, or stored, on special computers called _____.

13 Site _____ ensures that a website is secure, updated and working properly.

True or false questions

1 Webpages are written in HTML.

2 HTML tags are case sensitive.

3 A server-based website is on the server and not on your computer.

4 Webpages can be created using application software such as Excel.

5 All HTML tags are surrounded by the two characters, < and >.

6 The text between the <HEAD> tag and the </HEAD> tag is displayed in the browser window.

7 Word has a built-in HTML translator that can automatically convert any text, graphics or hyperlinks that you insert into your Word document into a web-compatible format.

8 Dreamweaver® is an example of web-authoring software.

9 The IMG tag in HTML inserts an image into a web page.

10 The attribute background-colour changes the background colour to the selected colour.

11 Website maintenance is not essential to keep visitors coming back to a site.

Multiple-choice questions

1 A website is a collection of:

a sound files.

b animation files.

c graphic images.

d web pages.

2 Which of the following is **not** a major step in website publishing?

a Planning

b Designing

c Executing

d Hosting

3 Web pages can be created using:

    a application software.

    b a text editor program such as Notepad.

    c specialist web-creation software.

    d all of the above.

4 Websites can provide a convenient way of:

    a advertising.

    b purchasing items.

    c paying bills.

    d doing all of the above.

5 The design of a website depends on:

    a the amount of memory space available on your computer.

    b the purpose and intended users of the site.

    c the processing speed of your computer.

    d all of the above.

Short-answer questions

1 Define the terms 'website' and 'web page'.

2 List the five major steps in website publishing.

3 Describe how you would go about building a web page.

4 Define the term 'wireframe' and explain its importance in building a website.

5 List five basic components of a web page.

6 List four different categories of software which can be used to create web pages.

7 What are the different types of links you can create in a web page?

8 Use the tags covered in this chapter and those that you may have discovered yourself to create a web page about yourself.

9 Create a web page for your club using Microsoft Word.

10 Create a web page for the PTA of your school using HTML in Notepad or Microsoft Word.

11 Create a web page for your school using Wix.

12 Explain the term 'web hosting'.

13 Explain the purpose for maintaining a site.

Research questions

1 Make a list of five of the most-used website-building software. Place this information in a table under the following headings:

    * Name of software
    * Cost
    * Features offered
    * Support offered

2 Make a list of five of the top web-hosting companies and each one's cost for their service.

3 Your friends have created a website using HTML. When they open it in the browser on the computer at school, it seems to work fine. They would like to make the site available to everyone on the internet. Explain to your friends what they need to do to publish their website on the internet.

4 Maintaining a website is important to its success. A few steps to maintain a website are listed in this chapter. Conduct research to find out about other ways to maintain a website. Use the information to prepare a list of instructions someone may follow to maintain a website.

Crossword

Across

1   The extension that must be used to save a Word document as a web page

3   A step in creating a website to make sure it meets the purpose, user and technical requirements

4   A basic text editor program that you can use to create web pages

5   A type of bracket that surrounds HTML tags

6   A collection of related web pages linked together with hyperlinks and located in a web server

Down

1   This allows you to move to another point within a document or another document or a website by clicking on a word or image

2   A simplistic sketch and/or layout of a web page

STEM project

Your country will be hosting CARIFESTA next year. The Ministry of the Arts and Culture has a website that facilitates the upload of artwork and dance and music performances by schools to highlight emerging talent. This must be accompanied by a description of the item and information on the contributing students.

The principal of your school has asked your class to help with the uploading exercise and to do a walk-through of the uploaded items to the entire school after the exercise has been completed.

You are selected to be the lead person in this project. You may ask a classmate to play the part of the principal.

1   How do you and your classmates plan to approach this exercise? List your planning steps and the categories of possible items for uploading.

2   Prepare your implementation plan. Remember to include a template for the description of each item as well as the student information.

3   Share your implementation plan with your principal. What suggestions for improvement did you receive?

Hints

1   Brainstorm approaches to doing this exercise and list all ideas.

2   Review relevant content within the chapter.

3   Contact your country's Ministry of Arts and Culture to find out what it does to help highlight emerging talent.

Objectives

At the end of the chapter, you will be able to:

❏ connect frames in Microsoft Publisher

❏ import text from another application

❏ delete and add a page to your publication

❏ start a publication from a blank template

❏ change page sizes and orientation

❏ set margin and grid guides

❏ add a picture

❏ add a frame (textbox)

❏ add borders and shading.

In Book 1 of this series, you learned about some desktop publishing (DTP) basics, with particular reference to Microsoft Publisher. In this chapter, we will look at some of the more advanced features of Publisher.

Figure 8.1 Different types of publications can be designed in Publisher.

Connecting frames

Imagine that you have created a publication, for example a newsletter, and the article you have written cannot fit into the frame provided. If this happens, there is a feature that can help you with this. Microsoft Publisher displays a message (see Figure 8.2) asking if you would like to use text **autoflow**. This feature automatically reflows text, which may not give you exactly what you want. So, if you select 'No', then the text that cannot fit in the frame is placed in an **overflow** area. The icon ⊞ at the end of the frame shows that there is more text that cannot currently be seen (see Figure 8.2).

Did you know?

Paul Brainerd is credited for creating the term 'desktop publishing' in 1985. He was the founder of the Aldus Corporation that created PageMaker, which was one of the first widely-used types of desktop publishing software for the Mac® computer.

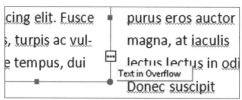

Figure 8.2 Text autoflow message

Figure 8.3 Linking group

Figure 8.4 The 'Pouring cup' icon connects one text box to another

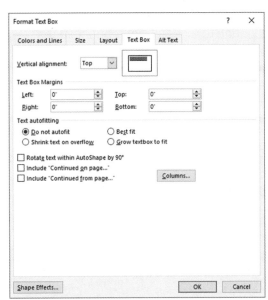

Figure 8.5 Format Text Box dialog box

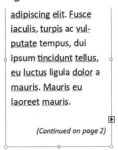

(Continued on page 2)

Figure 8.6 An example to show the use of 'Continued on page ...'

You have three options to try and bring this text into your document:

* **Increase the size of the frame:** Dragging the selection handles around the frame increases its size. However, increasing the size of the frame may not be possible, as there may not be enough room on the page to expand the frame and bring in all the text.

* **Decrease the size of the text:** This may work, but in many cases may not be desirable, as the text size may become too small, which would make the text difficult to read.

* **Continue the article in another frame:** This option means that you have to connect one frame to another, which would allow the text to flow from one frame into the next. The frames can be on the same page or on a different page.

Follow these steps to connect a frame using the Overflow icon:

1 Click in the frame with the Overflow.

2 Click the **Text in Overflow icon** on your frame or click on the **Create Link icon** in the Linking group of the Format tab for the text box (see Figure 8.3).

3 Click in the empty frame, and a mug will appear pouring letters into the frame (see Figure 8.4).

Here is the process to follow to connect a frame when the overflow message appears. If you click the **Overflow icon**, Publisher would have selected the next frame available for the overflow. If more frames are required, then Publisher moves to the next available frame. The process is continued until all the text is placed in frames. You can also select the frame for your text overflow.

You may also want to tell the reader that the text continues on another page. Follow these steps to do so:

1 Click on the last frame of the text on the first page.

2 Right-click and select **Format text box**; the Format Text Box dialog box will appear as shown in Figure 8.5.

3 Click on the **Text Box tab**.

4 Check the box Include "Continued on page ...".

5 You can also add the text 'Continued from page ...' to the beginning of the frame where the text continues by checking the box Include "Continued from page ..." (see Figure 8.6).

Figure 8.7 Newspapers use text flowing.

Importing text from another application

You have been typing directly into your publication. However, you can also add text to your publication that has been typed in Microsoft Word or any other word processing programs.

Follow these steps to import text from another application:

1   If you already have an existing document in Microsoft Word, open the document.

2   Select the text to be imported and choose **Copy** from the Edit menu.

3   Open the publication in Publisher.

4   Click in the frame you want to insert the text and choose **Paste** from the Edit menu.

5   Use Text Overflow to connect the frames if all the text does not fit into the single frame.

Deleting or adding a page

Often, you may need to add or delete a page from a publication. For example, you may want to produce a two-page newsletter, whereas the Publisher default setting for a newsletter publication is four pages.

Follow these steps to delete a page:

1   Right-click on the page you want to delete by clicking on the page thumbnail in the Page Navigation pane.

2   Select **Delete Page** from the pop-up menu; a message dialog box will appear asking whether you would like to delete the page (see Figure 8.8).

3   Confirm you would like to delete the page by clicking **Yes** or **No** if you changed your mind.

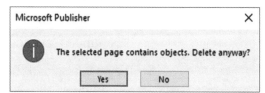

Figure 8.8 Delete Page message dialog box

Similarly, there will also be times when you want to add a page to a publication. Follow these steps:

1   Click where you want to insert the page.

2   Select **Page** from the Pages group of the Insert tab. From the drop-down menu select whether you would like to insert a blank page, or duplicate a page. Clicking **Insert Page** will open the Pages dialog box (see Figure 8.9) where you can enter the number of pages you want to insert.

3   Select whether you want to insert the page **before the current page** or **after the current page** and whether you want a blank or duplicated page (see Figure 8.10).

4   Click **OK**.

Figure 8.9 Insert Pages drop-down menu

Figure 8.10 Insert Page dialog box

Activity 1

1   Open Publisher.

2   Choose a newsletter template from Featured Publications or type newsletter in the search box and choose a newsletter.

3   Delete two or more pages from the publication so that you only have a two-page newsletter.

4   Delete the data in the 'Secondary story headline' frames.

5   Retrieve the document 'Responsibility' from www.hoddereducation.co.uk/interactanswers.

6   Copy and paste the article into the 'Secondary story headline' frame.

7   If the Overflow icon appears connect the frame to a frame on the second page.

8   Using Format Text box include the 'Continue on page …' text to the frame.

9   Change the heading of the Secondary Story Headline to 'A Time Spent Well'.

10 Enter your own text for the 'Lead Story' frames.

Starting from a blank publication

We will now look at creating a publication without using a template, by working from a blank publication. This option lets you decide what you want to produce, the size of page, whether you want the publication folded, and other details – giving you the exact form of the publication that you want.

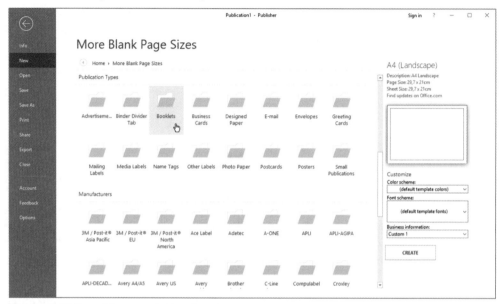

Figure 8.11 Possible newsletter layouts

Planning your publication

The type of publication that you want to produce determines the page size that you need, as well as the type of layout, which can be either landscape or portrait. You can also select the colour scheme, font scheme and Business Information.

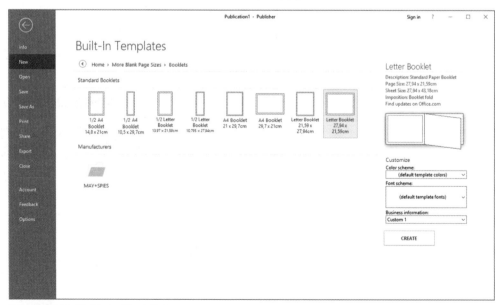

Figure 8.12 Built-In Templates

Follow these steps to work with a blank publication:

1   Choose **New** from the File tab. Click on **More Blank sizes**.

2   From the Publications Type section choose the type of publication: for example **Booklet**, **Postcards**, **Business cards**.

3   Choose the type paper, a preview of the type of fold and page dimensions appears on the right-hand side of the window, for example book fold, side fold or top fold, depending on your publication.

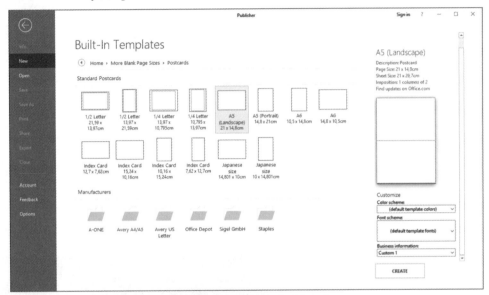

Figure 8.13 More blank pages, showing Blank Publications

Changing the page size and orientation

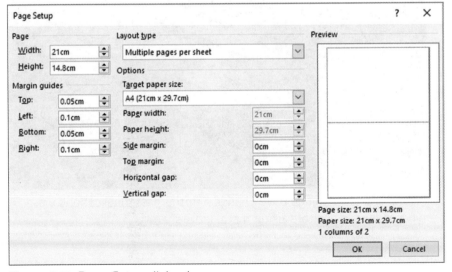

Figure 8.14 Page Setup dialog box

Follow these steps to change the page size and margins:

1   Choose **Margins**, **Orientation** or **Size** from the Page Setup group of the Page Design tab.

2   Select the orientation, either portrait or landscape.

3   Change the width and height to the dimensions you would like.

4   Adjust the margins.

You can also click on the **Dialog box launcher** of the Page Setup group to launch the Page Setup dialog box where you can make the changes (see Figure 8.14).

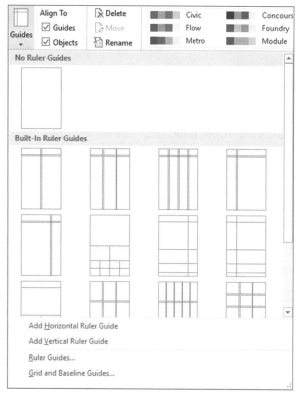

Figure 8.15 Margin Guides tab

Setting margin guides

Once you have selected your publication size, you will notice either pink or blue guidelines appearing on the page. These lines tell you where the margins are located, which helps you with the layout of your design. Changing your margin guides also changes your margins. If you do not want these margin guides to appear, you can set the margins to 0.

Follow these steps to set the margin guides:

1 Select **Guides** from Layout group of the Page Design tab.

2 Select the **Guide option** you desire (see Figure 8.15).

Or

3 Choose **Margins** from the Page Setup group of the Page Design tab and click **None**.

Figure 8.16 How things have changed: In the past, publications were typeset by compositors using metal letters.

Setting grid guides

If your publications require columns or rows, you can apply grid
guides to assist you in laying out your publication. You can select
from the list provided or set your own grid by:

1   Selecting **Grid and Baseline Guides** from the Guides
drop-down menu of the Layout group of the Page Design tab
(see Figure 8.17).

2   The Layout Guides dialog box will appear (see Figure 8.18).

3   Enter the number of columns and rows.

4   Click **OK**.

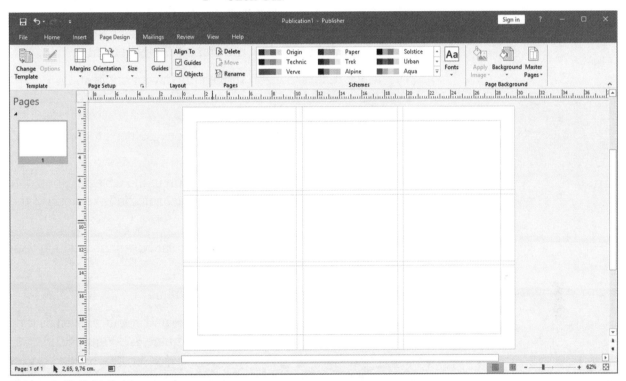

Figure 8.17 Grid Guides on document

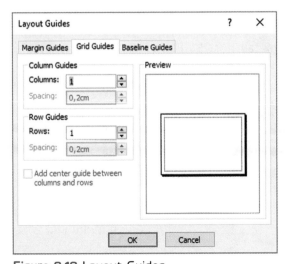

Figure 8.18 Layout Guides

Inserting a picture

When using a template, you can replace the graphic or image by double-clicking on the image or graphic. However, in a blank publication, you will need to insert the graphic in the position you want. Follow these steps to insert the graphic:

1   Click on the **Picture Placeholder** in the Illustrations group of the Insert tab icon.

2   Click and drag the Picture Placeholder frame to position on your page.

3   Expand the frame to the size of graphic you want.

4   Double-click on the **Picture Placeholder** and the Microsoft Clip Organizer window will appear. Click on **Search** or **Browse** on your computer for the graphic that you want.

5   Click **Insert** to insert the picture in your publication.

Adding a text frame

In order to add text to your publication, you need to insert a text frame. Follow these steps:

1   Click on the **Draw Text Box icon** in the Objects group of the Home tab or the Draw Text Box icon in the Text group of the Insert tab.

2   Click and drag the small rectangular box in the position you want the text to appear.

3   Enter your text by typing in the frame.

4   You can change the font, font size and colour, as well as the alignment of the text within the frame (see Figure 8.19).

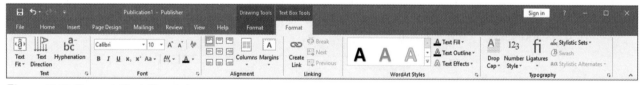

Figure 8.19 Format Text Box tab

Adding a border

In order to give your publication a finished look, you may decide to place a border around your text or your page.

Follow these steps to add a border:

1   Select **Borders & Accents** from the Building Blocks group of the Insert tab.

2   A drop-down menu will appear where you can select your border.

Note!
You can move and resize your graphic to your liking.

Note!
You can also click the **Line/ Border Style icon.**

3   You can also select the **Building Blocks group Dialog box launcher** and select **Borders & Accents** folder (see Figure 8.20)

4   Select a border and click **OK**.

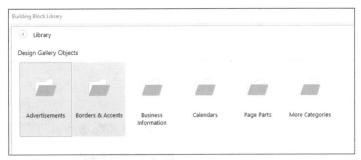

Figure 8.20 Building Block Library

To create a border around a page or object

You can also create a border around a page by using the Rectangle tool. Follow these steps:

1   Select the **Rectangle icon** from the Shapes drop-down menu of the Objects group on the Home tab. Or select the **Rectangle icon** from the Shapes drop-down menu of the Illustrations group on the Insert tab.

2   Click and drag to create a rectangle around your page or object.

3   On the Format tab, select **Shape Styles Dialog box launcher**. The Format Auto Shape dialog box will appear (see Figure 8.21).

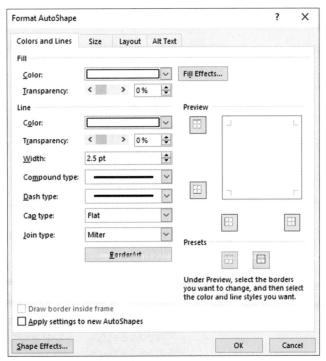

Figure 8.21 Format Auto Shapes

4   You can change the width, colour, dash type or change the line to BorderArt. By selecting **BorderArt**, the BorderArt, dialog box will appear (see Figure 8.22).

5   You will need to remove the fill colour or adjust the transparency of the colour of the rectangle in order to see what is behind it.

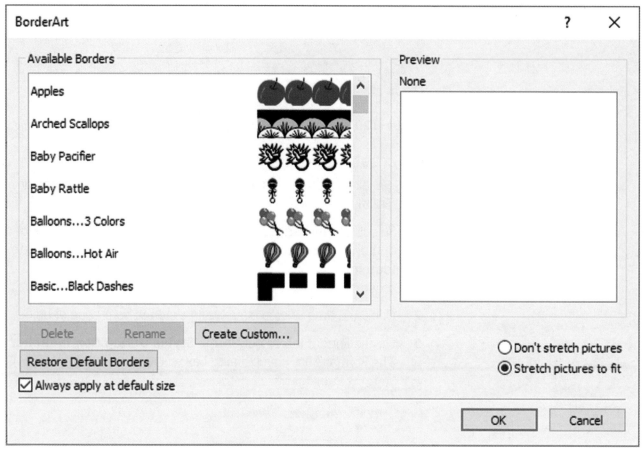

Figure 8.22 BorderArt dialog box

> ## Activity 2
>
> 1   Create a Greetings card from a blank publication.
>
> 2   Insert a border using the Rectangular tool icon and a graphic on the front page.
>
> 3   Insert a text frame on the front page and add the text 'Happy Birthday'.
>
> 4   On page 3 of the greetings card insert a text frame and include the following text:
>
> > 'Happy Birthday, have a great day! If only I could look as young as you!'

Summary 8

1 In Microsoft Publisher, text that cannot fit in a frame is placed in an Overflow area.

2 To handle an overflow you can do one of three things: increase the size of the frame, decrease the size of the text or connect the frame to another frame.

3 Publisher allows you to add 'Continued on page …' and 'Continued from page …' to indicate that part of the text is on another page.

4 You can import text into Publisher from other word processors such as Microsoft Word.

5 You can delete and add pages to a publication.

6 You can create a blank publication from the many types that are offered as standard in Publisher.

7 Margin and grid guides assist in the laying out of a publication.

8 You can insert pictures, add text frames and add borders to your publication.

9 Adding a border can give a publication a finished look.

Questions 8

Copy and fill in the blanks questions

| layout | margin guides | pink | margins | blue |

_____ are lines that tell where the margins are located. These _____ or _____ lines assist you in the _____ of your design. Changing the measurement of these lines also changes your _____.

True or false questions

1 A grid guide indicates where the margins are in a publication.

2 An overflow area holds text that cannot fit into a text frame.

3 You cannot adjust the margins by changing the margin guides.

4 Borders can only be used to frame a text frame.

5 You can import text from another application such as Microsoft Word into Microsoft Publisher.

6 You cannot delete or add a page once a publication type is selected.

7 Publisher allows you to add 'Continued on page …' when two frames are linked.

8 Connecting two frames allows you to see the overflow text.

Multiple-choice questions

1 From which menu can you adjust the margins and page orientation?

  a Edit

  b File

  c Page Setup

  d View

2 From which menu can you change the settings of the grid guides?

  a Arrange

  b File

  c Edit

  d Table

3 This icon ⊡ is known as the:

   a autoflow icon.

   b overflow icon.

   c text link icon.

   d text box icon.

4 This icon ▶ is known as the:

   a autoflow icon.

   b text link icon.

   c text box icon.

   d picture frame icon.

5 In order to add the following text to a frame 'Continued from page …' you need to:

   a right-click and choose Format Text Box.

   b select Format from the Font menu.

   c choose Continued from page … from the Edit menu.

   d type it in at the top of the text frame.

Short-answer questions

1 List the three options for allowing text to fit into a frame and explain in what context each option would work.

2 Explain the difference between margin guides and grid guides.

3 Your neighbour has decided to sell his puppies and he has stuck flyers all over the neighbourhood. Below is a copy of the flyer he produced. Identify four features that can be used to improve the flyer. Redesign the flyer using Microsoft Publisher.

Pups for Sale
3 weeks old, brown and black puppies,
vaccinated, pure breed German Shepard
Price: $400.00
Phone contact: Jason Smith 664-7622

Research question

You have applied for a job in a marketing company. In the interview, the manager gives you this scenario: 'You have been hired to promote our client's book by designing its cover, as well as other promotional documents. How would you use your knowledge of desktop publishing to create and promote our client's book? Explain and justify your choice of design elements.'

Hints

1 What is the first thing you would do?
2 What software would you use to design the book covers?
3 Which design elements would you use on the book cover?
4 What other promotional documents would you suggest be produced?
5 What are a few design elements you would include in the products?
6 Explain some guidelines that you would consider when producing a publication.

Crossword

Across

1. Publisher allows you to use text from other software by _____ it.

6. This icon connects one frame to another. (two words)

7. You can add or _____ a page from a publication.

8. You can add this to give a finished look to a publication.

Down

2. You can use this shape to create a border around a page.

3. You can create a publication without using a template by starting from a _____ publication.

4. Text that cannot fit in the frame is placed in this area.

5. These elements help with the layout of a publication.

STEM project

Your form teacher, who manages the production of the school magazine each year, appoints you as the editor of a special 25th anniversary edition of your school magazine. You have been tasked with planning all the details for a new full-colour magazine that must be published in six months. Your publishing team consists of a group of classmates.

1. You hold a meeting with your publishing team to plan what to do. What are the main issues you plan to discuss? What other issues are raised by the publishing team?

2. With the help of your publishing team, put together a step-by-step plan for producing the magazine. You may include a timeline for quick referencing.

3. When you present your plan to your teacher, she advises that she wants the following changes:

   * Class photographs must fit onto a maximum of seven pages, although there are 16 forms/grades and your original plan was to allocate one page per form/grade.
   * A select number of teachers' biographies from the year the school started (only typed versions are available for most) must be included.
   * Newspaper clippings on the school's greatest achievements must be included.

4. What adjustments do you need to make to your plan to ensure that your form teacher's wishes are carried out?

Hints

1. List the key features of a school magazine.
2. Interview students and teachers on the features they would like to see in the 25th anniversary edition of the school magazine.
3. Refer to the chapter as you and your publishing team work out your plan.

Objectives

At the end of the chapter, you will be able to:

❏ add speaker notes

❏ print your presentation

❏ create a slide master

❏ make an effective PowerPoint presentation.

In the *Interact with IT* Book 2, we looked at how to create a Microsoft PowerPoint presentation and include graphics and sound, as well as use a template, transitions and animations. In this chapter, you will learn how to add speaker notes and print out your presentation. You will also find out how to create a master slide.

Adding notes – speaker's notes

When speakers and presenters use PowerPoint, they often like to make additional notes just for themselves, containing further details that remind them of what they plan to say about specific points during the presentation.

These kinds of notes can be created in the Notes pane of the Normal view. You can also click on the Notes icon ≜ Notes in the bottom right-hand corner of the screen, which allows you to expand the Notes section. The audience will not see the notes during the slide show, but the speaker can print out the notes for their own benefit. On the printout, the speaker's notes normally appear below the printed slide. In this way, the speaker can look at their printout and see both the slide and the notes.

Activity 1

You are going to add speaker notes to your slides. Follow these steps:

1 Retrieve the presentation 'My environment'.

2 Add an appropriate graphic to one of your slides.

3 Add one slide of your own to the presentation before the last slide.

4 Add speaker notes to each of your slides.

5 In the Slide Sorter view, move the third slide to the second position.

6 Save your presentation.

7 Display your presentation as a slide show using the Slide Show view in the lower right-hand corner of your screen, or by choosing **From Beginning** from the Start Slide Show group of the Slide Show tab.

Printing your presentation

As we saw earlier, printing your presentation can be useful if you have added notes to it, so that you can refer to them as you give your speech. Printing your presentation can also be useful if you want to give a copy of it to your audience to take away with them and study in their own time. You can select whether you want to print each slide on a separate page or a number of slides on one page, for a shorter handout.

Follow these steps to print your presentation:

1   Select **Print** from the File tab; the Print dialog box will appear (see Figure 9.1).

2   Select **Slides or Handouts** from the Full Page Slides drop-down menu.

3   Selecting **Slides** will print a single slide on each page, selecting **Handouts** allows you to choose how many slides will be printed on a page.

4   From the Full Page Slides drop-down menu select the number of slides per page and whether you want it to be printed horizontally or vertically.

5   Click **OK** to print.

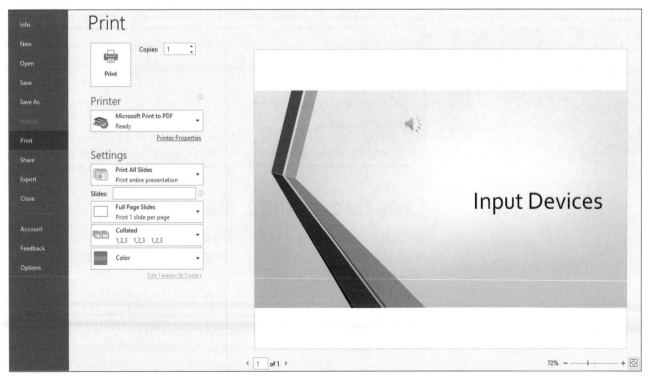

Figure 9.1 Print dialog box

Figure 8.21 Note pages

Follow these steps to print your speaker notes or outline:

1 Select **Print** from the File tab; the Print window will appear.

2 Select **Note Pages** or **Outline** from the Full Page Slides drop-down menu (see Figure 9.2).

3 Click **OK** to print.

Figure 9.2 Full Page Slides drop-down menu

Activity 2

You are going to print your presentation. Follow these steps:

1 Retrieve the presentation 'My environment' you saved from the earlier activity.

2 Print the presentation so that six slides appear on one page.

Creating a slide master

You can create a slide that acts as a template to give your entire presentation the same design elements. It affects every slide in your presentation. This slide can contain your company's logo, the background design, the font colour and the font type that needs to appear on every slide. This slide is called the **slide master**. It saves you from having to repeatedly format every slide in your presentation with the same design, such as colour, background, font, animation, and so on. You can pre-design how each of the layouts will look.

Follow these steps to create a slide master:

1 Select **Slide Master** from the Master Views group of the Views tab (see Figure 9.14). The side pane with various layout options will appear.

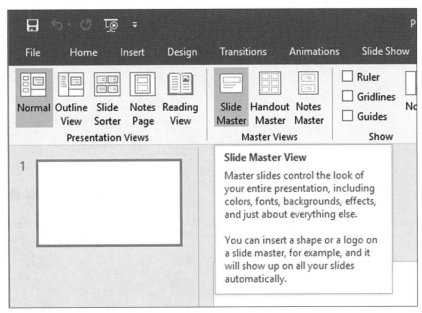

Figure 9.3 Master View group

2 Select the **Slide Master** slide. It is the largest and first slide in the pane (see Figure 9.3).

3 Make the changes you want to this slide and the other layout slides (see Figure 9.4).

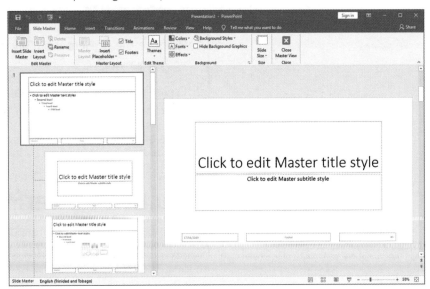

Figure 9.4 Slide Master

* You can modify the background, so that all your slides will have the same background.

* You can add a logo or a watermark
* You can rearrange the **placeholders** on the Slide Master, and all the slides with that layout will adjust according.
* You can customise your text and adjust the font type, font colour and font size on the Slide Master and the other slide layouts.
* You can even create your own slide layouts that look different from the Slide Master using a different background or theme.

4   When you are finished with your changes, select **Close Master View** from the Slide Master tab.

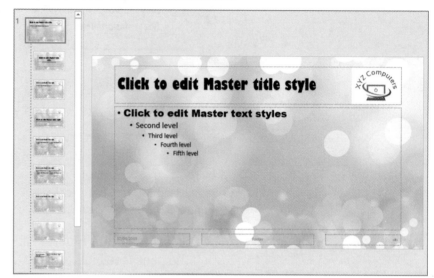

Figure 9.5 Changes to Slide Master and Layout slides

Activity 3

1 Retrieve the presentation 'My environment' you saved from the earlier activity.

2 Create a Slide Master for the presentation, and change the background, font, effects and placeholders.

3 Save and display your presentation.

Effective PowerPoint presentations

The purpose of creating a presentation is to get a message across to your audience. You may want to explain something or express an idea. Presentations can be exciting, fun and effective, and hold the audience's attention throughout, or they can be boring, unimpressive and ineffective, and perhaps even leaving the audience confused about what is being presented.

Here are some guidelines to keep in mind when you develop your presentation to ensure that it is interesting, fun and effective.

Guidelines for presenting

Remember these points:

* Plan carefully what you want to say and do your research.
* Practise and time your presentation.
* Speak clearly and enunciate your words. Do not rush your presentation by speaking too quickly as your audience will struggle to hear and understand you.

Guidelines for slides

Remember these points:

* Use design templates.
* Make sure your slides have standardised colours and styles.
* Make sure that slides include only essential information.
* Use contrasting colours on slides.
* Limit the number of slides in your presentation, because too many slides can confuse your audience.

Guidelines for text

Remember these points:

* Know your audience. Are you going to present to adults or children? Your audience will indicate the type of language (simple or more complex) that you will need to use.
* Try to limit the number of words on a line. Generally, you should have six to eight words per line and six to eight lines on a slide. As you place more words on a line, the text becomes smaller and your audience may not be able to see the information.
* Try to avoid long sentences, as they may become difficult for your audience to read.
* Pay careful attention to your use of font sizes, as they are important. Font sizes should generally range from 25 to 48 points. Larger font sizes in a presentation usually indicate more important information.
* Avoid using fancy fonts, as they can be hard to read.
* Make sure that the text colour contrasts with the background. Text colours that are very similar to the background colours are difficult to see and read.
* Avoid writing words with all capital letters, as they are difficult to read.
* Avoid using abbreviations and acronyms unless you explain them somewhere in your presentation, as the audience may not understand what they mean.

Guidelines for graphics and clipart

Remember these points:

* Make sure that the graphics and clipart enhance and complement the text, and do not overwhelm it.
* Check that the graphics and clipart relate to both the topic being presented and the information on that particular slide.
* Try to use no more than two graphics per slide.

Transitions and animations

Remember these points:

* Use animations and transitions only if they enhance your presentation, as they can be distracting.
* Avoid using too many animations and transitions, as they can confuse and distract your audience.
* Make sure that any animations and transitions are consistent, as many different types of animation on one slide can be distracting.

Sound and music

Remember these points:

* Add sounds only if they enhance and improve the quality of your presentation.
* Keep in mind that the sound you hear on your laptop or desktop may not be loud or clear enough to be heard by an audience in a large room.

Figure 9.6 Follow these guidelines to make sure that your presentation is interesting, fun and effective.

Summary 9

1 Speaker notes can be used by presenters to make additional notes containing further details to remind them about what to say about a specific point during a presentation.

2 Printing slides can be useful for looking at your presenter notes, or for handing out copies of your presentation to your audience.

3 You can print each slide on a separate page or a number of slides on one page, using the Handouts option in the Print dialog box.

4 A Slide Master is a slide that allows you to set a pre-designed theme, including elements such as background colours, fonts, effects and placeholders, which will apply to every slide in your presentation.

Questions 9

Copy and fill in the blanks questions

1 On the slide printouts, the _____ _____ appear below the printed slide.

2 A _____ _____ acts as a template to give an entire presentation the same _____ elements.

3 Rearranging the _____ on the _____ _____ adjusts all slides with that layout accordingly.

True or false questions

1 Speaker's notes can be created in the Notes pane of the Normal view.

2 You can only print six slides on a page.

3 You cannot print speaker notes; you can only print slides.

4 The audience will be able to see the speaker notes during a presentation.

5 A Slide Master does not affect the entire presentation.

6 Rearranging the placeholders on the Slide Master will cause all the slides with that layout to adjust according.

7 Too much animation can be a distraction in your presentation.

8 Text colours that are similar to the slide background are easy to see and read.

Multiple-choice questions

1 The Notes pane allows you to:

   a create your slide show.

   b add an animation to your slide.

   c add additional comments about the slide for the presenter.

   d determine if an audience will like your presentation.

2 To see how your presentation will look once it is printed, click:

   a Note Pages.

   b Preview.

   c Handouts.

   d Slide Master.

3 A Slide Master contains:

   a preset text boxes.

   b design elements to give slides a consistent appearance.

   c preformatted objects.

   d all of the above.

4 Which of the following is not an effective guideline to follow when creating a presentation?

    a Use consistent animations.

    b Use as many graphics as possible.

    c Use contrasting colours.

    d Be mindful of the sound quality.

Short-answer questions

1 What are speaker notes and how can they be used by a presenter?

2 Explain the purpose of using a Slide Master template.

3 List three guidelines for including sound, animation and transitions in presentations.

4 List five guidelines to follow for an effective presentation.

Create a slide presentation

Create a ten-slide presentation on one of the following topics:

1 Protecting our pets

2 Conserving electricity

3 Conserving water

4 The bee and the hummingbird are responsible for over 90% of the world's pollination.

5 Forms of transportation (air, land, water)

6 Evacuation drill in my school

7 Folk music in my country

8 Reviving the folk tales (folk stories told in my country)

9 Making my home more environmentally-friendly

10 A tradition in my family (who started it, how was it passed down through the generations)

STEM project

Continuing your STEM Project from Chapter 8, your form teacher has asked you and your publishing team to prepare a PowerPoint presentation showing samples of the items from the school magazine. She wants you to present this to the school principal and other staff members. You will have 15 minutes to deliver this presentation and answer any questions at the end. (*Note to teacher: Invite the principal and staff to view the presentation.*)

1 Using your new knowledge on transitions and animations from *Interact with IT* Book 2, organise a publishing team discussion on the items and features that you think would be suitable and effective for this presentation. Take notes of all ideas discussed.

2 Due to the time constraint, what are three major features you intend to use in your presentation? Why did you select these features?

3 Prepare your presentation, making sure all members of your publishing team contribute.

4 Show your presentation to the principal and other members of staff. Document all questions asked at the end of the presentation. Answer questions as they are asked and ask for some more time for you and your team to provide answers to any questions you cannot answer on the spot.

Hints

1 Review the chapter and list all of the features you can possibly use in your presentation.

2 Do a practice run of your presentation to make sure it's length is within the 15 minutes allocated.

3 Use the questions asked to help you plan similar projects in the future.

10 3D drawing with Paint

Objectives

At the end of the chapter, you will be able to:

❏ create 3D shapes such as 3D doodles, 3D objects and 3D models

❏ modify 3D graphics by colouring, adding textures and effects

❏ create mixed-reality 3D images

❏ crop your 3D image

❏ record and playback your creation of a 3D graphic.

Microsoft Paint is a program included with each Windows release that allows you to create and customise graphs. In the *Interact with IT* Book 1, you learned about the basics of how to draw with Paint, concentrating on 2D drawings. Two-dimensional (2D) drawings or objects only have height and length – in other words they are flat. An example of 2D is a drawing on a piece of paper.

In this chapter, you will learn how to do 3D drawings with Paint. You will look at 3D shapes and how to create, modify, crop, record and playback 3D graphics.

Figure 10.1 A 2D drawing of an owl

Figure 10.2 A 3D drawing of a puzzle cube

Drawing in 3D

When you draw in three dimensions or 3D, the object that you are drawing uses three axes:

✳ The *x*-axis or horizontal axis
✳ The *y*-axis or vertical axis
✳ The *z*-axis, which represents the width or depth.

An object is said to be three-dimensional or 3D if it has length, height and width. A 3D object drawn on a piece of paper appears as if it is coming out of the paper.

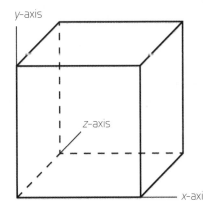

Figure 10.3 A 3D object – a cube

Did you know?

The word 'toggle' means to switch from one effect or state to another when a button, or in this case the icon, is selected.

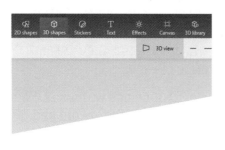

Figure 10.4 3D View tool

3D View tool

The 3D View tool toggles the 3D graphic in and out of the drawing canvas (see Figure 10.4).

Drawing using 3D shapes

You have a few options to choose from when drawing with 3D shapes. You can choose 3D doodles, 3D objects and 3D models or you choose to explore additional shapes from the Open 3D library.

3D doodles

The 3D doodles tool allows you to draw draw curved lines in 3D and use the drag points to modify the shape of the curve. As shown in Figure 10.5, the three options that you have when using this tool are the:

* tube brush
* sharp edge
* soft edge.

| tube brush | soft edge | sharp edge |

Figure 10.5 3D doodles

Follow these steps to draw 3D doodles:

1. Select the **3D shapes tool** and the 3D shapes panel will appear.

2. Select the **Tube brush** from the 3D doodles section (see Figure 10.10).

3. Place your mouse pointer on the canvas and drag to draw your doodle.

4. Adjust the drag points to change the shape of the drawing.

3D objects

The 3D Objects tool allows you to create some basic geometric shapes that you would usually find in your maths class. These shapes include cubes, cylinders and pyramids, as well as others.

You can rotate the 3D object along any of the axes (x-axis, y-axis or z-axis – see Figure 10.7). The 3D objects panel allows you the option to change the attributes of the object, such as the colour and material. It also allows you to flip the object horizontally or vertically.

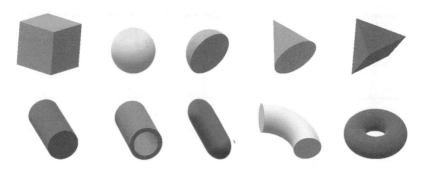

Figure 10.6 Samples of the 3D objects available

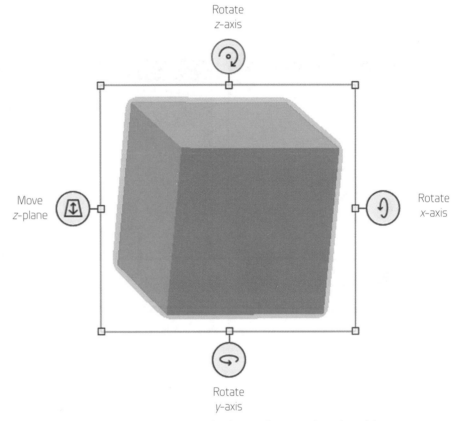

Figure 10.7 A 3D object showing the icons for rotating the object along the axes

Follow these steps to create and rotate 3D shapes:

1   Select the **3D shapes tool** and the 3D shapes panel will appear.

2   Select the cube object from the 3D objects section (see Figure 10.10).

3   Place your mouse pointer on the canvas and drag to draw the size of cube you want.

4   Rotate your object along each of the axes to get the perspective that you desire.

Figure 10.8 3D models of a woman and a dog

Exercise 1

1 Create a 3D doodle artwork using two out of the three doodle shapes.

2 Use three of the 3D objects available to create a new shape.

3 Combine a 3D doodle shape and a 3D object to create a 3D graphic.

3D models

The 3D Models tool gives you five basic models to choose from: a man, a woman, a dog, a cat and a fish (see Figure 10.8). However, there are many more 3D models available in the Open 3D Library (see Figures 10.9 and 10.10), which is located online.

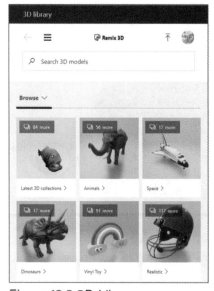

Figure 10.9 3D Library

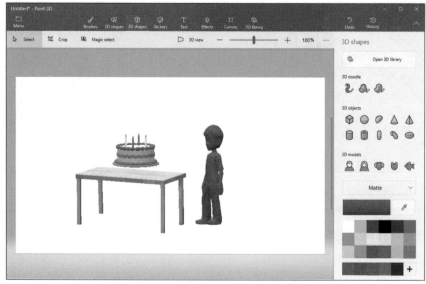

Figure 10.10 Models downloaded from the 3D library

Follow these steps to create and rotate 3D models:

1 Select the **3D shapes tool** and the 3D shapes panel will appear.

2 Select the woman model from the 3D models section.

3 Place your mouse pointer on the canvas and drag to draw the size of cube you want.

4 Rotate your object along each of the axes to get the perspective that you desire and click on your canvas to complete your drawing.

5 Select the dog model from the 3D models section and repeat steps 3 and 4.

Colouring a 3D model

Many models may not be in the colour that you want. You can choose to paint or colour the model using the Brushes tool.

Follow these steps to paint or colour a 3D model:

1 Select the **Brushes tool** and the brushes panel will appear.

2 Use the Watercolour brush tool or Marker tool to colour your model.

3 Zoom in on your object and adjust the thickness of the brush as needed, in order to paint the object.

4 Rotate the object as needed to paint or colour its entire surface.

5 Use the Eraser tool if you get the colour on other parts of the model where that colour should not appear.

Adding stickers to your model

Stickers are tiny forms of clip art that can be added to both your 2D and 3D objects and models. You can add eyes, mouth and nose stickers or even glasses to a face. You can also apply textures to a fish or a dog model.

Follow these steps to add stickers to your model:

1 Click on the **3D shapes** tool and the 3D shapes panel will appear.

2 Choose the 3D model of the dog, and place it on your canvas.

3 Make your model large.

4 Rotate the model so that it is facing directly towards you.

5 Click on the **Sticker tool**.

6 Add the mouth and the sunglasses to your 3D model (see Figure 10.11).

Adding textures to your model

Adding textures allows you to change the surface of an object, such as adding fur to a dog, scales to a fish or a wood texture to a table.

Follow these steps to add textures to your model:

1 Click on the **3D shapes** tool and the 3D shapes panel will appear.

2 Choose the 3D model of the dog, and place it on your canvas.

3 Make your model large.

4 Click on the **Sticker tool** and the sticker panel will appear

5 Click on the **Texture icon** and select an appropriate texture for the dog from those available (see Figure 10.12). You can also download or import your own graphics to use as textures.

Figure 10.11 Sticker of dog nose and glasses added to a 3D model

Note!

You can also adjust the opacity of the sticker. For example, it is possible for you to adjust the opacity of the glasses to see the eyes of the dog in the Figure 10.11.

Figure 10.12 Dog with a downloaded fur texture

Creating 3D text

We can create 3D text similar to WordArt in Microsoft word using the 3D text tool. We have already looked at 2D Text in the *Interact with IT* Book 2.

Follow these steps to create 3D text:

1 Click on the **Text tool** and the Text panel will appear.

2 Click on the **3D Text icon**.

3 Change the attributes of the text by changing the font, font size, colour, style and alignment.

4 Type your text into the text box.

5 Click anywhere on the canvas once your text is complete.

6 Rotate your object as needed (see Figure 10.13).

Figure 10.13 3D text

Exercise 2

Design a room using the 3D Library. Use stickers and textures to enhance the room, and label your room using 3D text.

Adding effects

The Effects tool allows you to add a filter colour, which adjusts how lighting of different colours, as well as the position of the lighting source, will affect the object. For example, if light shines on the object from the bottom, then the top of the object will appear dark.

Follow these steps to add effects:

1 Click on the **Effects tool** and the Effects panel will appear (see Figure 10.14).

2 Select a filter.

3 Drag the Light tool around the light wheel to change the position of the light source.

The Canvas tool

The Canvas tool is like a sheet of paper. It allows you to observe your 3D object or model in a 2D space or a single plane. You can flip the canvas, rotate it and make it transparent.

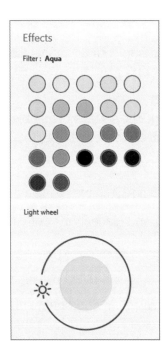

Figure 10.14 Effects panel

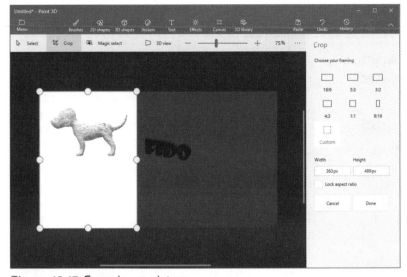

Figure 10.15 Cropping a picture

Figure 10.16 The History tool

Figure 10.17 Saving as a video

The Cropping tool

The Cropping tool allows you to change the size of the canvas. You can increase or decrease the size of the canvas. It allows you to cut out or remove the outer portions of an image that you do not want (Figure 10.15).

The History tool

The History tool keeps track of every step you have made while creating your 3D object or model. The History Slider allows you to replay every step you have taken in creating your drawing (see Figure 10.16).

You can export these steps as a video by clicking Save As and selecting Video. This exports the file as an MP4 that can be opened and viewed on any media player. Recording your movements or steps allows for the animation of your object. For example, you can record while you rotate or move an object and the object will appear to move when you play back the video (see Figure 10.17).

Mixed Reality tool

The Mixed Reality tool allows you to place your 3D model into a real space. Once you click this tool, a 3D Viewer opens and your device camera places your 3D Model into the live image. You can record a video of your model in the live background shot or take a picture of it (see Figure 10.18). This view is also called augmented reality. It is where computer-generated objects, text and sound are superimposed on the real world.

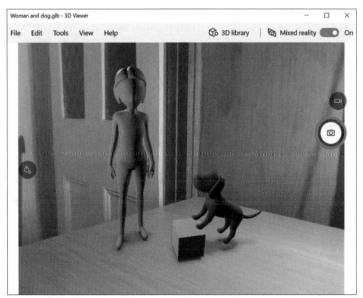

Figure 10.18 A mixed-reality picture, showing a 3D model interacting with the real world

Summary 10

1 A three-dimensional (3D) object has length, height and width, and exists in a plane with three axes: x-axis, y-axis and z-axis.

2 You can draw 3D shapes such as 3D doodles, 3D objects and 3D models in 3D Paint.

3 You can colour 3D models using the Brushes tool.

4 Stickers are tiny forms of clip art that can be added to both your 2D and 3D models.

5 Textures such as scales and fur can be added to the surface of any object.

6 3D Text, which is similar to WordArt, can be created using 3D Text tool.

7 The Effects tool lets you add a filter colour, which adjusts how lighting colours and the lighting source position will affects the object.

8 The Canvas tool lets you observe your 3D object or model in a 2D space or single plane.

9 Cropping cuts out or removes the outer portions of an image that you do not want.

10 The History tool keeps track of every step you make while creating your 3D object or model and the history slider allows you to play it back as a video.

11 The Mixed Reality tool superimposes your 3D drawing into a space in the real world.

Questions 10

Copy and fill in the blanks questions

1 A three-dimensional object has _____, _____ and _____. It exists on the _____, _____ and _____ axes.

2 The _____ _____ tool allows you to place a 3D object into a real environment. This is also called _____ reality.

True or false questions

1 You cannot cut unwanted parts from a picture.

2 The Effects tool allows you the change the position of the light source.

3 You cannot colour a 3D drawing.

4 You can record your actions while creating a 3D model and play it back as a video.

5 You cannot rotate any 3D graphic along the x-axis, y-axis or z-axis.

6 Using the Brushes tool allows you to colour 3D objects.

Multiple-choice questions

1 The graphic shown in Figure 10.19 tells you that you are using the:

a soft edge brush.

b marker brush.

c tube brush.

d sharp edge brush.

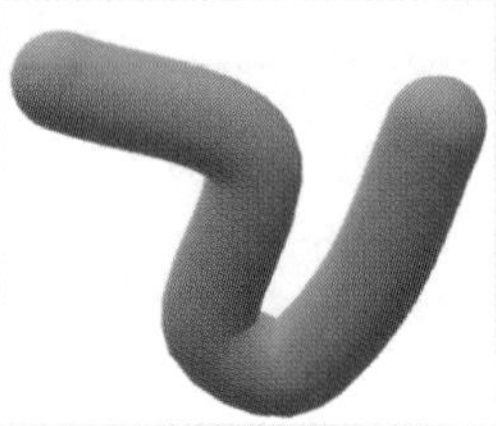

Figure 10.19

2 All the tools are available to draw 3D graphics except for

a 3D objects. b 3D models.

c 3D text. d 3D car.

3 Placing a 3D object or model into a real space requires the use of which tool?

a Paint brush tool

b 3D model tool

c The History tool

d The Mixed Reality tool

Short-answer questions

1 Explain the concept of a mixed-reality graphic.

2 Give one reason to use the History Slider to playback or create a video of your 3D graphic.

3 What makes an object three dimensional?

Crossword

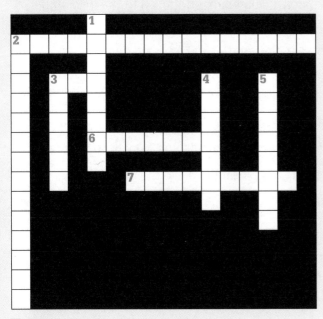

Down

1 Adding this to the surface of your object makes it look different

2 An object that exists on a single plane and has only height and length (two words)

3 This allows you to observe your 3D model in a 2D space

4 This tool allows you to paint or colour your objects

5 Small forms of clip art that can be added to your models

Across

2 An object that has length, height and width (two words)

3 You can _____ out unwanted parts of an image.

6 This lets you add a colour filter and lighting source to the object.

7 The term for placing a digital object into a space in the real world

Research question

3D paint can be used to create augmented-reality art. Explain and demonstrate using 3D paint what is augmented-reality art.

STEM project

In the early 1990s and 2000s when one heard of creating a work of art, one would imagine an artist, with pencil, paint and paper. This has now evolved to three-dimensional (3D) computerised drawings. Your school's Art and Design teacher has asked you to do a comparison table on the techniques involved and visual impact when drawing by hand compared to creating a 3D mixed-reality drawing. You can select any of the following themes to produce sample drawings for demonstrating your comparison: country scene with persons and animals, video arcade with persons and objects or a group of friends socialising at an eating place. Each student will be expected to produce their own comparison table but can discuss and plan in groups.

1 Write a paragraph stating exactly what you will be doing for your Art and Design teacher.

2 Discuss the advantages and disadvantages of using the 3D drawing with Paint software compared to using paper and paint to create a work of art. Record the points discussed for use in your comparison table.

3 Create two pieces of artwork on one of the themes given. Use this artwork to produce your comparison table, which you can present using any of the multimedia formats you prefer.

4 Present your artwork and comparison table to a group of your classmates. What feedback did you receive?

5 Give an opinion on which method produces more impactful art and give at least two reasons for your opinion.

Hints

1 What are possible headings for your comparison table?

2 Select a theme you will enjoy working on.

11 Problem solving and algorithm development (2)

✳ Objectives

At the end of the chapter, you will be able to:

❑ draw a flowchart for simple algorithms

❑ explain what is a finite loop and an indefinite loop

❑ explain what is a terminal or sentinel value

❑ develop algorithms using the FOR–NEXT statement

❑ develop algorithms using the WHILE–DO statement.

In *Interact with IT* Book 1, you were introduced to the following steps involved in problem solving:

1 Define the problem. Start with a clear understanding of what the problem is.

2 Analyse the problem (determine what to do to solve it).

3 Decide on the results to achieve.

4 Consider ways to achieve the result, and select the best option.

5 Develop a method or algorithm to solve the problem.

In Book 2, you learned how to write simple algorithms using narrative, refine the narrative to pseudocode, and create flowcharts. You also examined two of the three control structures, sequencing and selection, as well as comparison statements, such as IF–THEN and the IF–THEN–ELSE statements, and how to use them to solve simple linear mathematical problems. Let us review the important points to remember.

We can represent an algorithm in the following three ways:

As a **narrative**, using English statements to describe the solution to the problem
As a **flowchart**, which is a visual representation of the solution using specific symbols and arrows
As **pseudocode**, which (as the name implies: 'pseudo' – fake code) is not the actual program code, but closely resembles it.

The three types of control structures are:

sequencing instructions, where the instructions are executed line by line
selecting and comparison instructions, where the instructions are executed based on a particular choice
repeating or looping instructions, which involve the repeating of a piece of code.

In this chapter, you will learn how to write algorithms/pseudocode/flowcharts using the third control structure, which is repeating and looping instructions, such as the FOR–NEXT and WHILE–DO statements.

Before we start, let us review some facts about constants and variables.

> Constants are data that do not change, but remain the same during the execution of a program or algorithm, for example: 5, Jack
>
> Variables represent the values that change during the execution of a program or algorithm. There are numeric variables and literal or string variables. Variable names are assigned to locations in memory that hold the variable. Variable names should represent the data that is stored, for example: Num, StudentName where Num represents a number and StudentName represents a student's name.

Repeated instructions

In computing, as well as in real life, there are occasions where you may need a set of instructions to be repeated until a condition is met.

Here is an example from a real-life situation. John is running a bath for his younger brother; he wants the temperature of the water to be 35°C. However, after he adds hot water to the bath water, the temperature of the water rises to 50°C. He adds cold water a cup at a time and checks to see if the temperature of the water has gone down to the required temperature. He repeats this until the temperature drops to 35°C. The flowchart for this process is shown in Figure 11.1.

Figure 11.1 John repeated the process of adding cold water and checking the temperature until the bath water was 35°C.

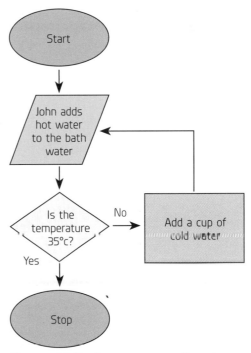

Figure 11.2 Bath temperature flowchart

Exercise 1

1 You are asked to help someone total a number of receipts. Their starting total is set to $0.00. To begin with, the amount on the first receipt is entered. After this, the person responds 'yes' or 'no' to the question: 'Are there any more receipts to add?' If the answer is 'yes', then another receipt is read and the amount is entered and added to the total. If the answer is 'no', the total is printed. Figure 11.3 shows the flowchart symbols necessary to solve this problem. Rearrange them into a workable solution.

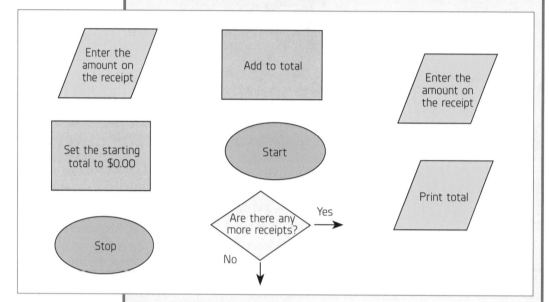

Figure 11.3 Flowchart symbols

2 Create a flowchart to show the following loop. Read the name and age of a child until you find the child who is older than 12 years.

When a statement or instruction or a group of statements or instructions are repeated, this is called a **loop**. As we saw in the first example, John adds a cup of cold water and checks to see if the temperature is 35°C, he does this repeatedly until the temperature is 35°C.

The two types of loops are a **finite loop** and an **indefinite loop**. A finite loop is where the instructions are repeated a fixed number of times. An indefinite loop is where the instructions are repeated an unspecified number of times.

In the case where John is adding a cup of cold water, he does not know how many cups he has to add for the temperature to reach 35°C, so he adds one at a time and checks the temperature. In this case, John has to look out for a particular value – the temperature of 35°C.

This value is called a **sentinel/terminal value** and is needed to stop the process. In the example, this value causes John to stop adding cold water. For a computer program, a sentinel or terminal value causes the program to exit the loop. It can also be called a **lookout value**, because if the data being entered ever becomes equal to that value, the computer exits the loop.

Counting

In scenarios such as those we have just been looking at, there is a need to use a counter to keep track of the iterations – in other words how many times instructions are repeated. An iteration is one execution of a set of statements. This counter can be part of a condition that stops the instructions from repeating. When the value of the counter becomes equal to a particular value, the instructions stop. For example:

<Counter variable> = <Counter variable> + 1

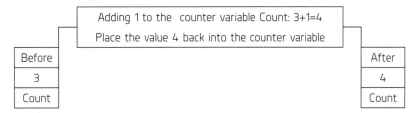

Figure 11.4 Incrementing a counter

This example simply states that 1 is added to the value of the counter variable and the result is placed back into the counter variable. The choice of name for the counter variable can be based on what is being counted. In Problem 1, the name 'NumBoys' is used for the number of boys.

Problem 1

A boxing ring admits only a certain number of boys. Read the name of the boy and count the number of boys. Print the number of boys.

Solution

Question	Algorithm (rough)	Algorithm refined	Algorithm refined further
What is the input instruction?	Prompt and enter the name of the boy	Prompt and enter Name	PRINT "Enter the name of a boy" READ Boy Name
What is the processing instruction?	Add 1 to the number of boys	Number of boys = number of boys + 1	NumBoys = 0 NumBoys = NumBoys + 1
What is the output instruction?	Display the number of boys	Output Number of boys	Print NumBoys

Cumulative totals

Figure 11.5 The cumulative total determines the final number of wickets taken.

It often becomes necessary to keep adding values to a current total to get a new total. This is called a **cumulative total**, which for example, is used to keep track of the total wickets taken by various bowlers on a cricket team:

bowler 1: 2; bowler 2: 1; bowler 3: 3 and so on.

<Cumulative Total> = <Cumulative Total> + <Variable>

It is important to set the initial Cumulative Total variable to 0 before the values are added. This is called **initialising** the variable. At the end of the match, each bowler's wickets have been added in turn to the Cumulative Total to get the final number of wickets taken.

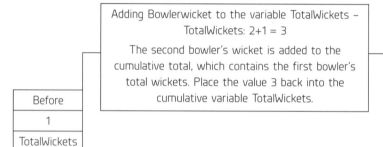

Adding Bowlerwicket to the variable TotalWickets – TotalWickets: 2+1 = 3

The second bowler's wicket is added to the cumulative total, which contains the first bowler's total wickets. Place the value 3 back into the cumulative variable TotalWickets.

Before
1
TotalWickets

After
3
TotalWickets

Figure 11.6 Cumulative totals

Problem 2

A bus picks up passengers at several stops along its route. Read the number of passengers picked up at a stop and add it to the total number of passengers picked up in one day. Print the total number of passengers.

Solution

Question	Algorithm (rough)	Algorithm refined	Algorithm refined further
What is the input instruction?	Prompt and enter the number of passengers at a stop	Prompt and enter number of passengers at stop	PRINT "Enter the number of passengers at a stop" READ NumPassengers
What is the processing instruction?	Add number of passengers at a stop to the total number of passengers	Set total number of passengers to 0. Total number of passengers = total number of passengers + number of passengers at stop	TotalPassengers = 0 TotalPassengers = TotalPassengers + NumPassengers
What is the output instruction?	Display the total number of passengers	Output total passengers	Print "Total Number of Passengers"

Exercise 2

Write algorithms to solve the following problems:

Figure 11.7 The cumulative total determines the total number of passengers.

1 Buses leave a station. Read the bus number and count the bus. Print the answer.

2 Buses leave a station. Read the bus number, bus destination and count the bus. If the bus is going to St Lucy, then also count the buses going to St Lucy. Print the number of buses leaving the station and the number of buses going to St Lucy.

3 A number of buses leave a station every day. Read the bus number and count the bus. Add the number of buses to the total number of buses that leave the bus station for the week. Print the total number of buses.

4 An airplane leaves an airport at regular intervals during the day. Read the flight number and count the flights. Print the number of flights.

5 An airplane leaves an airport at regular intervals during the day. Read the flight number and count the flights. Add the number of flights to the total weekly flights. Print the total number of flights.

WHILE–DO statement

In a WHILE–DO statement, the computer executes a set of statements or instructions repeatedly for as long as a given condition is true. This statement is used when you do not know beforehand how many times the statements within a loop are to be repeated. This explains why the WHILE–DO statement is used for indefinite loops.

Here is how it works:

* In the WHILE–DO statement, the condition is tested; if it is true the instructions within the WHILE and ENDWHILE are executed until the condition becomes false, then the loop is exited.
* Statements or instructions appearing before the WHILE–DO statement are carried out once.
* The statements after the ENDWHILE are carried out once. The ENDWHILE marks the end of the WHILE–DO statement.
* If, however, after carrying out the instructions before the loop, the condition in the WHILE loop is tested and is false, the computer skips the instructions within the while loop and continues with the statements after the ENDWHILE.
* The trigger that causes the loop to stop is called a lookout value, a terminating value or sentinel value.

In summary:

WHILE <Condition> DO

    <Statements>

ENDWHILE

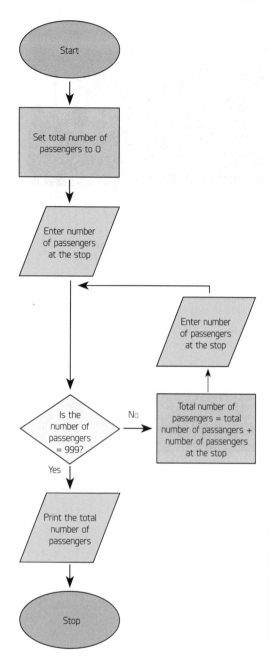

Figure 11.8 Flowchart for Problem 3

Problem 3

A bus picks up passengers at several stops along its route. Write an algorithm to read the number of passengers picked up at each stop, and add it to the total number of passengers. Calculate the total number of passengers picked up in one day if the data is terminated by the user entering a value of 999. Print the total number of passengers.

Solution

Algorithm rough

Set the total number of passengers to 0

Prompt and enter the number of passengers at the stop

WHILE number of passengers at the stop is not equal to 999 DO

Total number of passengers = total number of passengers + number of passengers at the stop

Prompt and enter the number of passengers at a stop

ENDWHILE

Print "Total Number of Passengers"

Algorithm refined

Total number of passengers = 0

Prompt and enter the number of passengers

WHILE number of passengers <> 999 DO

Total number of passengers = total number of passengers + number of passengers

Prompt and enter the number of passengers

ENDWHILE

Print "Total Number of Passengers"

Algorithm further refined

Total Passengers = 0

Prompt and Input number of passengers

WHILE number of passengers <> 999 DO

Total passengers = total passengers + number of passengers

Prompt and Input number of passengers

ENDWHILE

Print "Total Number of Passengers"

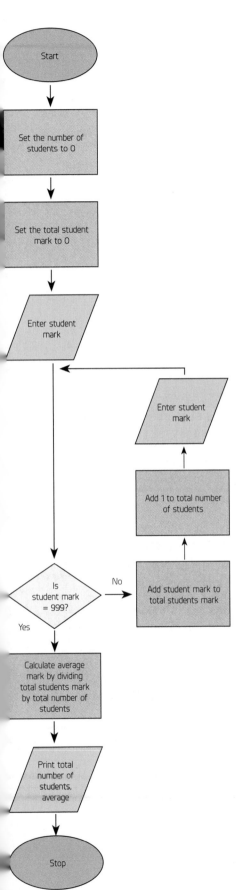

Figure 11.9 Flowchart for Problem 4

Problem 4

Write an algorithm to enter the marks students obtained in English, and count the number of students in a class. Calculate the average English mark of the group of students if the data is terminated by the value 999. Print the number of students in the class and the average mark of the students.

Solution

Algorithm rough

Set the number of students to 0

Set the total students marks to 0

Prompt and enter student mark

While the student mark is not equal to 999 DO

Add the student mark to total students mark

Add one to the total number of students

Prompt and enter next student mark

ENDWHILE

Find the average of the students mark by dividing the total students mark by the total number of students

Print the number of students and the average mark of the students

Algorithm refined

Total number of students = 0

Total students marks = 0

Prompt and enter student mark

While the student mark <> 999 do

Total students mark = total students mark + student mark

Total number of students = total number of students + 1

Prompt and enter student mark

ENDWHILE

Average mark = total students mark / total number of students

Print number of students, average mark

Algorithm further refined

Total students = 0

Total marks = 0

Prompt and enter student mark

While student mark <> 999 do

Total mark = total mark + student mark

Total students = total students + 1

Prompt and enter student mark

Endwhile

Average mark = total mark / total students

Print total students, average mark

Exercise 3

1 Create a flowchart and write an algorithm for the following problem. Enter the marks obtained by students in a given subject, and find the highest mark. The data entered is terminated by 999.

2 Write an algorithm to find and print the sum of a list of positive integers. The number of integers is not known in advance. The procedure is terminated by the value 0.

3 Write an algorithm to read the employee number, rate of pay and the hours worked by employees, and calculate their salary. The number of employees is not known in advance. The procedure is terminated when the employee number 0 is entered.

4 Write an algorithm to find the average age of students. The number of students is not known in advance. Print the average age of the students. The data is terminated when the age 199 is entered.

5 Develop a flowchart and write an algorithm to find and print the square and cube of a number entered. The data is terminated by the number 0.

FOR–NEXT statement

In the FOR–NEXT statement, the loop is controlled by a counter that increases each time the set of instructions is executed. This statement is used for finite loops. It is used when the amount of times a set of instructions has to be repeated is known.

> FOR <Counter Variable> = <Beginning value> TO <Ending value> DO
>
> > <Statements to be repeated>
>
> NEXT

OR

> FOR <Counter Variable> = <Beginning value> TO <Ending value> DO
>
> > <Statements to be repeated>
>
> ENDFOR

Example:

> For Counter = 1 TO 4 DO
>
> > <Statements to be repeated >
>
> NEXT

When this statement is executed, the counter variable is initially set to the beginning value, in this case, 1. After the execution of the instructions between the FOR and the ENDFOR or FOR and NEXT, the counter variable is increased by 1. The instructions are repeated and the counter variable increases until it becomes equal to the ending value, in this case, 4. So the instructions are repeated four times.

Note!

The variable in the FOR–NEXT statement is a counter variable that keeps track of the number of times the loop is executed.

Problem 5

Write an algorithm to enter the English mark of 10 students in a class. Calculate the average English mark of the students. Print the average mark of the students.

Solution

Algorithm rough

Set the total student mark to 0

FOR number of students = 1 TO 10 DO

Prompt and enter the student marks

Add the student mark to the total

students mark

NEXT

Find the average of the students mark by dividing the total students mark by 10

Print the average mark of the students

Algorithm refined

Total student mark = 0

FOR number of students = 1 TO 10 DO

Prompt and enter student marks

Total students mark =0

total students mark + student mark

ENDFOR

Average students mark = total students mark divided by 10

Print average mark of the students

Algorithm further refined

Total mark = 0

FOR NumStudents = 1 TO 10 DO

Prompt and enter student marks

Total mark = total mark + student mark

ENDFOR

Average = total mark / 10

Print average

The FOR…NEXT statement can be used to crea and print a table.

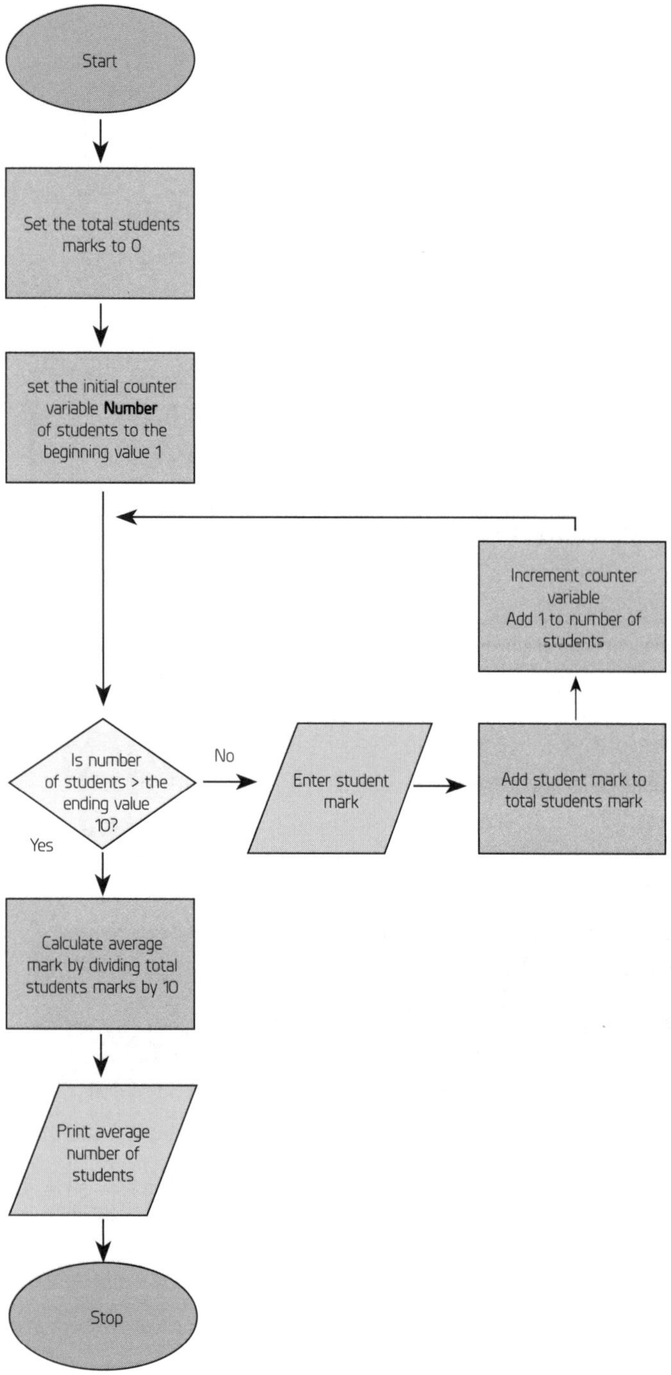

Figure 11.10 Flowchart for Problem 5

Problem 6

Print a table to find the square of numbers 1 to 10.

Solution

Algorithm rough

Output the heading Number and Square

For Number = 1 to 10 do

Calculate square by multiplying the number by itself

Print Number, Square

ENDFOR

Algorithm refined

Print "Number", "Square"

For Number = 1 to 10 do

Square = Number * Number

Print Number, Square

ENDFOR

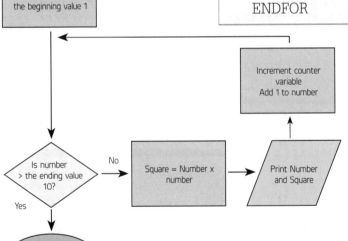

Figure 11.11 Flowchart for Problem 6

* In this case Number becomes set to the initial value 1.
* The first time through the loop, Square becomes equal to Number * Number which is 1 * 1.
* Then the Number and Square are printed.
* The second time through the loop, Number becomes set to 2 and the Square is calculated and printed.
* This continues until Number becomes equal to the ending value which is 10.

Exercise 4

1 Write an algorithm to find the average age of 10 students.

2 Create a flowchart and write an algorithm to find the sum of all numbers between 2 and 20 inclusive.

3 Write an algorithm to print a table of the cube of numbers 10 to 20.

4 Write an algorithm to read the employee number, rate of pay and hours worked by 15 employees, and to calculate their salary.

5 Write an algorithm to print a 3-times table for numbers 1 to 12.

Summary 11

1 When a statement or instruction or a group of statements or instructions are repeated in computer programming, this is called a loop.

2 A finite loop is where the instructions are repeated a fixed number of times.

3 An indefinite loop is where the instructions are repeated an unspecified number of times.

4 The trigger or value that causes the loop to stop is called a lookout value, a terminating value or a sentinel value.

5 It is important to set the initial cumulative total variable to 0 before the values are added. This is called initialising the variable.

6 In the WHILE–DO statement, the computer executes a set of statements or instructions repeatedly for as long as a given condition is true. This statement is used for indefinite loops.

7 In the For–NEXT statement, the loop is controlled by a counter that increases each time the set of instructions are executed. This statement is used for finite loops.

8 Syntax is specific rules and statements of that particular computer language, much like rules in grammar in English or any other human language.

Questions 11

Copy and fill in the blanks questions

1 Adding values to a current total is described as _____ totals, while adding 1 to a counter is known as _____ the counter.

2 _____ are statements that can be repeated a number of times. The two types are _____ and _____.

True or false questions

1 When instructions are repeated this is called a loop.

2 A lookout value is also called a sentinel value.

3 The FOR…NEXT loop is an example of an indefinite loop.

4 The instructions within a finite loop are repeated a fixed number of times.

5 When a variable is set to a particular value at the beginning of a program, this is called initialising the variable.

Multiple-choice questions

1 A value that stops a loop from repeating is called all of the following except for:

a terminal.

b lookout.

c finish.

d sentinel.

2 Statements within the WHILE…DO loop are executed as long as:

a the condition is false.

b the condition is somewhat false.

c the condition is somewhat true.

d the condition is true.

3 A finite loop is executed:

a an indefinite number of times.

b a fixed number of times.

c an unspecified number of times.

d when the number of times is unknown.

Short-answer questions

1 What is the difference between a finite loop and an indefinite loop?

2 Flour is sold at $40.00 a bag. Write a program using QBASIC to input an order number and the quantity ordered. Calculate the cost of the order. Print the order number, quantity and cost.

3 Identify the lines that are errors in the following algorithm. Rearrange the algorithm so that it makes sense.

```
1  Set Total to 0
2  Prompt and enter the number
3  WHILE number >= 5 DO
4  Set number to 0
5  Total = Total + (Number * 2)
6  ENDWHILE
7  Print total
8  Add 1 to number
```

Research question

Have you seen television shows where the hero of the show has been stuck in an infinite loop in time? Do you think that indefinite loops happen in the real world? Create a scenario where it is possible to be stuck in an indefinite loop and then explain how to exit this loop.

STEM project

A national sports group is scouting for new national talent in cricket, football, and track and field. It wants to set up trials in as many school districts as possible to identify athletes in the above categories between the ages of 12 and 16 years. Your school will be sending a number of athletes to the district trial for your region and your class is currently using problem-solving and algorithm development to help develop a recordkeeping system for the scores and times of each school athlete. You and a group of your classmates are preparing a presentation on how your record system will work and are planning to share it with this national sports group as a way to help them keep accurate records on the athletes for all the trials. (*Note to teacher: Divide the class into project groups of no more than five students.*)

1 What are three possible questions to ask that can help develop a meaningful recordkeeping system for this scenario? Explain the steps that you and your group use to produce these questions.

2 For each question, use an algorithm to work out a solution. You must use algorithms with the FOR–NEXT and WHILE–DO statements and use at least one flowchart in your solution for any one of the questions.

3 Select one question and decide on the presentation method best suited to it and its corresponding algorithm and solution. Prepare your presentation. Ensure that all group members take part and document the part that each person plays.

4 Show your presentation to another group and ask them to evaluate it. What feedback did you receive? How can you use this feedback to improve your presentation? If you chose to ignore any feedback, what was your reason for doing so?

Hints

1 List all the important items that must be in a useful recordkeeping system for school athletes, for example, full name, date of birth, sport engaged in, scoring method, and so on.
2 Explain what an algorithm is, in your own words. What is the difference between a rough and a refined algorithm?
3 List any assumptions that you have made.

```
        PlaceAsideUserInstalledFontsW

End Sub

Private Sub FindAndLoadInstalledF

    ReDim Preserve InstalledFonts
    Dim dArrayCountNothing As Boo
    Dim i, j As Integer
    For i = 0 To MasterCategoryFo
        For j = 0 To AllFonts.Get
            If MasterCategoryFont
                If dArrayCountNoth
                    dArrayCountNot
                Else
                    ReDim Preserve
                End If
                InstalledFontsCate
            Else
                'NOT A MATCH, WHIC
            End If
        Next
    Next
```

Figure 12.1 Visual Basic is a 4GL high-level computer language.

Different generations of programming languages

Computer languages can be classified according to whether they are low level or high level.

* **Low-level languages** are machine-dependent. Different brands of computer use different program codes.
* **High-level languages** are independent of the machine. They are not specifically designed for any one brand of computer.

Many computer languages have been developed and have evolved over the years. They can be classified according to five different generations of computer languages.

First-generation (1GL) – a low-level language

The first-generation computer language is a machine language that is written using 1s and 0s, that is, binary code. This low-level machine language is the only instruction that the CPU understands and can obey or execute directly without having to translate it.

Second generation (2GL) – a low-level language

The second-generation computer language is an assembly language written using mnemonic codes, which are short codes that suggest their meaning and are therefore easier to remember. Typical codes might be: LDA, STO, ADD, and so on.

Third generation (3GL) – a high-level language

The third-generation computer language has been designed to be even easier for people to understand. This high-level language uses English words and symbols and is therefore easy to write. Examples include Pascal, Basic, **QBasic**, C, and so on.

Fourth generation (4GL) – a high-level language

The fourth-generation computer language was designed for the development of commercial business software. It uses English-like statements that are very user-friendly, which makes these programs even easier to write than the earlier ones. This reduces the time that it takes to write programs. Examples include SQL, RPG-II, Visual Basic, and so on.

Fifth generation (5GL) – a high-level language

Fifth-generation computer languages are designed to build specific programs that help computers to solve specific problems. These languages are essentially 4GLs with a knowledge base (a large store of information about a topic). The 5GLs are used mainly in artificial intelligence. Examples include Prolog and Mercury.

Coding a program using the Visual Basic programming language

After developing an algorithm for solving a problem we need to express the algorithm using a programming language. This requires the use of the specific syntax of that programming language. **Syntax** means the specific rules and statements of that particular computer language, much like rules in grammar of English or any other human language.

C programming language

One of the more common programming languages is called simply, 'C'. Developed by Bell Laboratories in the USA (now AT&T) it is one of the most popular languages in use today.

Many other programming languages have evolved from C, such as C++ and Java. An example of the programming code to add two numbers using C is as follows:

```
#INCLUDE <STDIO.H>
MAIN ()
{
    INT Num1, Num2, Sum;
    Read (Num1, Num2);
    Sum = Num1 + Num2;
    Printf (Sum);
}
```

Note that a computer does not actually understand C or other programming languages: a **compiler** or **interpreter** is needed to convert these programs into the language that the computer understands, which is machine code (binary ones and zeros).

After the conversion or compilation, the program is executed. An interpreter does this directly (on the fly) and is consequently slower than a compiled program.

Simple coding for the QBSIC programming language

The BASIC language (Beginner's All-purpose Symbolic Instruction Code), as its name suggests, was designed for beginners to use. It is a language that is more accessible than 'C'. Visual Basic is a version of the BASIC programming language. We will now look at simple coding for the QBASIC programming language.

An example of the programming code required to add two numbers using QBASIC is:

```
INPUT Num1
INPUT Num2
Sum = Num1 + Num2
PRINT Sum
```

Let us first look at the QBASIC prompting statements. Here is a simple example:

Syntax: PRINT <String>

Example: PRINT "Enter student name"

Output: Enter student name

In this chapter, we will look at coding in Visual Basic programming language. Visual Basic has the following structure. It is divided into four distinct parts:

* The Module header (or program header)
    - The Subroutine block (or program block)
    - The Subroutine terminator
* The Module terminator.

A basic program structure looks like this:

```
Module <name of program>
    SUB Main ( )
        <Block of instructions>
    END SUB
End Module
```

The following example shows the programming code required to add two numbers using Visual Basic:

```
MODULE AddTwoNumbers
'This program reads the two numbers and finds the sum
SUB Main ( )
    DIM Num1 AS Integer
    DIM Num2 AS Integer
    DIM Sum AS Integer
    CONSOLE.WRITELINE ("Enter a value for Num1")
    Num1 = CONSOLE.READLINE ( )
    CONSOLE.WRITELINE ("Enter a value for Num2")
    Num2 = CONSOLE.READLINE ( )
    CONSOLE.READKEY( )
    Sum = Num1 + Num2
    CONSOLE.WRITELINE ("Sum " & Sum)
END SUB
END MODULE
```

Keywords

Keywords, also called reserved words, have special meaning in a programming language:

* They are predefined.
* They can only be used in a specific way.
* They cannot be used as variable names.

Keywords in Visual Basic

The keywords in Visual Basic are:

MODULE   SUB   READLINE   WRITELINE

READ   WRITE   CONST   CONSOLE

Identifiers in Visual Basic

Identifiers are names given to variables, constants and types. They are also the names given to the program. The following rules govern how these names are written:

* They must begin with a letter.
* They can be followed by an alphanumeric character, which is either a letter or a number.
* They can contain an underscore (_).
* They cannot contain any of the following characters as these have special meaning in the Pascal language: ~ ! @ # $ % ^ & * ( ) + ` – = { } [ ] : " ; ' < > ? , . / |
* Visual Basic is not case-sensitive, which means that text written in all caps or the first letter capital or all lower case is considered to be the same. For example, NUM, Num and num are regarded as the same. For clarity in this Student's Book, we will put keywords in all capitals to differentiate them from variable names or identifiers.

Note!

An identifier can be any length. However, it is not advisable to use too long a name for an identifier as a number of standard compilers only take the first 8–16 characters of an identifier.

Data types in Visual Basic

A data type allows the computer to know what kind of data to process. In order for the computer to manipulate the data and treat the data types in a specific way, they need to be part of a specific group. Visual Basic uses the data types shown in Table 12.1.

Table 12.1 Data types in Visual Basic

Data type	Keyword	Explanation
Integer	INTEGER	Whole numbers
Real/Floating Point	LONG	Contains numbers with decimals, for example 3.4
Character	CHAR	Holds a single character but must be enclosed in single quotes, for example 'a', 'H', '+'
Boolean	BOOLEAN	Can have either one of two values TRUE or FALSE
String	STRING	This is a string of characters enclosed in double quotes, for example "Smith"
Double	DOUBLE	Floating point numbers but with greater accuracy, for example 3.415632

Note!

An undeclared constant or variable within a program will cause a syntax error.

In programming languages, we need to declare constants and variables. When we declare a constant or a variable within a program, we are informing the compiler to expect these particular words and how to treat with them. In other words, the declared constants and variables are of a particular type and can only be used in a particular way.

Declaring constants

Values declared in the CONST section cannot be changed during the course of the program. If the constant declaration is placed within a module and prefixed with the keyword PUBLIC, it makes the constant available to other modules within the program.

Syntax:

CONST <identifier> AS <datatype> = value

PUBLIC CONST <identifier> AS <datatype> = value

Example:

CONST Name AS String = "Jonathan"

CONST Year AS Integer = 2019

CONST Pi AS Long = 3.14

CONST Pi AS Double = 3.141592653589

Declaring variables

Syntax:

DIM <identifier> AS <datatype>

DIM <identifier> AS <datatype>, <identifier> AS <datatype>, <identifier> AS <datatype>

DIM <identifier> AS String * n (where n is the number of characters)

Example:

DIM Age AS Integer

DIM Sum AS Integer

DIM Average AS Long

DIM Grade AS Char

DIM Fail AS Boolean

DIM Num1, Num2, Sum AS Integer

DIM Name AS String

DIM Name As String * 10 (Note: In this example, the Variable Name can only be 10 characters long)

DIM Name As String, Age As Integer, Fail As Boolean

Assignment statement

A variable is assigned the results of a calculation. In Visual Basic, the assignment symbol is the equal sign (=).

Syntax:

<identifier> = <actual calculation>

Example:

Area = (Base * Height)/2

F = 32 + ((9*C)/5)

Mathematical operators

Visual Basic uses the mathematical operators shown in Table 12.2.

Table 12.2 Mathematical operators

Operator	Operation	Operand value	Resulting value
+	Addition or positive	REAL or INTEGER	REAL or INTEGER
−	Subtraction or negative	REAL or INTEGER	REAL or INTEGER
*	Multiplication	REAL or INTEGER	REAL or INTEGER
/	Division	REAL or INTEGER	REAL

Visual Basic prompting statements

Prompting statements usually appear before input statements to indicate to the user what data needs to be entered via the keyboard. They are output statements.

Remember that Visual Basic is not case sensitive. For readability, this book places the keywords in uppercase. The keyword CONSOLE allows you to see the output on your screen.

Syntax:
```
CONSOLE.WRITE ("String")

CONSOLE.WRITELINE ("String")
```

Example:
```
CONSOLE.WRITE ("Enter student name")

CONSOLE.WRITELINE ("Enter student name")
```

Difference between WRITE and WRITELINE

WRITE places the cursor at the end of the output while WRITELINE places the cursor at the beginning of the next line.

```
MODULE StudentInfo

SUB Main ( )

        CONSOLE.WRITE ("Enter student name")

END SUB

END MODULE

The output will be:

Enter student name _
```

However, in order for you to see the output, you need to pause the output screen. You need to include CONSOLE.READKEY( ) or CONSOLE.READLINE ( )

```
MODULE StudentInfo
SUB Main ( )
      CONSOLE.WRITELINE ("Enter student name")
      CONSOLE.READKEY ( )
END SUB
END MODULE


The output will be:
Enter student name

_
```

Visual Basic input statements

Input statements take data from the standard input (usually a keyboard).

Syntax:
  <identifier> = CONSOLE.READ ()
  <identifier> = CONSOLE.READLINE ()

Example:
  Name = CONSOLE.READ ()
  Name = CONSOLE.READLINE ()

Difference between READ and READLINE

READ accepts data on the same line, while READLINE reads the
first set of data values, discards the other values on the line and
waits for the user to input a value. In Visual Basic, only one set of
data should be read in one statement.

Example:
  Data: Michael 19

Code	Result
Name = CONSOLE.READ ( )	Michael
Age = CONSOLE.READ ( )	19
Name = CONSOLE.READLINE ( )	Michael
Age = CONSOLE.READLINE ( )	

Visual Basic output statements

Syntax:
  CONSOLE.WRITE (identifier)
  CONSOLE.WRITELINE (identifier)
  CONSOLE.WRITE ("String" & identifier)
  CONSOLE.WRITELINE ("String"& identifier)
  CONSOLE.WRITELINE (identifier & identifier)

Example:
  CONSOLE.WRITE (Name)
  CONSOLE.WRITELINE (Name)
  Example of Concatenation (concatenation
  is the joining of two things)
  CONSOLE.WRITE ("My name is " & Name)
  CONSOLE.WRITELINE ("My name is " & Name)
  CONSOLE.WRITELINE (FirstName &" "&
  LastName)

module areaofrectangle 'this program reads the base and height of a rectangle and calculates and prints the area

sub main ( ) dim base, height, area as integer console.writeline ("enter the base of the rectangle") base = console.readline () console.writeline ("enter the height of the rectangle") height = console.readline () area = (base + height) *2 console.writeline ("the area of the rectangle is = " & area) console.readkey( ) end sub end module

Syntax:
  Identifier = calculation

Visual Basic calculation statements

At this point it is important to develop good programming or coding styles. Although no indentation is required when writing any program, indentation makes a program easier to read and understand (see the example below). A lack of indentation makes it difficult for someone else to modify, maintain or even debug the program. You may even have difficulty finding errors in the program. Therefore, it is good practice to develop proper coding habits and styles such as:

* using tabs and spacing to indent blocks of code
* grouping blocks of code together
* using suitable variable names (something that represents what is being stored)
* using suitable comments to explain parts of your program
* using all caps for keywords
* using an underscore as a separator for variables with multiple names, for example student_name, or first letter caps, for example, StudentName.

The box above to the left shows code without indentations and without the keywords in all caps. The example below shows this same code with indents and caps.

Example:
  Area = (Base + Height) * 2

Example: Visual Basic program

MODULE AreaofRectangle

'This program reads the base and height of a rectangle and calculates and prints the area

SUB Main ( )

  DIM Base, Height, Area AS Integer

  CONSOLE.WRITELINE ("Enter the Base of the rectangle")

  Base = CONSOLE.READLINE ()

  CONSOLE.WRITELINE ("Enter the Height of the rectangle")

  Height = CONSOLE.READLINE ()

  Area = (Base + Height) *2

  CONSOLE.WRITELINE ("The area of the rectangle is = " & Area)

  CONSOLE.READKEY( )

END SUB

END MODULE

Exercise 1

1 Write a program to find and display the total and average of three numbers.

2 Write a program to find and display the area of a rectangle.

3 Write a program to find and display the square of a number.

4 Write a program to input the name of an item and price. Calculate the discount on this price at 15% and the discounted price. Display the price, the discount and the discounted price of the item.

IF–THEN construct

Syntax:

IF <condition> THEN

    Instructions

END IF

Example 1 algorithm

PRINT "Enter a student name"

READ Name

PRINT "Enter the student age"

READ Age

IF Age < 12 THEN

    PRINT "You are too young for this programme"

ENDIF

Example 1 Visual basic program

MODULE Programme_Age

SUB Main ( )

    'This program reads the age of the student and says whether they are too young

    DIM Age AS Integer

    DIM Name AS String

    CONSOLE.WRITELINE ("Enter the name of the student")

    Name = CONSOLE.READLINE( )

    CONSOLE.WRITELINE ("Enter the age of the student")

    Age = CONSOLE.READLINE( )

    IF (Age < 12) THEN

        CONSOLE.WRITELINE ("You are too young for this programme")

    END IF

END SUB

END MODULE

Example 2 algorithm

Print "Enter a number"

Read Num

If Num > 10 THEN

    Answer = Num * 10

ENDIF

PRINT "Answer is", Answer

Example 2 Visual basic program

MODULE CalculateNum

SUB Main ( )

    'This program reads a number and multiplies it by 10

    DIM Num AS Integer

    DIM Answer AS Integer

    CONSOLE.WRITELINE ("Enter a number")

    Num = CONSOLE.READLINE( )

    IF (Num >10) THEN

        Answer = Num * 10

    END IF

    CONSOLE.WRITELINE ("Answer is" & Answer)

END SUB

END MODULE

IF-THEN-ELSE construct

Let us look at the Example 1 algorithm from earlier. A syntax of the IF-THEN-ELSE construct and an example of the code is shown below.

Syntax:
```
IF <condition> THEN

    <instructions>

ELSE

    <instructions>

END IF
```

Example 1 algorithm

PRINT "Enter a student name"

READ Name

PRINT "Enter the student age"

READ Age

IF Age < 12 THEN

    PRINT "You are too young for this programme"

ELSE

    PRINT "You are accepted into the young leaders programme"

ENDIF

Example 1 Visual Basic program

MODULE Programme_Age

SUB Main ( )

    'This program reads the age of the student and says whether they are too young

    DIM Age AS Integer

    DIM Name AS String

    CONSOLE.WRITELINE ("Enter the name of the student")

    Name = CONSOLE.READLINE( )

    CONSOLE.WRITELINE ("Enter the age of the student")

    Age = CONSOLE.READLINE( )

    IF (Age < 12) THEN

        CONSOLE.WRITELINE ("You are too young for this programme")

    ELSE

        CONSOLE.WRITELINE ("You are accepted into the young leaders programme")

    END IF

END SUB

END MODULE

Note!

Comments can be placed anywhere within a program since they are not executed.

Let us look at the Example 2 algorithm from earlier.

Example 2 algorithm

Print "Enter a number"

Read Num

If Num > 10 THEN

    Answer = Num * 10

ELSE

    Answer = Num + 2

ENDIF

PRINT "Answer is", Answer

Example 2 Visual Basic program

```
MODULE CalculateNum
SUB Main ( )
    'This program reads a number and multiplies it by 10 if
    greater than 10 otherwise
    'adds 2
    DIM Num AS Integer
    DIM Answer AS Integer
    CONSOLE.WRITELINE ("Enter a number")
    Num = CONSOLE.READLINE( )
    IF (Num >10) THEN
        Answer = Num * 10
    END IF
    CONSOLE.WRITELINE ("Answer is" & Answer)
END SUB
END MODULE
```

Exercise 2

1 Persons under four feet in height are not allowed to ride the rollercoaster. Write a program to read a person's height and if the height is less than four feet, and output 'Sorry you are not allowed to ride the rollercoaster'.

2 Persons are awarded reward points depending on how much money they spend on their purchase; if they spend $5.00 they are awarded 1 reward point. Read the person's amount spent and calculate the points rewarded for that purchase. Add the points to the person's total reward points. Print the person's total reward points.

3 Write a program to input a number N. If the number is greater than 50 subtract 10 from the number, otherwise multiply the number by 2 and add 5. Print the number and the result.

4 Write a program to determine the average age of students in a class of 20. Read the age of each student and print the average.

FOR–NEXT statement

Syntax:

FOR \<Variable name\> = \<Beginning value\> TO \<Ending value\> DO

   \<Action to be repeated \>

NEXT

Example 3 algorithm

```
TotalMark = 0

FOR NumStudents = 1 TO 10 DO

    INPUT "Enter student mark", StudentMark

    TotalMark = TotalMark + StudentMark

ENDFOR

Average = TotalMark /10

PRINT "The average mark for the students is:", Average
```

Example 3 Visual Basic program

```
MODULE AverageStudentMark

SUB Main ( )

    DIM        NumStudents, TotalMark, StudentMark AS Integer

    DIM AverageMark AS Double

    TotalMark = 0

    FOR NumStudents = 1 TO 10

        CONSOLE.WRITE ("Enter student mark")

        StudentMark = CONSOLE.READLINE ()

        TotalMark = TotalMark + StudentMark

    NEXT

    AverageMark = TotalMark/NumStudents

    CONSOLE.WRITELINE ("The average mark for the students
    is: " & AverageMark)

    CONSOLE.READKEY ( )

END SUB

END MODULE
```

WHILE–DO statement

Example 4 algorithm

```
PRINT "Do you want to find another student average? (y/n)"
READ Answer
WHILE Answer = "y" DO
    PRINT "Enter student first mark"
    READ Mark1
    PRINT "Enter student second mark"
    READ Mark2
    Average = (Mark1 + Mark2)/2
    PRINT "Student average mark", Average
    PRINT "Do you want to find another student average? (y/n)"
    READ Answer
ENDWHILE
```

Example 4 Visual Basic program: Option 1

```
MODULE AverageStudentMark
SUB Main ( )
    DIM  Mark1, Mark2 AS Integer
DIM Average AS Long
DIM Answer AS Char
CONSOLE.WRITELINE ("Do you want to find another student average? (y/n)"
Answer = CONSOLE.READLINE( )
console.WRITEline ("Enter student first mark ")
Mark1 = CONSOLE.ReadLINE ( )
console.WRITEline ("Enter student second mark ")
Mark2 = CONSOLE.ReadLINE ( )
WHILE (Answer = "y")
    Average = (Mark1 + Mark2)/2
    CONSOLE.WRITELINE ("Student average mark is " &
    Average)
    CONSOLE.WRITELINE ("Do you want to find another
    student average? (y/n)"
    Answer = CONSOLE.READLINE( )
END WHILE
END SUB
END MODULE
```

Example 4 Visual Basic program: Option 2

```
MODULE AverageStudentMark

SUB Main ( )

    'This program takes into account whether the user types
    capital or common y for yes

    DIM  Mark1, Mark2 AS Integer

    DIM Average AS Long

    DIM Answer AS Char

    CONSOLE.WRITELINE ("Do you want to find another student
    average? (y/n)"

    Answer = CONSOLE.READLINE( )

    console.WRITEline ("Enter student first mark ")

    Mark1 = CONSOLE.ReadLINE ( )

    console.WRITEline ("Enter student second mark ")

    Mark2 = CONSOLE.ReadLINE ( )

    WHILE (Answer = "y") OR (Answer = "Y")

        Average = (Mark1 + Mark2)/2

        CONSOLE.WRITELINE ("Student average mark is " &
        Average)

        CONSOLE.WRITELINE ("Do you want to find another
        student average? (y/n)"

        Answer = CONSOLE.READLINE( )

    END WHILE

END SUB

END MODULE
```

Exercise 3

Write the Visual Basic code for the following:

1 Buses leave a station. Read the bus number and count the bus.
   Print the answer.

2 Buses leave a station. Read the bus number and count the bus.
   If the bus is going to St Lucy then also count the buses going to
   St Lucy. Print the number of buses leaving the station and the
   number of buses going to St Lucy. Hint: Use the 'While' Construct.

▶ **Exercise 3 continued**

3 A number of buses leave a station every day. Read the bus number and count the bus. Add the number of buses to the total number of buses that leave the bus station for the week. Print the total number of buses.

4 An airplane leaves an airport at regular intervals during the day. Read the flight number and count the flights. Print the number of flights.

5 An airplane leaves an airport at regular intervals during the day. Read the flight number, count the flight and count the flights going to Jamaica. Print the number of flights leaving the airport and the number of flights going to Jamaica.

6 An airplane leaves an airport at regular intervals during the day. Read the flight number and count the flight. Add the number of flights to the total weekly flights. Print the total number of flights.

7 Write a program to enter the marks of students and find the highest mark. The data entered is terminated by 999.

8 Write a program to find and print the sum of a list of positive integers. The number of integers is not known in advance. The procedure is terminated by the value 0.

9 Write a program to read the employee number, rate of pay and the hours worked by employees, and to calculate their salary. The number of employees is not known in advance. The procedure is terminated when the employee number 0 is entered.

10 Write a program to find the average age of students. The number of students is not known in advance. Print the average age of the students. The data is terminated when the age of 199 is entered.

11 Write a program to find the average age of 10 students.

12 Write a program to find the sum of all numbers between 2 and 20 inclusive.

13 Write a program to print a table of the cube of numbers 10 to 20.

14 Write a program to read the employee number, rate of pay and the hours worked by 15 employees, and to calculate their salary.

15 Write a program to print a 3-times table for numbers 1 to 12.

Summary 12

1 A compiler or interpreter converts the programs into the machine language of the computer that you are using, which is the language that the computer understands.

2 The BASIC (Beginner's All-purpose Symbolic Instruction Code) language was designed for beginners to use.

3 The C programming language was developed by Bell Laboratories in the USA (now AT&T) and is one of the more popular languages.

4 Keywords, also called reserved words, have special meaning in a programming language. Identifiers are names given to variables, constants and types.

5 Comments are pieces of code that are not executed during the running of a program and help to explain the action in the program.

Questions 12

Copy and fill in the blanks questions

Copy the sentences and use the words below to fill in the blanks. Note that some words may be used more than once.

interpreter	syntax	algorithm
machine code	compiler	
computer program		convert

We need to _____ the _____ to a _____ using programming language. Specific _____ is required when converting the algorithm to a particular programming language. _____ is the specific rules and statements of that particular computer language. A _____ or _____ is required to _____ the programs into _____ of the computer you are using. _____ is the language that the computer understands.

Multiple-choice questions

1 BASIC stands for:

a Beginner's All-purpose Symbolic Instruction Code.

b Beginner's Associative Signal Instruction Code.

c Basic Associative Signal Identification Code.

d Basic All-purpose Symbol Identification Codes.

2 A compiler:

a converts a program in C to a program written in BASIC.

b converts a program to machine language.

c determines if a program is ready to be read by the computer.

d instructs a user how to write a program.

3 In Visual Basic programming language, CONSOLE.READ:

a reads information typed on the keyboard by the user.

b displays the information typed by the user.

c clears the screen.

d cleans the screen.

4 Which of the following is the correct Visual Basic code for producing the following output?

Jack Smith is: 25

a CONSOLE.PRINT ("Jack Smith is:", Age)

b PRINT "Jack Smith is:", Age$

c OUTPUT Jack Smith is: 25

d CONSOLE.WRITE ("Jack Smith is:" & Age)

True or false questions

1   C is the name of a type of instruction.

2   A comment cannot be written anywhere in a program.

3   A comment in Visual Basic may be enclosed using { and }.

4   A comment cannot be enclosed using (* and *).

5   The & is an operator in Visual Basic.

6   Semi-colons are not at the end of a statement in the Visual Basic programming language.

Short-answer questions

1   Explain the purpose of a compiler.

2   Write a program using Visual Basic to calculate the simple interest on savings in a bank. The program should allow the user to input the principal, rate and time, and output the principal and the interest earned. Simple interest = (Principal x Rate x Time)/100.

3   Write a program using Visual Basic to convert kilograms (Kg) to pounds for values 1 to 20 kilograms. Display the amount in kilograms and pounds, for example: 1 Kg = 2.2 pounds

Research question

1   Conduct research to find information on at least five other programming languages. Draw up a comparison table with brief descriptions of each programming language, as well as the following information for each one:

   a   The popularity of the programming language

   b   The ease with which the programming language can be used

   c   The function for which the programming language is generally used.

2   Which one of these programming languages can be useful to you as a student? Give two reasons for your selection.

STEM project

Continuing your STEM project from Chapter 11, you and a group of your classmates have been tasked with coding one of the algorithms that you have developed. You will be explaining how it works to members of the national sports group, many of whom are not very knowledgeable about programming, but are enthusiastic about having computerised trial records.

You decide to write coding to find the highest cricket scorer in your region. You and you group will be given 15 minutes to deliver your explanation and the members of the national sports group will ask any questions they may have after that. Your aim is to prepare an explanation that will not require further questions afterwards.

1   Write the algorithm and the Visual BASIC program for entering the number of runs scored by students in a cricket trial to find the highest scorer. Do this on PowerPoint slides.

2   Write the oral explanation you will give as the slides are shown. Ensure that you include explanations of key terminology.

3   Demonstrate your presentation to another group of classmates. What feedback did you receive?

4   How can you improve your presentation based on feedback received?

Hints

1   Research how cricket runs are currently recorded in similar trials.

2   Ensure that you use appropriate words and logical sentences in your oral explanation.

3   Keep your explanation within the specified time given.

4   Anticipate possible questions and answer these within your explanation.

Introduction to programming with Scratch

Objectives

At the end of the chapter, you will be able to:

❑ identify elements in the Scratch window

❑ create simple Scratch programs

❑ convert algorithms to Scratch programs.

What is Scratch programming?

Scratch programming is a visual block-type programming language. It visually represents blocks of code that can be dragged and pieced together to write a program.

In this chapter, we will look at using Scratch programming to code some of the algorithms we wrote earlier.

Scratch uses what is known as a Sprite, which is a computer graphic that moves on the stage or canvas area based on the written program.

The Scratch program offers a variety of sprites to choose from (see Figure 13.1).

Figure 13.1 The Sprite library

Did you know?

Scratch programming was developed to teach children as young as eight years old how to write program code.

The Scratch window

The Script tab displays the Script Editor where the block programming language is dragged to write your Scratch program. There are ten menus, or groups of blocks, on the Scripts tab. Table 13.1 contains an explanation of each one.

Table 13.1 Explanation of the Scripts tab menus

Menu (blocks)	Colour of menu (blocks)	Function
Motion	Blue	Controls movement of the Sprite
Look	Purple	Changes the appearance of the Sprite
Sound	Pink/Magenta	Controls the sound
Pen	Dark green	Allows the Sprite to control its pens
Data/List (variable block)	Orange/Dark red	Allows you to manage variables
Events	Brown	Triggers or senses an event
Control	Gold	Controls the scripts
Sensing	Light blue	Detects when an action takes place
Operators	Light green	Scripts mathematical equations and the handling of strings
More blocks	Pink	Custom-made blocks that hold pre-defined codes or procedures for selected Sprites. For example, LEGO scripts that can be used for LEGO robots that use Scratch programming.

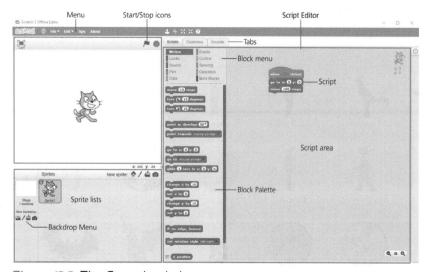

The Sprite Costume tab displays the Costume Editor, where you can change the colour, look and feel of your sprite. The Sound tab displays the Sound Editor, where you can add and edit sound for your sprite by either recording your own sound or uploading an already saved sound file.

Figure 13.2 The Scratch window

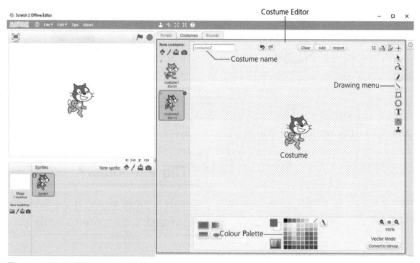

Figure 13.3 Costume Editor

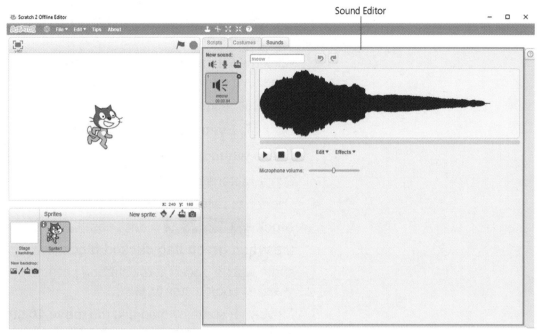

Figure 13.4 Sound Editor

Moving your sprite

You can move your sprite in the Canvas or Stage area by building simple scripts using the block scratch code.

You will use coordinates to tell the sprite how to move. The coordinates are given based on their position in relation to the *x*-axis and *y*-axis. For example, coordinate (0, 0) is the centre of the stage where the *x*-axis and the *y*-axis intersect (meet). The sprite can move along the *x*-axis from −240 to +240 and along the *y*-axis from −180 to +180 (see Figure 13.5).

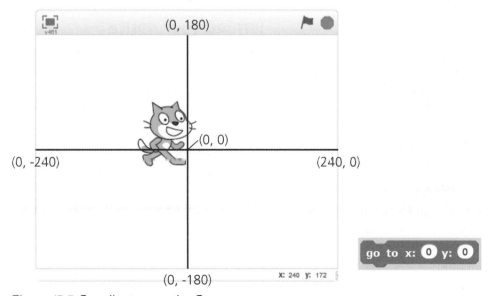

Figure 13.5 Coordinates on the Stage

Creating a program to move your sprite

You can create a program to move your sprite. Follow these steps:

1 Click the **File menu** and select **New**. This creates a new project where you can enter the project name.

2 Enter the name 'CreateSquare'.

3 Click the **Events menu** �Events on the Script Editor tab. Drag a **when green flag clicked block** when clicked to the Script Editor area.

4 Click on the **Motion menu** ▪Motion▪. Drag the **go to x: 0 y: 0 block** go to x: 0 y: 0 to the Script Editor area and snap it into the **when green flag clicked block** (see Figure 13.6). Your sprite will be placed at the starting position on the *x*-axis and *y*-axis at coordinates (0, 0).

5 Move your sprite by dragging the **move 10 steps block** to snap into the bottom of the script. Change the value 10 to 100 (see Figure 13.7). The **move 10 steps block** tells the sprite to move 10 points from its current position. Therefore, changing the value to read **move 100 steps** will move the sprite 100 points in the direction in which the sprite is facing.

Figure 13.6 The script with the 'when green flag clicked' and coordinates blocks snapped together

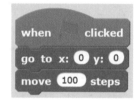

Figure 13.7 Changing the value of the 'move 10 steps' block

Turning your sprite

In order to create a square, your sprite has to change direction and turn to face the bottom of the stage area and move the same distance as before. Follow these steps:

Click the **Motion menu**. Drag the **turn clockwise 15 degrees block** to snap to the bottom of the 'move 100 steps' block. Change 15 degrees to 90 degrees. Add a 'move 10 steps' block and change the 10 to 100 (see Figure 13.8).

Add the 'turn clockwise' and 'move' blocks so that you have four pairs of 'move100 steps' and turn clockwise 90 degrees' (see Figure 13.9).

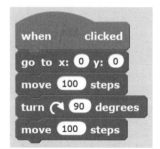

Figure 13.8 The script with the additional 'turn clockwise' and 'move' blocks added

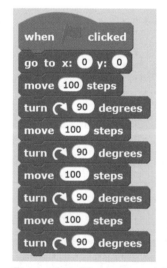

Figure 13.9 The script with four pairs of 'turn clockwise' and 'move' blocks added

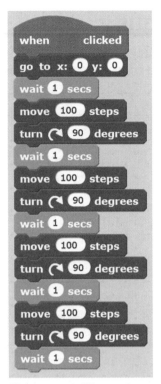

Figure 13.10 The script with the 'wait 1 secs' blocks added

If you run your program by clicking on the **green Start flag** in the Stage or Canvas area, you will not actually see your sprite move. This is because the program is executed so quickly that you cannot notice the movement. In order to actually see your sprite move, you need to add a wait time to your sprite script. You can do this by adding a **wait 1 secs block** [wait 1 secs] from the Control menu [Control] after each turn (see Figure 13.10).

Looping

You will notice that a number of steps in your script have been repeated. The 'wait', 'move' and 'turn' blocks have been repeated four times. You can make your script more economical and shorter by using the repeat loop. Follow these steps:

1 Drag the four sets of repeated 'wait', 'move' and 'turn' scripts away from the bottom of the script.

2 Drag a **repeat 10 block** to the bottom of the first 'wait 1 secs' block. Change the number of times to repeat from 10 to 5.

3 Drag one set of 'move', 'turn' and 'wait' blocks inside the 'repeat' block (see Figure 13.11).

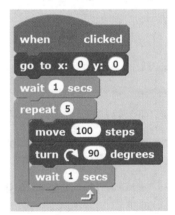

Figure 13.11 The script with the 'repeat 5' block added

4 Run your program by clicking on the **green Start flag** in the stage or canvas area.

Deleting unused script blocks

If you have dragged Script blocks to the Script Editor area and you want to remove or delete them, drag the blocks back to the Block Palette.

Sequence instructions

Now that you have learned how to operate within the Scratch environment, we can explore how to convert some algorithms to Scratch programs. Look at the following algorithm:

> WRITE "Enter a value for A"
>
> READ A
>
> PRINT "Enter a value for B"
>
> READ B
>
> PRINT "Enter a value for C"
>
> READ C
>
> Total = A + B + C
>
> PRINT Total

To create a Scratch program for this algorithm, you need to start by creating the variables. You learned about variables in Chapter 12 in *Interact with IT* Book 2. A variable is a value that changes during the execution of a program or algorithm.

Follow these steps to create a Scratch program for the given algorithm:

1   Click on the **File menu** and select **New**. This creates a new project where you can enter the project name. Enter the name 'FindTotal'.

2   Click the **Events menu** `Events` on the Script Editor tab. Drag a **when green flag clicked block** `when   clicked` to the Script Editor area.

3   Click the **Data menu** `Data` on the Script Editor tab and click **Make a Variable**. Enter the variable name 'A' in the box. The icon ☑ Ⓐ will appear in the Script Block Palette. Make a variable for every variable name in your algorithm, which would be: 'A', 'B', 'C' and 'Total'.

Note!

You can create a variable that can be used by all sprites or by one particular sprite. If you check the box next to the variable, names will be set to the answers and will appear in the Stage or Canvas area.

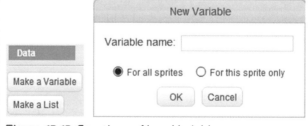

Figure 13.12 Creating a New Variable

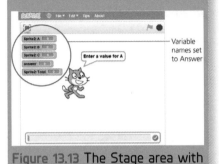

Figure 13.13 The Stage area with the Question and input box

4 We need to ask and receive information from the user, so we need to display information on the screen and receive information from the keyboard.

5 Click on the **Sensing menu** and drag the **ask What is your name and wait block** to the Script area. Change 'What is your name' to 'Enter a value for A' (see Figure 13.14).

6 Drag the **set Total to 0 block** from the Data menu. Click on the drop-down arrow and select the **Variable 'A'**. Drag the **answer block** to join the **set A by 1 block** (see Figure 13.14).

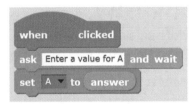

Figure 13.14 The script with the 'answer' block added

7 Repeat for each input variable (see Figure 13.15).

8 Drag the **change Total by 1 block**  from the Data menu. We need to add the three variables together, so we need to select from the **Operators menu** `Operators`. Combine the Add operator and the variables to create A + B + C. You can also combine more than one operators block (see Figure 13.16).

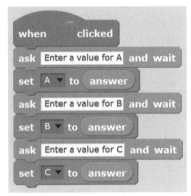

Figure 13.15 The script with the 'ask' and 'answer' blocks for all the variables

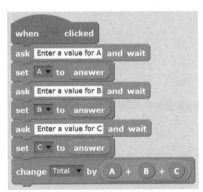

Figure 13.17 The script with the 'Change Total' block combined with the operators block

Figure 13.16 Three operators blocks combined

9 Drag the **change Total by 1 block** from the Data menu and combine it with the Operators block (see Figure 13.17).

10 Run your program by clicking on the **green flag**.

11 Drag the **say Hello block** from the Looks menu `Looks` to let the sprite display the value in the stage area. Change 'Hello' to 'Total' (see Figure 13.18).

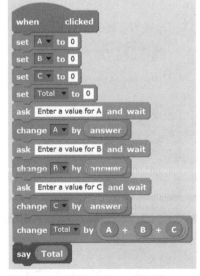

Figure 13.18 Setting variables to 0 or initialising the variables.

Conditional statements

IF–THEN construct

Activity 1 shows how to write an algorithm that uses the IF–THEN construct and convert it to a Scratch program.

▶ Activity 1

Write an algorithm to read the number of days a person has been using a demo and display the message 'Time Up' if the number of days exceeds 12.

Here is the algorithm:

> WRITE "Enter the number of days of demo use"
>
> READ Days
>
> IF Days > 12 THEN
>
>   WRITE "Time Up"
>
> ENDIF

Here is how to write the script for this algorithm (see Figure 13.19):

1 Create the name 'Variable Days' in the Data menu.

2 Drag the **when green flag clicked block** from the Events menu to the Script area.

3 Drag the **set Days to 0 block** and snap to the **when green flag clicked block** from Events menu.

4 Drag and snap the **ask what is your name and wait block** from the Sensing menu and change the question to: 'What is the number of days of demo use?'

5 Drag the **change days by 1 block** from the Data menu and snap to combine with the 'answer' block from the Sensing menu.

6 Drag the **if-then block** from the Control menu and snap to combine with the 'greater than' operator
Days > 12 from the Operator menu.

7 Drag the **say hello block** and change 'Hello' to 'Time Up', and then combine with the 'if–then' block.

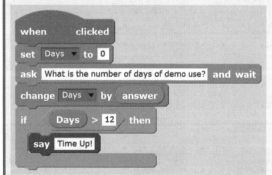

Figure 13.19 Script for algorithm in Activity 1

IF–THEN–ELSE construct

Activity 2 shows how to write an algorithm that uses the 'IF–THEN–ELSE' construct and convert it to a Scratch program.

▶Activity 2

The National Lottery Control Board gives out bonuses based on the amount of sales by their sales representatives each month. Once the sale is greater than $5 000.00, a bonus of $500.00 is given; otherwise a bonus of $20.00 is given. Read the sales amount and print the bonus.

Here is the algorithm:

READ Sales

Bonus = 0

IF Sales > $5000 THEN

    Bonus = $500.00

ELSE

    Bonus = $20.00

ENDIF

PRINT "Bonus", Bonus

Here is how to write the script for this algorithm (see Figure 13.20):

1 Create a new project and name it 'SalesBonus'.

2 Drag the **when green flag clicked** block from Events menu to the script area.

3 Select the **Data menu** and create your variables 'Sales' and 'Bonus'.

4 Select the **ask to enter the sales amount** from the Sensing menu.

5 Select the **if–then–else block** from the Control menu.

6 Select the **greater than block** from the Operator menu and enter the answer '> 5000'.

7 In the 'then' part of the 'if–then–else' block from the Data menu, insert the 'change Bonus by 500' block.

8 In the 'else' part of the 'if–then–else' block from the Data menu, insert the 'change bonus by 20' block.

9 Select the **say–for 2 secs block** from the Look menu and add the word 'bonus'.

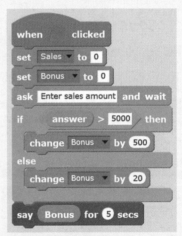

Figure 13.20 Scratch script for Activity 2's algorithm

Note!

The Join Operator links together two strings or a string and a variable. You can use this feature to display text combined with a variable (see Figure 13.21).

join hello world   join count Count

Figure 13.21 Join operator

Looping or repeating

We initially looked at looping when we had to repeat the movement of the sprite to draw a square. In Activities 3, 4 and 5, we will look at how to how to write algorithms that use looping and convert them to Scratch programs. In Scratch, the 'while do' loop, the 'repeat–until' loop and the 'for–next' loop can all be written using the 'repeat–until' block.

Activity 3

Write an algorithm to enter the passenger name and count the number of passengers travelling on a flight. Calculate the total paid for the flight if a fee of $300.00 per person is paid. Print the total collected and the number of passengers. The data is terminated by the passenger name "Nomore".

Here is the algorithm:

```
Count = 0
REPEAT
      PRINT "Enter Passenger Name"
      READ Name
      Count = Count + 1
UNTIL Name = "Nomore"
Total_Collected = Count * $25
PRINT "Total Collected = ", Total_Collected
PRINT "Number of Passengers =", Count
```

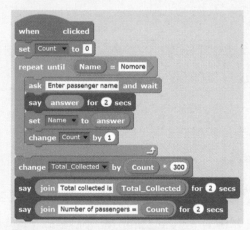

Figure 13.22 Scratch script for Activity 3's algorithm

Here is how to write the script for this algorithm (see Figure 13.22):

1 Create a new project and name it 'Passengercount'.

2 Drag the **when green flag clicked block** from Events menu to the script area.

3 Select the **Data menu** and create your variables 'Count', 'Name' and 'Total_collected'.

4 Select **set count to 0** from the Data menu.

5 Select the **repeat–until block** from the Control menu.

6 Select the **equal to block** from the Operator menu and enter 'Name = Noname'. Drag 'Name' from the Data menu to the operator block. Combine this block with the 'repeat until' block.

7 Select the **ask Enter the passenger name** from the Sensing menu.

8 Select the **set Name to answer block** from the Data menu.

9 Select the **change Count by 1** from the Data menu.

10 Attach the 'change Total_collected by 1' from the Data menu block to the bottom of the 'repeat until' block.

11 Combine 'count * 300' from the Operator menu with the 'change Total_collected by 1' block.

12 Select the **'say...for 2 secs' block** from the Look menu and combine with the 'Join' from the Operator menu.

13 Enter 'Number of passengers =' on the 'join' block and add 'Count' from the Data menu.

Activity 4

Write an algorithm to enter the age and count the number of students in a class. Calculate the average age of the group of students if the data is terminated by the value 999. Print the number of students in the class and the average age of the students. Here is the algorithm:

PRINT "Enter the student's age"

READ Age

Count = 0

WHILE Age <> 999 DO

    Total = Total + Age

    Count = Count + 1

    PRINT "Enter the student's age"

    READ Age

ENDWHILE

Average = Total/Count

PRINT "Number of students:", Count

PRINT "Average age of students:", Average

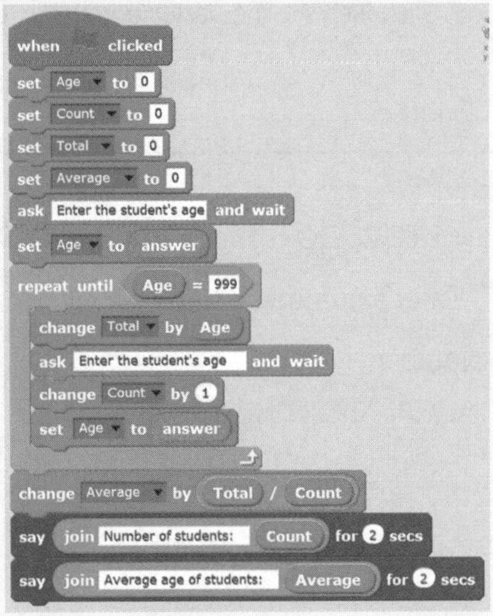

Figure 13.23 Scratch script for Activity 4's algorithm

Here is how to write the script for this algorithm (see Figure 13.23):

1 Create a new project and name it 'AverageAge'.

2 Drag the **when green flag clicked block** from Events menu to the Script area.

3 Select the **Data menu** and create your variables 'Age', 'Count', 'Total' and 'Average'.

4 Select **Age, Count, Total** and **Average** from the Data menu and set them to 0.

5 Select **ask to enter the Student's age** from the Sensing menu.

6 Select the **repeat–until** block from the Control menu.

7 Select the **equal to block** from the Operator menu and enter 'Age = 999'. Drag the 'Age' variable from the Data menu to the Operator block. Combine this block with the 'repeat until' block.

8 Select **change Total by Age** from the Data menu.

9 Select the **ask Enter the student's age block** from the Sensing menu.

10 Select the **change Count by 1 block** from the Data menu.

11 Select the **set Age to answer** from the Sensing menu.

12 Attach the 'change Average by 1' block from the Data menu to the bottom of the 'repeat until' block.

13 Combine the Total/Count from the Operator menu with the 'change Average by 1' block.

14 Select the **say…for 2 secs block** from the Look menu and combine with the 'join' block from the Operator menu.

15 Enter 'Number of students =' on the 'join' block and add 'Count' from the Data menu.

16 Select the **say…for 2 secs block** from the Look menu and combine with the 'join' from the Operator menu.

17 Enter 'Average age of students =' on the 'join' block and add 'Average' from the Data menu.

Activity 5

Write an algorithm to read 10 numbers and print the lowest. You need to choose an initial value for 'Lowest' so that any number entered would be lower than that value. You cannot choose 0 (zero) as an initial value for 'Lowest' because, of the 10 numbers entered, it may not be the lowest value. The variable 'Count' is chosen as the variable counter to keep track of the number of times the instructions are executed.

Here is the algorithm:

```
Lowest = 999999
FOR Count = 1 TO 25 DO
    PRINT "Enter a number"
    READ Number
    IF Number < Lowest THEN
        Lowest = Number
    ENDIF
ENDFOR
PRINT "The lowest number entered is:", Lowest
```

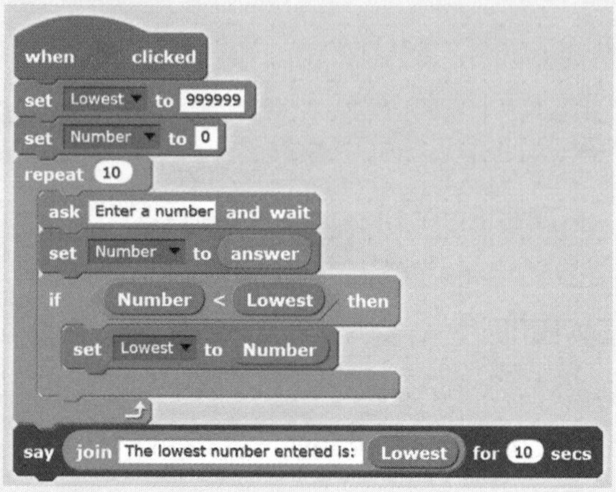

Figure 13.24 Scratch script for Activity 5's algorithm

Here is how to write the script for this algorithm (see Figure 13.24):

1 Create a new project and name it 'LowestNumber'.

2 Drag the **when green flag clicked block** from the Events menu to the Script area.

3 Select the **Data menu** and create the variables 'Lowest' and 'Number'.

4 Select the **repeat 10 block** (we use this because we know the number of times we have to repeat and can enter the value) from the Control menu.

5 Select the **ask Enter a number block** from the Sensing menu.

6 Select the **set Number to answer block** from the Sensing menu.

7 Select the **if–then** block from the Control menu.

8 Combine the 'Number < Lowest' from the Operator menu, where 'Number' and 'Lowest' are taken from the Data menu.

9 Attach the 'set Lowest to Number' to the 'if–then' block from the Data menu.

10 Select the **say…for 2 secs block** from the Look menu and combine with the 'join' block from the Operator menu.

11 Enter **The Lowest number entered is**: on the 'join block' and add 'Lowest' from the Data menu.

Summary 13

1 A sprite is a computer graphic that moves on the Stage or Canvas area based on the written program.

2 The Costume Editor allows you to change the colour, look and feel of your sprite.

3 The Sound Editor allows you to add and edit sound for your sprite.

4 The Script Editor allows you to drag your block programming code together to write your Scratch program.

Questions 13

Copy and fill in the blanks questions

1 The _____ editor allows you to add and edit sound for your sprite.

2 Scratch programming language is a _____ _____ type language.

True or false questions

1 You cannot change the colour of your sprite costume.

2 You can record your voice as a sound for your sprite.

3 You can drag blocks of code together to create a program in Scratch.

4 You cannot use variable names in a Scratch program.

Multiple-choice questions

1 Your new teacher has written a program to accept the input from the user's keyboard (see Figure 13.25). The variable that holds the input is called 'Value'. What would be the final data stored in the variable value after the program has been run?

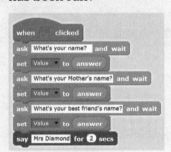

Figure 13.25

a Your name

b Your best friend's name

c Hi Mrs Diamond

d Your mother's name

2 A programme is written to compare two numbers and to subtract or multiply if one number is greater than the other. What will the sprite say if the user entered 5 for R and 4 for S after the program is run? (See Figure 3.26.)

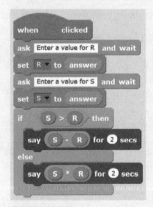

Figure 3.26

a 20   b 1

c 5   d 4

3 Which of the following is **not** a variable used in this program (see Figure 13.27)?

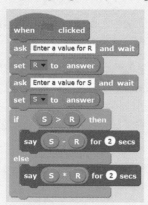

Figure 13.27

a Answer   **b** R

c 2   **d** S

Short-answer questions

1 Explain what the costume editor does.

2 Explain how to use coordinates to position a sprite on the Stage Area.

3 What does the 'answer' block from the Sensing menu do?

Project

1 Create a Scratch program using two sprites in which these two sprites are speaking to each other, asking and answering questions about themselves such as:

  ✳ What is your name?
  ✳ Where do you live?
  ✳ What are your hobbies?

2 Create a Scratch program to draw a kite using the coordinates of the stage and the blocks of code in the Motions menu.

STEM project

You are excited about including Scratch programming in your future presentations. Select one of your presentations from a previous chapter to include a sprite or sprites.

1 Write a paragraph stating which presentation you have selected and giving at least two reasons for this selection. Select an appropriate sprite or sprites.

2 Decide on the appropriate part(s) of the presentation for the inclusion of the sprite(s). Say why you have selected these parts.

3 Write the algorithm for the inclusion of the sprite and its features. Create your Scratch program and include it in your presentation or part of your presentation.

4 Show your Scratch program to your classmates. Assess the impact of the sprite(s) from the reactions of your classmate. Ask your classmates' opinions on the impact of the sprite(s).

Hints

1 Look at online or television advertisements that have sprites. Assess how effective they are.
2 Select a sprite or sprites that is/are relevant to the presentation and use for impact but not to overwhelm the presentation.

14 Computing careers (3)

✳ Objectives

At the end of the chapter, you will be able to:

❑ identify some IT skills used by people whom are not IT specialists

❑ name some traditional IT specialists

❑ identify IT career opportunities in new and emerging IT fields

❑ identify the qualifications needed for these IT careers

❑ state the job functions of the various personnel in these IT careers

❑ state some benefits of certification and identify some IT certification vendors.

IT skills needed by non-IT professionals

Computers have changed the way in which we do our jobs, and have also created new employment opportunities.

Most office workers today interact with computers, and their jobs have changed to make full use of this useful technology. Secretaries, lawyers, doctors and sales people all need to be computer literate. They have to do tasks such as send emails, use the intranet in their organisation, type and print letters on word processors and enter, update and even protect data on certain files. Other skills required for many positions include being able to use spreadsheets and presentation software, as well as being to find information on the internet. Even such diverse professions as postal workers, clergy and politicians are using modern technology to enhance the way their jobs are done.

Career opportunities for IT specialists

The opportunities that exist for IT specialists range from traditional Information, Communication and Technology (ICT) department jobs to the more recent additions to the computer job industry in new and emerging IT fields.

Traditional IT careers in ICT departments

A company or organisation may have one or more IT specialists. A large traditional computer department may have several IT specialists such as an ICT manager, a network administrator, technicians, data entry operators, IT trainers and a web master, among others. The next section includes a brief summary of the different careers in a traditional and non-traditional ICT departments, which we discussed in detail in the *Interact with IT* Books 1 and 2.

Figure 14.1 Office works such as secretaries need to be computer literate.

Figure 14.1 Office works such as secretaries need to be computer literate.

The following traditional career opportunities are available in ICT departments:

* **Information-systems (ICT or data-processing) managers** are responsible for planning, coordinating, managing and staffing the information systems department of a large organisation.
* **Systems analysts** are in charge of developing a system from start to finish. They analyse the problem to find a solution, and then develop, implement and test the system. They usually work to a budget and may have a team of individuals working with them.
* **Programmers** develop both application and system software. They discuss program specifications with systems analysts, write programs, test and debug programs (correct errors), document the program (using manuals or internal comments), update it, repair it, modify it and further develop existing programs.
    * **Computer programmers** can be divided into two categories, relating to the types of programs they develop.
        - **Application programmers** write software to meet end-user requirements such as typing, drawing, calculating and gaming, and may produce applications such as payroll programs, science programs and word-processing programs.
        - **Systems programmers** write systems software, such as programs to monitor and control peripheral devices such as printers, speakers and WiFi cards or adapters.

Figure 14.2 A computer programmer

* **Network administrators** create, manage and secure computer networks in their organisation. They troubleshoot problems, issue passwords to individual users and allow access to the system by setting up user accounts. They start and shut down the network and can also restrict users' access to certain files, folders and websites.
* **Database administrators (DBAs)** administer and manage a company's database. This involves the efficient storage, retrieval, customisation and archiving of data.
* **Operations managers** are in charge of the daily operations of the computer department. They supervise the use and maintenance of computer equipment, supervise the receiving and preparation of data, schedule processing activities, allocate duties to staff and consult with the data processing manager.
* **Computer operators** monitor and control the central computer system (or console) by starting up and shutting down the system and responding to messages from the system. They also perform routine maintenance, such as cleaning drives, loading input and output systems such as tape drives or paper in printers, and keeping logs on system performance.

* **Data-entry operators** enter data into the system from source documents (documents used for recording data that is to be later fed into the computer). They keep records of the data that they have entered and verify that data.

* **Help or service desk specialists or technicians** assist and support users have an issue or problem with their computer system, hardware or software. They do this either over the phone, via email or chat, or in person. They work closely with IT department personnel to resolve issues that may need more knowledge or expertise than they possess. They also troubleshoot problems and advise on a course of action.

* **File librarians** organise a company's data files and software by cataloguing and storing the tapes and disks. They maintain and protect the company's data, and also clean and inspect the data storage media.

* **Data security analysts / Data security specialists** look after the security and protection of the company's data. They protect the company's computer systems against threats from hackers, viruses, power outages, fraud, theft and invasion of privacy.

* **Computer consultants** are required to give an independent and objective opinion on how ICT can be used to meet the needs of an organisation. They are usually contracted for a short period of time to provide technical assistance to an organisation in areas such as systems analysis, design and programming, in the formation or upgrading of a data processing department.

Figure 14.3 A file librarian

* **Web-page designers / Web developer** build and maintain websites using programming languages such as HTML and Java. They maintain and improve web pages.

* **Web masters** are specialists whose responsibilities range from monitoring internet traffic on the web server to answering queries about website operations. Their duties may include that of a web designer or someone who updates the web pages.

* **Computer engineers** design components, test and assemble them. Items such as microprocessors and circuit boards, as well as computer peripherals, are examples of these components.

* **Software engineers** are specialists who design or create software. They may not write actual programming code but they must be competent in programming. They work together with both the business and the programmers, explaining the business functions to the programmers and the technology to the non-technical personnel.

Figure 14.4 A computer engineer

Figure 14.5 A mobile app developer

* **Computer technicians**, sometimes called computer repair technicians, are called when a computer system is not working as it should. They maintain, repair and install hardware and software. Computer technicians may be employed as part of an organisation or can be outsourced, that is they may have their own business and be called to perform a service (independent service providers).
* **Software testers**, also called software test engineers, are hired by companies to do quality control tests on the software they produce. Their aim is to find any bugs in the program.
* **Software trainers**, also called IT trainers, design, develop and deliver training courses to individuals and organisations on a variety of software applications.
* **Multimedia artists and animators** develop moving pictures with the use of computers for use in game development, use on the internet, in movies and television. They may work with a web developer or designer or a programmer to develop their design.
* **Mobile app developers** have one of the fastest-growing IT careers in the world. The growth and advances in mobile technology has resulted an explosion in the development of software specifically designed for mobile devices.

New and emerging careers in the ICT industry

As the ICT industry expands and computers become more entrenched in our society, ICT skills will continue to change and be in great demand. These new and emerging IT fields provide many ICT career opportunities, which we will discuss in this chapter.

The gaming industry

The gaming industry is expanding rapidly and has created a range of new jobs. These include games programmer, games artist, games designer, animator and games tester. Multimedia artist and animators, their job function and qualifications were discussed in Book 2.

Gaming programmers

Games programmers, similar to other software programmers, write and code software using a variety of programming languages to create video games. These programmers usually work as part of a team to write the program.

Educational qualifications	Duties
Qualifications needed to become a computer programmer are a bachelor's degree in computer science or computer engineering, or any other relevant programming courses. Games programmers must have good problem-solving and analytical skills. Depending on the size of the company, games programmers may also function as game designers, game artists and game testers.	• Write and code software for the game. • Oversee the game testing. • Work with the game designers, game artists and game testers.

Game artists

A game artist creates the visual elements of a video game. They combine artistic and technical skills, for example, classical art with computer and graphics design.

Educational qualifications	Duties
• People employed as games artists can obtain their qualifications from a number of courses offered at the level of associate, bachelor's or master's degrees. • A multimedia artist usually will have formal training in art, drawing, illustration or a related area. Many game artists study anatomy in order to produce characters that are lifelike.	• Sketch and develop designs into either 2D or 3D graphics forms. • Create artwork for websites, packages, and promotional materials. • Listen to feedback from testers and modify designs. • Creates and builds characters, objects and environments of the game.

Game designers

A game designer conceptualises the game concepts, storyline, characters, setting and game play, ways to win or lose the game, difficulty levels and the user interface. They work as part of a team with game artists, game programmers and game testers.

Educational qualifications	Duties
The qualifications for this job may be ordinary level passes and a good knowledge of computers, although some jobs may require a bachelor's degree in video game design or computer science. Creativity is also an important attribute of a game designer, as is the ability to tell a story. A key skill of a game designer is the ability to work as part of a team. An asset for a game designer is the ability to understand programming languages used in game development and animation/3D modelling software.	• Create the storyline and biographies of the characters in the game. • Script and storyboard the game. • Create the setting, rules, props, modes of play, environment and characters for the game. • Determine what the game's intended audience wants from the game through market research. • Create the prototypes with the assistance of the game team (game artist, programmers and testers) • Train testers to play the game. • Use feedback from testers to modify the game. • Document the game design process. • Conduct the design reviews.

Game testers

Game testers play games to determine if there are any bugs in the game, which they then document and report. They make recommendations about how to improve the game before it is sold or launched to the general public.

Educational qualifications	Duties
Although no specific qualifications are needed to become a game tester, knowledge of computers and qualifications in computer science, maths and physics at an ordinary level or 'A' levels are assets. A game tester also has to have good analytical and problem-solving skills and the ability to pay attention to detail.	• Test different levels and versions of the game. • Record problems found while playing the game and make suggestions or recommendations to the game designer. • Check the game for copyright infringement (its similarity to other games). • Determine what caused the bugs in the game. • Determine if the instructional manual is user friendly and accurate. • Check for errors such as spelling and graphics in the game, in the packaging and in the instructions manual. • Check if the game works according to the designer's specifications. • Write a report about any bugs found in the game and submit this to the designer.

Other careers in the ICT industry

Here are some examples of other careers in the ICT industry.

Technical writers

A technical writer converts technical and complex information into an easy to understand, simple language. They create user manuals, instructional manuals on how to assemble equipment, training manuals, customer service training guides and technical reports using simple, easy to comprehend language.

Educational qualifications	Duties
The qualification required to become a technical writer is a bachelor's degree in computer science, English, communication, journalism or a related field. Good writing skills and excellent communication skills are essential requirements for a technical writer.	• Create easy-to-use instructional guides with the help of the technical staff • Utilise videos, diagrams, drawings, animations, photographs and charts to make the instructional material more understandable. • Choose the most appropriate medium to deliver the message to the intended audience such as manuals, instructional videos, and so on. • Determine what the end-user needs from the technical document and write accordingly. • Create documents for products. • Revise documents based on feedback or as problems arise. • Use feedback about the usability of the documentation from customers, designers and manufacturers.

E-commerce management specialists

E-commerce is a new and rapidly expanding field of study. It combines business studies/education with management of information systems. An e-commerce specialist deals with online business transactions such as internet banking, electronic funds transfer, buying and selling on the internet, mobile commerce, internet marketing, and so on.

Educational qualifications	Duties
• Although very few universities have specialised degrees in e-commerce because it is a relatively new field, employers accept bachelor's degrees in business and management, information systems, management information systems or related fields. Qualifications in marketing are an asset. E-commerce specialists must have a good understanding of social media and strategies surrounding their use. • An e-commerce management specialist also must have good written and verbal communication skills, as they will have to communicate their ideas to both upper management and their staff.	• Develop and carry out strategic online marketing plans. • Collaborate with content developers on website design and website advertising. • Conduct market research. • Compile budgets for projects. • Interview and train new recruits. • Supervise the e-commerce department. • Present project designs to upper management.

Robotics engineers

A robotics engineer designs and constructs or creates robots and robotic systems with the aid of computer-aided design and drafting (CAD and CADD) tools. They may use 3D modelling software or 3D printing to make prototypes of their designs. They are involved in research and development of robotic systems to assist in many fields.

Figure 14.6 A robotics engineer using a laptop to program a robot

Educational qualifications	Duties
The qualifications needed are usually a bachelor's degree in computer engineering, mechanical or electrical engineering, computer science and robotics engineering as offered by some universities. A robotics engineer has current knowledge of what is taking place in the field of artificial intelligence (AI). Therefore, knowledge and current information on AI is an asset for a robotics engineer. Good communications skills are also an asset, as a robotics engineer is usually part of a team involved in developing new systems.	• Create designs using CAD/CADD software. • Create software for robots and robotics systems to function. • Design machines that will manufacture/build the robots. • Create prototypes of the robot or robotic systems. • Analyse, detect and fix bugs in the robot or robotic systems. • Conduct research and development to improve or create new systems.

Computer forensics analysts

Computer forensics is a growing and rapidly expanding field, as computer crimes become more common. Computer forensic analysts (also called computer forensic technicians or computer forensic specialists) collect information from a variety of digital devices that can form part of legal court cases.

Educational qualifications	Duties
The required qualification is a bachelor's degree in computer science or information technology. Additional qualifications that would be useful would be courses in criminal justice and certification in computer forensics.	• Work closely with law enforcement or criminal justice organisations. • Determine how cybercriminals infiltrate computer systems. • Recover vital information, data and files that have been lost (hidden), deleted, damaged or altered from various storage devices, such as flash drives, hard drives, zip drives and cell phones. • Find evidence of illegal activities on the internet or computer. • Make sure that computers and computer networks are secure (computer forensics analysts are also security experts). • Analyse data for relevance to criminal case. • Testify in court about the information and procedures used to collect the information relevant to the case. • Format the data to be used in the legal proceedings.

Artificial Intelligence (AI) specialists

An AI specialist writes programs for computers to test hypotheses by using simulations based on how the human mind thinks or works. For example, a computer recognises patterns based on what is stored in memory in a similar way to that of the human brain.

AI is the part of computer science that focuses on the creation of machines that can react and perform intelligent tasks similar to people. This includes speech recognition and decision-making.

Educational qualifications	Duties
Qualifications required in this field are a bachelor's degree in computer science or computer engineering, in-depth knowledge of programming in several programming languages and systems analysis and a master's degree in computer science and/or psychology, anthropology and philosophy.	• Research scientists, who are generally responsible for designing and analysing information • Software engineers and software analysts • Software development managers, and C and Java software programmers or developers • Information security engineers or specialists.

Virtual reality specialists/augmented reality specialists

As virtual reality technology becomes more and more popular, a relatively new career is that of the virtual reality specialist or augmented reality specialist. The potential for the use of virtual reality technologies in a variety of fields such as medicine, gaming, biotechnology, tourism and real estate has caused this field to grow rapidly.

Virtual reality specialists uses a combination of the real environment and computer-generated information, thereby creating an environment in which the user can get experience in completing a task. In other words, the user has a simulated experience.

Educational qualifications	Duties
The qualifications required to become a virtual reality specialist are a bachelor's degree in computer science or game design. Other recommended qualifications include art, psychology and video production and editing.	• Collaborate with graphics artist, animators and multimedia specialist to develop graphics. • Provide technical support and training. • Provide recommendations on equipment needed. • Ensure security of the system. • Develop and maintain efficient code for the system. • Schedule and conduct experiments and demonstrations. • Develop and provide instructional learning material.

Figure 14.7 A cryptographer

Cryptographers

Cryptography is the writing and the solving of codes. It is the conversion of ordinary text into an unintelligible format for the purpose of secrecy to prevent the message from being read by persons for whom the message is not intended. Cryptographers are persons who develop cyphers, algorithms and security systems to encrypt important and sensitive information. They are highly analytical and have a great knowledge and understanding of mathematical theories, which helps in the creation and breaking of codes and cyphers.

Educational qualifications	Duties
Cryptographers usually require a bachelor's degree in computer engineering, computer science or mathematics. Relevant qualifications and knowledge of the related programming languages such as Java, C++, C# and Python are also necessary. Some jobs may accept non-technical degrees. However, a large amount of experience in the field is necessary. Masters and PhD degrees in computer science are an advantage and can be required for promotion to higher levels within an organisation.	• Ensure that financial data is protected and only available to the authorised user, by writing algorithms to disguise or hide information such as credit card, account and financial information. • Encrypt and protect computers and networks from hackers and cyberterrorists. • Encrypt sensitive and important information from being copied, edited or deleted. • Test systems or software for areas of possible intrusion by hackers and cyber terrorists. • Find ways to intrude and access data.

Cloud architect

Cloud technology (called the cloud and cloud storage) is one of the fastest-growing fields in the 21st century. It consists of storage, servers, software and computing services. Organisations can choose to save or back-up their data with a cloud storage company instead of on their premises. One of the newest ICT careers is that of a cloud architect. A cloud architect is responsible for developing and implementing cloud technology and cloud security policies for an organisation and its users.

Figure 14.8 A cloud architect manages cloud systems.

Educational qualifications	Duties
The qualification required to become a cloud architect is a bachelor's degree in computer science, software engineering or a related degree. Additional qualifications, such as a Master's in Business Administration (MBA), are an asset and can be required for more advanced positions. Some companies such as IBM and Microsoft offer their own certification suited to their particular products.	<ul><li>Design and set up cloud storage and computing systems.</li><li>Manage cloud systems.</li><li>Set up security policies for use and access of cloud systems.</li><li>Implement updates to cloud systems.</li><li>Ensure that the cloud systems are stable, safe and accessible at all times.</li></ul>

Health IT specialists

Health IT specialists install and maintain the computer system, software and patient health information (data) in a health facility.

Educational qualifications	Duties
The qualifications for this field are a degree in computer science and a related medical field such as medical coding, nursing, radiology, and so on. Some universities offer specialised degrees, such as a bachelor's degree in health information technology. Qualifications in information management systems are also an asset for this profession.	<ul><li>Build, implement and maintain electronic health systems for the health facility.</li><li>Monitor and secure patients' data.</li><li>Monitor the privacy, accuracy and efficiency with which patients data is communicated or shared with authorised personnel.</li><li>Manage patient data and data quality.</li><li>Report and analyse patient data.</li></ul>

Bioinformaticians

Bioinformatics is the combination of biology, health sciences, medicine or any related medical field, and information technology. This field includes biochemists, biophysicists, pharmacists, biomechanical engineers, biostatisticians, geneticists and so on, who combine their work and research with the field of information technology.

Educational qualifications	Duties
Bioinformaticians usually need a bachelor's degree in their area of study or a medical degree. In some cases, a master's degree or PhD is required along with information technology or computer science qualifications.	<ul><li>Create algorithms and computer software to perform statistical analysis of data and identify and classify biological systems such as DNA sequences.</li><li>Oversee other scientists in the department.</li><li>Design clinical trials for new medication.</li></ul>

Figure 14.9 Aerial photographs are one form of data that a geospatial analyst examines to conserve resources.

Geospatial analysts

Geospatial analysts examine a wide range of environmental and geographical data including geographic information system (GIS) data, aerial photographs, satellite data, soil and map geographic data in an attempt to compare past and present information, discover potential problems, effectively manage and conserve resources and plan for the future.

Geospatial analysts are employed in many fields, such as construction industry and, environmental protection agencies, and city and urban planning. They act as consultants for companies that work with scientific and environmental data.

Educational qualifications	Duties
The qualifications needed to become a geospatial analyst are a bachelor's degree in information technology and science, geography, environmental science, forestry and engineering. Qualifications or good aptitude in mathematics is an important asset.	• Create maps, tables and reports using GIS technology. • Research and analyse data from current literature and those collected from aerial photographs, satellite data, soil and other environmental data. • Create presentations and reports and communicate analytical results and processes. • Consult with clients to discuss results from the analysis of geospatial data.

ICT careers and certification related to green technologies

The phrase 'going green' means to try and lead a more environmentally-friendly lifestyle that will protect the environment and sustain the natural resources for our generation and future generations. Many jobs share the same goals of reducing their harmful impact on the environment. Careers in the ICT industry promote a green environment by:

* producing green ICTs, which means producing environmentally-friendly ICT products
* using ICTs to make other activities greener, which means to use ICTs to produce other materials in order to reduce the consumption of natural resources.

Green technologies, such as energy-efficient buildings, smart power grids, wind and solar power, and cellulosic biofuels, as well as the occupations that set up these technologies, now need green ICT skills.

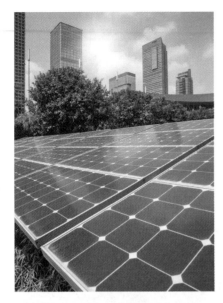

Green jobs in the ICT sector are a result of the direct production of ICT products and services, for example, the production of microprocessors, computers and peripherals that would reduce the sector's impact on the environment. Many of these jobs employ the principles of 'Reduce, Reuse, Recycle' to reduce the impact on the environment.

Any IT professional or IT user can now become certified as a 'Green IT Professional' by doing an additional course and training offered in Green ICT and Sustainability through several universities, as well as through online programs.

Certification

As new IT jobs are created and technology keeps advancing, people need to show that they are qualified in certain areas to remain current or to take advantage of new jobs opportunities.

Certification is evidence that you have taken a course to keep up with the technology or that you are capable in a new field. Degrees (bachelor's, master's and doctorates) offered by universities are the highest IT level certification that you can obtain. Other certifications are offered by well-respected organisations or examining bodies, such as Microsoft, CompTIA, Cisco, HP, IBM and Oracle, or by local colleges. These organisations offer certificates or diplomas.

A degree usually takes about three years to complete and does not have to be renewed. It consists of several related courses, as well as others like mathematics and English, and it is very expensive.

The other certifications can take only a few months to a year to complete. They focus almost entirely on a particular area of study and may give precise hands-on training. These are cheaper than degrees and are more attractive to young adults and beginners. Two such certifications are CompTIA Security + and MCSD.

* The CompTIA Security+ certification teaches a person about the structure and organisation of different networks, network security methods and controlling access to the network. Network security certification is in high demand because of increasing threats to computer security.
* The letters 'MCSD' stand for Microsoft Certified Solutions Developer. This certification provides training on how to use Microsoft technologies to create business applications or programs that can be used over a network and to develop web applications to use over the internet.

Figure 14.10 Green technologies

Reasons for IT certification

The three major reasons to get IT certification are credibility, marketability and personal development.

Credibility

Certification indicates to employers or clients that you have a certain amount of knowledge, skill, proficiency and experience in a certain area. It shows your abilities and expertise.

Marketability

Certification can give you an advantage over someone who is not certified. It also indicates to an employer that you are committed to your field of study and you are willing to develop yourself in that area. The right certification also improves your chances of promotion and a salary increase. It can also indicate to potential clients that you are an expert in your field and promote client trust.

Personal and professional development

Certification can help you to improve and update your skills in the particular area or field. It allows you the opportunity to be certified in new ways of doing things. It confirms your expertise and can give you the personal satisfaction of knowing that you have the ability to perform the task expertly.

Benefits of IT certification

Certification has the following benefits:

* It increases your chances of getting a job or a promotion.
* It demonstrates to the employer that you are willing to learn and improve or enhance your skills.
* Customers may prefer working with companies that have certified individuals, which means that you are more likely to be hired if you are certified.
* It requires that you learn the content thoroughly, which is good for you and your employer.
* It increases respect for you and your ideas, as you are considered more knowledgeable.
* Some certification allows you to become a member of their group of certified and skilled professionals. You can get help from this group when you have a problem or can learn new methods or ideas from what members share with the group.

Did you know?

Cloud architects, on average, earn higher wages than building architects.

Salary range for IT professionals

In the USA, salaries for IT professionals range from $42 000 to $110 000 a year. The average salary is $62 000 a year, which works out to $5 000+ a month.

Summary 14

1. Employees who are not IT specialists are expected to have IT skills, such as typing and printing from a word processor, data entry and updating of files, send emails, saving and retrieving files, and being able to use the organisation's intranet.

2. A gaming programmer writes and codes software for video games.

3. A games artist creates the visual elements for the games, such as the characters, setting and environment.

4. A games designer thinks up the game concepts, storyline, characters, setting and game play, ways to win or lose a game, difficulty levels and the user interface.

5. A game tester plays games to find and document any bugs.

6. A technical writer creates user manuals, instructional manuals on how to assemble equipment, training manuals, customer service training guides and technical reports using simple, easy to comprehend language.

7. An e-commerce specialist deals with online business transactions, such as internet banking, electronic funds transfer, buying and selling on the internet, mobile commerce and internet marketing.

8. A robotics engineer designs and constructs or creates robots and robotic systems with the aid of computer-aided design and drafting (CAD and CADD) tools.

9. A computer forensics analysist or computer forensics technician collects information from a variety of digital devices that can form part of legal court cases.

10. An artificial Intelligence (AI) specialist writes programs for computers to test hypotheses by using simulations based on how the human mind thinks or works.

11. A virtual reality or augmented reality specialist uses a combination of the real environment and computer-generated information to create an environment in which the user can gain experience in completing a task.

12. A cryptographer develops cyphers, algorithms and security systems to encrypt important and sensitive information.

13. A cloud architect is responsible for developing and implementing cloud technology and cloud security policies for an organisation and its users.

14. A health IT specialist is responsible for the installation and maintenance of the computer system, software and patient health information (data) in a health facility.

15. Bioinformaticians combine their fields of study in biology, health sciences, medicine or other medical-related fields with the field of information technology.

16. A geospatial analyst examines a wide range of environmental and geographical data to compare past and present information, discover potential problems, effectively manage and conserve resources and plan for the future.

17. A green ICT professional promotes green environments by producing green ICTs products or using ICTs to make other activities more environmentally-friendly.

18. Certification in an IT field has several advantages, including increasing your chances of getting a job or a promotion and the public's confidence in you or the company you work for. Certification may be a degree from a university, or diplomas and certificates from colleges and popular examination bodies in the technology field.

Questions 14

Copy and fill in the blanks questions

1 A _____ is responsible for staffing, planning and managing the information systems department of a large organisation.

2 A _____ is in charge of developing a computerised system for a client or business from start to finish.

3 A games designer has to work together with the game _____, _____ and _____.

4 The IT specialist who creates and builds characters, objects and environments of the game is a _____.

5 A company that requires some files converted to an unreadable format needs the services of a/an _____.

6 A games programmer must have good _____ and _____ skills.

7 _____ is the part of computer science that focuses on the creation of machines that can react and perform intelligent tasks similar to humans.

8 This IT specialist, a _____, examines environment and geographical data, including aerial photographs, satellite data, and soil and geographical maps, to look for potential problems in an area.

True or false questions

1 Ordinary jobs nowadays usually require basic computer skills.

2 You can get a certification from Microsoft.

3 CompTIA and Cisco certification is obtained from a university.

4 A systems analyst can be assisted by a computer consultant.

5 A games designer comes up with ideas for the storyline, characters, setting and the rules of the game, while the games artist draws or creates the characters, props and setting for the game.

6 A technical writer does not require good communication skills, as he does not come into contact with the public.

7 Cryptographers write algorithms to disguise or hide information such as credit card information, account information and financial information.

8 Cybercriminals need the internet to commit crime.

Multiple-choice questions

1 What is the minimum qualification you need to be a games tester?

   a Bachelor's degree   b Diploma

   c Certificate   d Nothing

2 All of the following are benefits of certification except for:

   a giving you job security, as it increases your chances of getting a job or a promotion.

   b making you more eligible to become the manager.

   c drawing customers to you or your company.

   d providing you with entry into an elite group of certified and skilled professionals.

3 Who is assigns IT work to staff on a daily basis?

   a ICT manager

   b Operations manager

   c Network administrator

   d Programmer

4 One of the fastest-growing IT careers is a:

   a computer technician.

   b robotics engineer.

   c mobile app developer.

   d computer consultant.

5 For a career as a robotics engineer, you need a bachelor's degree in:

a computer engineering.

b mechanical or electrical engineering.

c robotics-engineering.

d any of the above.

6 A games designer does all of the following except for:

a sketch and develop graphical designs in 2D or 3D format.

b train testers to play the game.

c use feedback from testers to modify the game.

d document the game design process.

7 In a small company, which computer specialist may have to do the job of the games designer, game artist and game tester?

a Technical writer

b Artificial Intelligence (AI) specialist

c Games programmer

d Virtual reality specialist

8 Which specialist does not work with the environment or human biology?

a Cloud architect

b Health IT specialist and green ICT specialist

c Geospatial or analyst

d Bioinformatician

9 The work of a cryptographer involves a part of the functions of these two specialists:

a Technical writer and artificial intelligence (AI) specialist

b Programmer and data security specialist

c Virtual reality specialist and geospatial professional

d Software tester and file librarian

10 Which of the following statements are correct?

> **i** A web developer builds, maintains and improves websites.
>
> **ii** A web master monitors internet traffic on given websites, answer queries about site operations, and perform the duties of a web developer.
>
> **iii** A computer engineer designs and creates hardware and software for the computer.
>
> **iv** A file librarian catalogues the company's DVDs, CDs, tapes and other portable storage media or devices and monitors the borrowing of these items.
>
> **v** A data consultant is only contracted to give technical assistance in the design of a new data processing department.

a i and ii only

b i, ii and iv

c i, ii, iii and v

d i, iii and v

Short-answer questions

1 List three specific IT skills you need as a high school student.

2 State three functions of a video game tester.

3 List four types of manuals or documents that a technical writer has to produce.

4 Name three types of online business transactions that an e-commerce specialist deals with.

5 Name four emerging technology specialists that require degrees.

6 An AI specialist has to take on the jobs of certain specialists in the AI field. List three of these specialists.

7 Why is the work of a geospatial analyst important?

8 Identify three differences in the qualification requirements between a game tester and a cryptographer.

Research questions

1 A robbery took place at a downtown store when no one was around. The thief broke through a glass door to get in and out.

    a State three pieces or types of evidence that a computer forensic technician could receive from a crime scene.

    b Name any devices used to capture this information.

2   **a** Define the term 'cloud storage'.

    b Give at least three advantages and two disadvantages of cloud storage.

3 Your school wants to computerise its library so that book enquiries can be made to find out if a book is in stock, its location in the library, the number of each book that the library has, the names and quantities of books borrowed and the ID number of the borrower, as well as other related matters. Students can go to one of four or five computerised stations to type enquiries. Books are scanned when borrowed, returned or newly added to the library's stockpile. List four IT specialists you think would be required for this project and briefly state one function that each one would perform.

4 Select two industries from this list below and explain at least three ways in which ICT skills can be utilised in the profession or industry.

> - Hotels   · Schools   · Banks
> - Government agencies
> - Insurance companies
> - Police stations
> - Custom and excise departments
> - Hospitals
> - Local businesses (realty investments, distributors, farmers, wholesalers)

5 Do research on IT courses that are offered at Technical Vocational Institutions or Community Colleges in your country. What are the prerequisites for applying to study these courses?

Project

You have applied for a job as a data security analyst and you are asked to prepare a résumé to present at the interview. Design a résumé using the security analyst qualifications and any additional information you think you will need to create the résumé.

Hint: Contact your English teacher for assistance.

STEM project

You are a Form 6 (Grade 12) student who has won an international technology competition by designing a Caribbean-based travel game. A new Caribbean gaming company has invited you to submit your resume for employment as a game designer, for possible employment after you have finished your schooling.

1 Make short notes about what you will include in your résumé. How do you plan to make your résumé stand out?

2 Do a template for your résumé and fill in the content.

3 Present your résumé to a trusted classmate and ask for feedback in terms of, for example, the appropriateness of the format, the relevance of the content, the impact and the ease of location of key information

4 How can you improve your résumé based on feedback from your classmate?

Hints

1 Do research into résumé formats and select one that you think suits you best.
2 List the reasons for your suitability for the job in order of their relevance and importance to the job.
3 Keep your résumé format for use when applying for jobs in real life.

Glossary

autoflow reflows text into another linked frame (DTP)

blog regularly-updated informational web page written by an individual

cell intersection of a row and column in a table or spreadsheet

chat rooms group of people with common interests communicating with one another interactively, in real time

column vertical set of cells in a table or spreadsheet

compiler pre-converts programs into the language that the computer understands, machine code

cumulative total keep adding values to a current total to get a new total

cybercrimes illegal acts committed online or via the internet

cybercriminals people who commit illegal acts online or via the internet

cyberbullying bullying (making someone feel sad, afraid or angry) using electronic or digital devices (by teenagers)

cyberstalking threatening or scaring someone using electronic or digital devices (by adults)

data integrity the validity of data. Data is said to have integrity if it is accurate and complete when it enters a system and does not become inaccurate after further processing

data security ways of ensuring data integrity using physical and software safeguards

database a database is a collection of related data about a particular subject (person, place or thing) stored together

database package a database package is a piece of software that enables you to organise and store related data together, so that specific pieces of information can be retrieved easily and quickly

device driver a software application that acts as a translator between the hardware device and the programs or operating systems that use it

directory a folder that is used to hold documents, programs, files and even subdirectories and subfolders

domain name system (DNS) a system that divides the internet into a series of domains, using a hierarchical naming system or tree structure to represent a host

download taking a file from a server or computer on one part of the internet and copying it to your computer or other storage device

dynaset a group of records that answers a query

email electronic mail, the most popular and widely used service on the internet

encrypt (encode) data encode (scramble) data during storage or transmission so that it cannot be understood by someone who does not have the encryption key or software to convert it back to its original form

electronic funds transfer (EFT) ability to transfer funds from one account to another electronically

field a field is an area reserved for a particular type of data

file a storage unit in a computer for storing data, information or commands

file management the process of creating, sharing and manipulating files in a computer system

file manager software on a computer with a graphical interface, where electronic files and documents are organised into folders

File Transfer Protocol (FTP) set of rules specifically for transferring files over the internet

firewall a program, a hardware device, or a combination of both that filters the information coming in through the internet connections to your computer system or network. It prevents unauthorised users from gaining access

folder a directory that is used to hold documents, programs, files and even subdirectories and subfolders

form a field is an area reserved for a particular type of data

form object an option you can select to create a form as a means of viewing data stored in a table or entering data in a database

freeware copyright software that can be copied as many times as you like for personal use.

hacker person who gains unauthorised access to a computer to steal information or cause damage

hierarchical structure a website split into several pages, linked by hyperlinks

high-level languages computer languages that are independent of the machine, as they are not specifically designed for any one brand of computer

HTML language that web browsers use to understand how to display the contents of a web page

hyperlink reference (an address) to a resource on the Web

home page   the first page that you open on a website, which has menus to link to other pages where most of the information is stored

industrial espionage   spying on competitors in order to steal confidential information about their products, formulae, systems, plans or processes

initialising (a variable)   setting a variable to zero before any operations are carried out on it

interpreter   directly converts programs into the language that the computer understands, machine code, 'on the fly'

loop   when a statement/instruction or a group of statements/instructions are repeated

loop, finite   where the instructions are repeated a fixed number of times

loop, indefinite   where the instructions are repeated an unspecified number of times

low-level languages   computer languages that are machine-dependent, with different brands of computer using different program codes

markup tags   tell a web browser how to display the web page that is made from the file

newsgroup   an online discussion forum that allows a group of people with common interests to communicate with one another

node   a unique address that identifies each computer on the internet, so that information can be sent to it

object   an option that you can select and manipulate

overflow   area that stores text if it cannot fit into a frame

podcast   online audio content delivered over the internet

post (a message)   messages from subscribers on bulletin boards

primary key   a primary key is a selected field in a table that uniquely identifies a record

public domain software   software that can be copied as many times as you like.

QBasic   a version of the BASIC programming language

query   a query is a means of storing and answering questions about information.

record   a record is a group of related fields pertaining to one person, place or thing.

report   a report allows data from a table or query to be displayed in a customised format

root drive   the highest or uppermost partition in the hard disk

row   horizontal set of cells in a table or spreadsheet

search engines   a website that allows users to find information quickly and easily; also sometimes called a web portal

sentinel/terminal/lookout value   required to cause a process to stop or exit a loop

slide master   slide that acts as a template to give your entire presentation the same design elements

syntax   the specific rules and statements of a particular computer language, much like rules in grammar of English or Spanish or any other human language

table   a table is a basic unit of a database

test audience   a group of people who match your intended audience who you invite to try out the website before it is published

thumbnail   a smaller version of an actual image

trade secrets   confidential or secret information that belongs to a company such as new product designs, unpublished prices of new products, formulae for new medicines, business plans for expansion into new markets, and new technology or systems

troubleshooting   a form of problem solving, which in computers means to find the source of the problem and come up with a solution to fix it

Trojan horse   program that performs a desired task, but also includes unexpected functionality

turnkey solution   a system, such as network security, billing or website design, which can be easily incorporated into a company's existing operations and processes

uniform resource locator (URL)   the address of an internet file

upload   send files to other computers on the internet

virus   program that activates itself unknown to the user and destroys or corrupts data

webcasting   The delivery of live or delayed sound or video broadcasts over the World Wide Web (WWW)

webinar   a seminar or lecture over the WWW, using graphics (often slides), text and even live voice, where the audience is able to interact with the presenter

web resources   anything on the World Wide Web that you can watch, read, listen to or interact with, such as videos, newspapers, podcasts and online quizzes

website   a collection of related web pages linked together with hyperlinks

wireframe   a simplistic sketch and/or layout of a web page

worm   self-replicating program that is self-contained and does not require a host program

Index

Page numbers in *italics* refer to tables and figures.

Acknowledgements

The Publishers would like to thank the following for permission to reproduce copyright material. Every effort has been made to trace or contact all copyright holders, but if any have been inadvertently overlooked the Publishers will be pleased to make the necessary arrangements at the first opportunity.

Photo acknowledgements

p. 3 *bl* © Scan Rail/Adobe Stock; **p. 8** *br* © Mehaniq 41/Adobe Stock; **p. 10** *br* © Andrey Popov/Adobe Stock; **p. 13** *tl* © Doc Rabe Media/Adobe Stock; **p. 29** *br* © Elnur/Adobe Stock; **p. 30** *cl* © Karunyapas/Adobe Stock; **p. 30** *bl* © Wavebreak Media Micro/Adobe Stock; **p. 31** *tl* © Metamor Works/Adobe Stock; **p. 31** *cl* © Ake 1150/Adobe Stock; **p. 32** *cl* © Andrey Popov/Adobe Stock; **p. 33** *tl* © Engage Stock/Adobe Stock; **p. 33** *cl* © Wavebreak Media Micro/Adobe Stock; **p. 34** *tl* © Koonsiri/Adobe Stock; **p. 34** *tr* © Raw Pixel.com/Adobe Stock; **p. 36** *tl* © Ball Ball 14/Adobe Stock; **p. 38** *bl* © Salita 2010/Adobe Stock; **p. 40** *tl* © KTS Design/Adobe Stock; **p. 45** *bl* © Hachette; **p. 51** *tr* © Raw Pixel.com/Adobe Stock; **p. 51** *br* © Kaprik Foto/Adobe Stock; **p. 52** *tl* © Designer 491/Adobe Stock; **p. 52** *bl* © Rocket Clips/Adobe Stock; **p. 53** *cl* © Zerbor/Adobe Stock; **p. 54** *tl* © Kalpis/Adobe Stock; **p. 54** *bl* © Highway Starz/Adobe Stock; **p. 55** *cl* © Monkey Business/Adobe Stock; **p. 56** *tl* © Tero Vesalainen/Adobe Stock; **p. 56** *bl* © JenkoAtaman/Adobe Stock; **p. 57** *bl* © Jam Design/Adobe Stock; **p. 58** *tl* © Raw Pixel.com/Adobe Stock; **p. 58** *bl* © Brian Jackson/Adobe Stock; **p. 59** *br* © See Less/Adobe Stock; **p. 61** *tl* © Joey Photo/Adobe Stock; **p. 69** *br* © Canjoena/Adobe Stock; **p. 100** *br* © Raw Pixel.com/Adobe Stock; **p. 118** *br* © Haywire Media/Adobe Stock; **p. 119** *tl* © Paul Pirosca/Adobe Stock; **p. 119** *cr* © Pure Solution/Adobe Stock; **p. 120** *cl* © Terove Salainen/Adobe Stock; **p. 121** *cl* © New Africa/Adobe Stock; **p. 123** *cl* © Nmedia/Adobe Stock; **p. 123** *bl* © Silver Tiger/123rf; **p. 123** *br* © Silver Tiger/Shutterstock; **p. 125** *bl* © Maicasaa/Adobe Stock; **p. 126** *tl* © Mego Studio/Adobe Stock; **p. 127** *tl* © Saquizeta/Adobe Stock; **p. 135** *bl* © E Pyton/Adobe Stock; **p. 136** *bl* © Victor Moussa/Adobe Stock; **p. 146** *cl* © Scan Rail/Adobe Stock; **p. 148** *tl* © Black Salmon/Adobe Stock; **p. 149** *bl* © Sikov/Adobe Stock; **p. 154** *tr* © Raw Pixel.com/Adobe Stock; **p. 155** *br* © Sergey Peterman/Adobe Stock; **p. 160** *br* © Collided/Adobe Stock; **p. 174** *br* © Goroden Koff/Adobe Stock; **p. 177** *tr* © Collided/Adobe Stock; **p. 190** *tl* © Nicholas Pitt/Alamy Stock; **p. 191** *tr* © John Barron/Alamy Stock; **p. 200** *bl* © Patrick Cheatham/Adobe Stock; **p. 233** *bl* © Rido/Adobe Stock; **p. 234** *cl* © Seventy Four/Adobe Stock; **p. 235** *cl* © Sir Travel Alot/Shutterstock; **p. 235** *bl* © Scan Rail/Adobe Stock; **p. 236** *tl* © Bongkarn/Adobe Stock; **p. 238** *bl* © Goroden Koff/Adobe Stock; **p. 240** *cl* © Alexander/Adobe Stock; **p. 241** *tl* © Goroden Koff/Adobe Stock; **p. 242** *tl* © Gerckens Photo/Adobe Stock; **p. 243** *tl* © Xiaoliangge/Adobe Stock; **p. 243** *cl* © Jezper/Adobe Stock; **p. 243** *bl* © 성수 한/Adobe Stock.

t = top, *b* = bottom, *l* = left, *r* = right, *c* = centre

Screenshot acknowledgements

pp. 6–7, 16–17, 20–25, 71–95, 101–115, 128–140, 154–164, 169–172, 177–184 © Used with permission from Microsoft. **p. 44** © Flickr. **p. 45** © LinkedIn® professional networking services. **pp. 63–64** © 2018 Google LLC, used with permission. Google and the Google logo are registered trademarks of Google LLC. **pp. 124–125** © Hachette. **pp. 143–147** © 2006-2019 Wix.com, Inc. **pp. 219–232** © Scratch is developed by the Lifelong Kindergarten Group at the MIT Media Lab. See http://scratch.mit.edu. Licensed under a Creative Commons Attribution-ShareAlike 2.0 Genericlicense (CC BY-SA 2.0).

Text acknowledgements

pp. iii, 3, 12, 16–28, 31, 38, 52, 62, 65, 69–118, 122, 125, 128–152, 156, 154–185, 218, 251–253 © Used with permission from Microsoft. **pp. 20, 52, 62, 65, 127, 128, 150** © Copyright © 2019 Adobe. All rights reserved. **p. 17** © Apple® Macintosh® is a trademark of Apple Inc. **pp. 17, 154** © Mac® is a trademark of Apple Inc. **pp. 17, 18** © OS X® is a trademark of Apple Inc. **pp. 17, 63** © iPhone® is a trademark of Apple Inc. **p. 18** © Finder® is a trademark of Apple Inc. **pp. 21, 26** © iCloud® is a trademark of Apple Inc. **p. 21** © 2007 - 2019 SpiderOak Inc. All rights reserved. **pp. 21, 26, 61–62, 127** © 2018 Google LLC All rights reserved. Google and the Google logo are registered trademarks of Google LLC. **p. 31** © Facebook © 2019. **p. 32** © iPod® is a trademark of Apple Inc. **pp. 41, 42** © located on ASCD's website: http://WWW.ascd.org/publications/books/study-guides.aspx. **p. 43** ©AppInventor.org is licensed under an Attribution-NonCommercial-ShareAlike 3.0 Unported License. **p. 43** © 2019 Discovery Education. All rights reserved. **pp. 43, 127** © GoDaddy® is a registered trademark of GoDaddy Operating Company, LLC. All rights reserved. **p. 43** © Weebly, Inc. **p. 43** © WordPress **pp. 43, 127–128, 143–152, 253** © 2006-2019 Wix.com, Inc. **p. 44** © Flickr. **p. 45** © Facebook © 2019. **p. 45** © Myspace.ge © All rights reserved. **p. 45** © TikiWiki® are registered trademarks of the Tiki Software Community Association+. **pp. 45, 47, 135** © Wikipedia and MediaWiki are trademarks of the Wikimedia Foundation and are used with permission of the Wikimedia Foundation. We are not endorsed by or affiliated with the Wikimedia Foundation. **pp. 45, 252** © LinkedIn Corporation 2019 **p. 53** © 2001-2019 Softpedia. All rights reserved. Softpedia® and the Softpedia® logo are registered trademarks of SoftNews NET SRL. **p. 53** ©2019 Secure by Design Inc. **p. 63** © Apple® is a trademark of Apple Inc. **p. 63** © 2019 Twitter, Inc. **p. 63** © iPad® is a trademark of Apple Inc. **p. 122** © 1994–2019 The Omni Group; Apple, MacBook, the Apple logo, iPad, and iPhone are trademarks of © Apple Inc., registered in the U.S. and other countries. App Store is a service mark of Apple Inc. **p. 122** © 1999-2019 by Visual Paradigm. All rights reserved. **p. 124** © Hachette. **p. 127** © Bookmark Your Life, All Rights Reserved. **p. 127** © 2019 CoffeeCup Software, Inc. **p. 127** © 1998–2019 by individual mozilla.org. **pp. 128, 150** © 2019 Webflow, Inc. All rights reserved. **pp. 128, 150** © 2005 – 2018 Axway, Inc. **pp. 128, 150** © Sitebuilder. **p. 140** © 2015 Joomla! **p. 149** © 2002-2019 bluehost inc. All rights reserved. **p. 149** © 2019 HostGator.com LLC. All Rights Reserved. **pp. 241, 243** © Courtesy of International Business Machines Corporation, © International Business Machines Corporation.